CALGARY CAVALCADE

Photo courtesy, Calgary Exhibition & Stampede Ltd.

CALGARY CAVALCADE

from FORT TO FORTUNE

by GRANT MacEWEN

Published by THE INSTITUTE OF APPLIED ART, LTD.

EDMONTON, ALBERTA

Printed by EVERGREEN PRESS (ALBERTA) LTD.

*To friends in the Canadian Club
who encouraged me to write the
Calgary story, this effort is respect-
fully dedicated.*

FOREWORD

Behind every Canadian city or community is a story well punctuated with humor, tradgedy and triumph. Too often it is unknown to residents or unappreciated by them. Inasmuch as the records of other years can be useful as well as entertaining, they should be safeguarded assiduously. "A wise nation preserves its records."

Attempting to capture essential segments in the Calgary story has been an enjoyable task. There is no suggestion, however, that the book which now emerges is an exhaustive treatise. Quite obviously, not all the captivating people who were important and colorful in the expanding community could be treated adequately. And in a book which began as an effort to set down the main reasons for Calgary's individuality, it was found necessary to leave to other writers the parts Calgary, like other Canadian communities, played in world wars, continent-wide depressions and matters of national consequence as much as local.

And, as always, the author is indebted to friends—many of them —to whom he appealed for information. Some were the patient people at the City Library; some were pioneers with good memories. The Glenbow Foundation helpfully loaned certain documents. Acknowledgement should be made, also, of the privilege of drawing freely from ancient newspapers—the *Calgary Herald* in particular, columns of which hold endless historic treasures about the City of the Foothills.

GRANT MacEWAN.

TABLE OF CONTENTS

TABLE OF CONTENTS

LIST OF ILLUSTRATIONS

"IT'S HARD TO BELIEVE"

Flying conditions were favorable and the evening flight from Winnipeg, April 27, 1957, was expected to arrive at Calgary on time. Overhead was a cloudless spring sky and a few thousand feet below were blackened fields telling that seeding operations were in progress across the wheat country.

"You might fasten your seat-belt," the stewardess instructed an old man showing more than usual interest in everything about him. "We'll be landing at your destination in a few minutes."

"In a few minutes? Golly, Miss, we just left Winnipeg about three hours ago."

"Yes, I know," she replied with an understanding smile. "It doesn't take long nowadays. See, there are the lights of the City and you can still see the outline of the mountains beyond. Beautiful sight!"

Peering through the window, the old man with shaggy grey hair and a youthful gleam in his big eyes, studied the sea of illumination extending across 60 square miles of city blocks. "Golly, is that Calgary?" he mumbled. "Beats all; danged if it doesn't."

"You've been here before?" the stewardess enquired as she placed her passenger's hat and coat beside him.

"Yes, I've been here before, Miss, but golly, golly, it wasn't like that. Do you know, Miss, I feel like I'm coming to visit a rich old man I haven't seen since he was a poor kid with pimply face and no shoes."

"You mean you knew Calgary when it was small?"

"Golly, Miss, you've got a nice face — and figure too. But pardon, you asked if Calgary was small when I first saw it. Say, you could have packed all the white men into this plane, and there weren't enough white women to keep the gossip circulating. No lights like those, I tell you. A few kerosene lamps stuck in shack windows but you could've blown the whole danged lot out with about four puffs."

The girl chuckled, wished she had started the conversation sooner but she had other passengers to attend. She wanted to ask

1

one more question, however. "Tell me, how long did it take you to travel from Winnipeg to Calgary the first time?"

"Four weeks. We came as far as we could on old Van Horne's train — rattled like a hay rack — and then we drove a team and wagon from Regina; 74 years ago, I figure. I was only eight years old — travelling with my father. I was exactly the same age as the Mounted Police fort down there beside the mouth of the Elbow River."

Reluctantly, the stewardess went about her duties, leaving the aged passenger to gaze at the new Calgary. "Hope that grandson or somebody's here to meet me," he mumbled. "I'd danged well get myself lost in that place."

Touching down at Calgary's McCall Field, named to honor the memory of Fred Robert Gordon McCall, "brilliant and courageous war ace of World War I," the big plane taxied to a stop under the lights of the new Municipal Air Terminal, acknowledged to be one of Canada's finest.

Facing the sign on the terminal wall: "Elevation 3545 feet," the old gentleman, walking toward the entrance, observed for all around him to hear: "Elevation's probably the only blessed thing somebody hasn't changed since I was here."

"Hi Grandfather! Oh Father!" came voices at the gate. They were from 17-year-old Sonny and his mother, who embraced the old timer and whisked him inside to await the release of his baggage.

"Pretty swell place, this!" was the man's first comment. "I suppose the mortgage is a swell one too."

"Lovely building! Yes, father. It was opened just a few months ago. But while we're waiting, there's a mural on this inner wall you should see — done by Artist Don Frache especially for the building. I think you'd appreciate it. There; you see it attempts to present the story of the West, Calgary particularly. Notice the fluffy cloud with an outline resembling the map of Canada? And the settlers with oxen and wagons plodding westward? But take a good look at the faces of the five men dominating the scene. Recognize any of them? There's Reverend John McDougall on the left, then Colonel Macleod of the Mounted Police, next is Chief Crowfoot, then an unidentified settler, and on the extreme right, Father Lacombe. They're supposed to have caught the vision of the City of Calgary. And there in the Valley of the Bow you see the city of their dreams rising into prominence — and the mountains as a backdrop. I like it."

"Grandfather," Sonny exclaimed, "that man they didn't name must have been you. He even looks like you. Do you think it's a good painting?"

"Don't ask me about paintings. Helped paint this old town one night when Bennett was elected to the Legislature of the Territories, but that's about as far as my experience went. I'll tell you, though; I knew Lacombe and Macleod and McDougall and I saw old Crowfoot once. Yes sir, four fine gentlemen, and the artist made the faces really look like them. He should've included another — Frederick Haultain, the Premier of the Territories. Now, there was a statesman. I wish those old lads could have been with me tonight to see their Calgary from the air. Golly, it was wonderful. Why it even made me take my eyes off that pretty little stewardess — blonde, limbs like an antelope and waist like . . ."

"Come Father, remember you're 82 now. We'll get your suitcase and be on our way. Tomorrow, Sonny's going to drive you around to see some of the landmarks, and maybe you'll see more blondes. By the way, tomorrow afternoon, there is the formal opening of the new Jubilee Auditorium. We're taking you to that. It's the smartest building you ever saw."

The following morning after consuming his customary two plates of oatmeal and observing that "a man shouldn't start the day without his prayers and his porridge," Grandfather was ready to tour a city he hadn't seen for more than half a century. "If it wasn't Sunday," he announced, "I'd buy a new hat — one big enough to hold a ration of oats for a work horse — like I see the Mayor of Calgary wearing in the pictures. But where do you intend to take me? If it's all the same to you, Sonny, let's start where Calgary started, at the place where the old fort stood. Don't suppose there's a danged thing left of it. That was where my father pitched our tent the day we arrived at the old shack-town, 74 years ago."

And so, they were on their way, the athletic young Calgarian driving the family car and the perky pioneer sitting proudly beside him. On 9th Avenue Grandfather remembered that as a young fellow he had earned his first wages, "right here, picking stones off this road — we called it Atlantic Avenue — 75 cents a day and I saved half a dollar every day. Golly yes!"

"Once we got the stones gathered up, all the boys with fast horses wanted to use this avenue for a race track. There were some good races, too. I remember Parson Tom's Thoroughbred being matched against a dark horse from the Sarcee Reserve. That was quite a race. The Thoroughbred had the breeding and the cayuse had the speed and the Indians were still drunk two days later."

Near the corner of 6th Street and 9th Avenue, South East, the two men left their car and paused to read the inscription on the huge boulder standing there as a monument: "This Stone Marks The Original Site Of The R.N.W.M.P. Barracks, 1874-1914."

"Sure I remember the fort. It wasn't very beautiful but that didn't matter. It was about 200 feet long and 150 feet the other way. The men's quarters were over there on the Elbow River side and the stables for 50 horses were on the Bow River side. Storehouses were on this west side. You see, Sonny, the buildings formed part of the fort walls and there was a drill ground at the centre. And a good lot of lads who lived there, trying to keep the settlers from worrying to death."

"Golly, I was a scared kid, one day just after we arrived. Chief Bull Head and his Sarcees came in, fair spoiling for fight. They came right into I.G. Baker's store and accused Joe LaRondale of taking a horse from the reserve. They had more shades of war paint than you'd find on a show-girl's dresser and they acted as though they were going to scalp Joe right there. The police had to make peace, but golly, I don't know how they did it."

"Now, just over there, on the south side of your 9th Avenue, was the Baker store. George Clift King had been in charge but he was setting up his own store when we came. That Baker store was a long, low shack that looked more like a cow-shed than a place of business, but it was just like a super-market to us. And across the Elbow, not far from the Bow, was the Hudson's Bay Company store, another log building. John Bunn ran it. Too bad somebody didn't think to keep that old building as a relic. They could have put it in the men's wash room of the present Hudson's Bay store, I imagine, and there'd still be plenty of space."

"See, most of the shacks and tents were on that east side of the Elbow when we came, but right after that the C.P.R. began building a station on the west side. Most people were mad as hungry hounds, but there wasn't much they could do about it; and after a lot of grousing most of them loaded their shacks on sleighs and hauled them across on the river ice."

"Before you want to go back to the car, let's take a walk a block or so west of this corner and I'll show you exactly where Calgary's first school building stood. I suppose it's been torn down too. That school started — I think it was February in 1884 and J. W. Costello was the teacher. I attended a little while — not long enough; but when a young fellow could earn 75 cents a day picking stones or pounding spikes in sidewalks, education was bound to suffer."

"Where do you want to go now, Grandfather?" Sonny asked.

"We might go east of the Elbow. If the William Pearce house is still standing I'd like to see it. After that you can take me where you like."

"Fine with me," was the reply. "When we're down this way we can stop at the Inglewood Bird Sanctuary where Colonel Walker once lived. And on the way back we might stop at the Fish Hatchery at the Calgary Brewery, and then the Zoo on St. George's Island. If you're like me, you could stay all day at the zoo. We're pretty proud of it, but we can't stay long because I'd like to show you the Reader Rock Garden beside the Macleod Trail, named after W. R. Reader who was superintendent of City Parks for nearly 30 years. There's a lot to see, but Mother wants us home in good time for lunch because there's the Jubilee Auditorium opening this afternoon."

"Yes, and if we're late, your mother'll think the blondes got me."

Driving home they crossed the Louise Bridge, Grandfather recalling the day in 1897 when the old Bow Marsh bridge built right there went out with the spring flood. "The river was a mile wide in places and quite a few houses floated away," he remembered.

Early in the day the old man and grandson stood to get a vision of the old fort with its log walls, dirt floors, sod roofs and generally primitive character. Now they were to see a symbol of the same district grown to maturity and riches, an ultra-modern auditorium capable of seating 2695 people, one of the finest in the world.

"So that's it?" Grandfather was properly impressed with the luxury and elegance in this five and one-half million dollar showpiece, a gift from the Province on the occasion of Alberta's Jubilee

"IT'S HARD TO BELIEVE

Year celebrated in 1955. Taking part in the dedication ceremony,
along with Chairman H. A. Webster, were His Honor J. J. Bowlen,
Lieutenant-Governor of Alberta, and himself a distinguished
pioneer; Honorable Ernest C. Manning, Premier of the Province;
and His Worship, Donald H. Mackay, Mayor of Calgary.

The magnificent building, like its counterpart in Edmonton,
covering one and one-half acres and dedicated to the memory of
Alberta's pioneers, impressed nobody more than the old gentleman
who was carrying a vivid mental impression of Fort Calgary.

"Golly, golly," he was whispering to himself. "To think it
could happen just 82 years after they built the fort, 74 years after
we drove in by wagon."

"Sonny," the old man whispered a little louder, "I wish those
old fellows in the picture — Lacombe and McDougall and Macleod
and Crowfoot could have seen this."

The grandson smiled. "At least the man who wasn't named
saw it. You saw it."

"Golly yes; I saw it. But Calgary shouldn't forget all that
happened in the years between the Fort and the Auditorium, all
the hard work and planning and hardship and progress — and
the heroes and heroines along the way. Golly, yes."

WHERE THE ELBOW JOINS THE BOW

On a bright day late in August, 1875, Inspector A. E. Brisebois and 50 Mounted Police rode across prairie now bearing the district name of Crescent Heights and halted on the high bank of the Bow River, about at the end of today's 2nd Street, North East. There they surveyed the expanse of natural beauty laid out on all sides, knowing at once they were close to destination and an opportunity to relax.

Behind them was "The Nose," that 4000-foot eminence known later as Spy Hill, atop of which Reverend John McDougall stood a few years before and saw more buffalo on the plains "than a hundred men could count in a day." Before them, extending picturesquely toward glistening mountains, were trees, grasslands and billowing hills. And off at the left was the point at which the Swift or Elbow River joined the Bow.

"Our first sight of this lovely spot," wrote a member of the troop, "was one never to be forgotten and one to which only a poet could do justice." Until that moment there was some doubt about the exact place to be chosen for the new fort; now there was none. The men were eager to cross the river and pitch their tents on the lightly-wooded ground in the angle of the two rivers. Riders as well as horses were weary, having been on the mosquito-infested trail more than twice as long as was contemplated when leaving Fort Macleod a full month before.

These young men, members of the recently-organized North West Mounted Police, had been in the country less than a year. Fort Macleod had been built on the Oldman River but there was need for additional outposts in this uneasy Indian territory. In the spring of 1875, men of the Force rode to the Cypress Hills to build what became known as Fort Walsh; and at the beginning of August, Police Scout Jerry Potts led the way for Inspector Brisebois and his troop carrying instructions to select a suitable site for a fort on the Bow River and prepare for building.

Assistant Commissioner J. F. Macleod remained behind to receive a message from Ottawa but later overtook his men at the Bow River, straight north of Fort Macleod. The message necessitated a change of plans; Major-General Selby-Smyth, Commander of the Canadian Militia, was in the West and anxious to meet Colonel Macleod at a designated point on the Red Deer River.

Instead of pursuing the search for a building site, the Mounties continued northward and, after another six days of riding, touched the Red Deer River directly south of Buffalo Lake. Before the police had time to groom their horses and themselves for the meeting, however, a courier rode in to inform Colonel Macleod that the General had decided to travel from Fort Edmonton by a more westerly route, less exposed to the eyes of belligerent Indians. His new proposal was to meet the police at the river crossing about two miles above the present City of Red Deer.

There beside the river, with more spit and polish than the buffalo country had witnessed before, the meeting was held and the police troops were formally inspected. The General then continued on his way southward, accompanied by Colonel Macleod and Jerry Potts. That left Brisebois and the men of F Troop to renew their original purpose. Their southerly course brought them to the Bow River close to the mouth of the Ghost and then along the stream to stop their tired and thin horses at the point mentioned, a few hundred yards east of the north end of today's Centre Street Bridge.

"That looks like the place," Brisebois commented with arm outstretched. "That must be the spot Jerry Potts told us about."

At once, Constable George Clift King was instructed to locate a suitable river-ford to take men and horses to the other side. King's horse took him across without mishap, about where the Langevin Bridge was built many years later, and thus King was the first of the Mounties to set foot on the site from which the city was to emerge. The same man had other distinctions; after taking discharge from the force two years later, he became manager of the I. G. Baker store at Fort Calgary, then the town's first postmaster, and in 1886 the town's mayor.

The other members of F Troop followed King across the river, hobbled their horses and began without delay to erect their tents close to the Elbow. All their first impressions were confirmed. "It was by far the most beautiful spot we had seen since coming West," one of the men related later.

Little wonder that such a location — offering firewood, clear glacial water, excellent makings for bows and arrows, and fish in the streams — carried Indian names meaning "Good Place For

Tepees." David One Spot, patriarch of the Sarcees, said so. Moreover, this was for long a place favored by those seeking to commune with the Great Spirit, and on many occasions through the years, Sun Dance lodges were erected right there where a modern city thoroughfare now conveys 10,000 motor vehicles a day.

Strolling inquisitively about their new camp ground before the sun disappeared behind the mountains, the police discovered that the area was not totally without human life. Sam Livingstone, who became the first farmer in the district, was squatting on the west side of the Elbow; and in the trees beside the river was a small buffalo-skin tent occupied by Missionary Father Joseph Doucet, not long out from France and attempting to bring the Christian religion to the Blackfoot tribes.

And to fire the curiosity of enquiring minds were other discoveries: the ashes of many campfires, some human bones picked free of flesh by coyotes, and, most intriguing of all, the rotted logs of what could have been a human habitation.

BATTLE-SCARRED KANOUSE LIVED THERE

Such a natural camp-site in the angle made by the two rivers could not escape the eyes of explorers and traders — and it didn't. The decayed remains of a log structure invited speculation.

Brisebois, knowing something of fur trade history, gleefully concluded that the rotten logs were those of Fort la Jonquiere, the exact location of which was long in doubt. It was a pretty theory and many people since Brisebois' time have been ready to accept it — that Calgary stands on the spot where French traders built their most westerly post on May 29, 1751. Wherever Fort la Jonquiere may have been built at that time, the Frenchmen were carrying out instructions "to establish a fort three hundred leagues" above the one then located where the Manitoba town of The Pas stands today.

Disappointingly, the weight of evidence is very much against the theory that the French were the first to choose the Calgary site. If they left their base now marked by the Manitoba town after the river was free of ice in the spring, they could not have paddled as far as the mouth of the Elbow River by the 29th of May. The late Professor Arthur Morton, highest authority on Western Canadian history, believed the post in question was only 200 yards west of La Corne's Fort, north of the present town of Kinistino in Saskatchewan. That would be sufficient to permit the boast that la Jonquiere was the most westerly of posts, and still leave the distinction of being the first white man to see the Canadian Rockies to Anthony Henday, who trekked across the West in 1754. And so one is obliged to conclude that the log ruins seen by Inspector Brisebois were those of something built by a trader from Fort Benton and not as ancient as the police officer chose to believe.

Probably the first white man to see the confluence of those mountain streams and camp nearby was David Thompson, whose name deserves letters of gold upon the pages of Western history. He was the young Welshman with a flair for mathematics — the 14-year old who went with the Hudson's Bay Company and, after 13 years of trading and exploring, offered his services to the rival North West Company and proved to be the greatest surveyor and maker of maps in his time. Moreover, he stands out as one of the sterling characters in the early West — reliable, generous, and opposed to the use of liquor in the Indian trade. That he died in poverty in Montreal after pawning his overcoat to buy food for his half-breed wife and himself, testifies to the shameful inadequacy of his rewards.

It was 33 years after Hudson's Bay Company Servant Anthony Henday saw the grandeur of the Rockies that young David Thompson rode south from Manchester House on the North Saskatchewan River to behold the spot from which the City of the Foothills would one day arise. On a meadow not far away — perhaps in the Springbank district — he met Piegan Indians and spent the ensuing winter with them.

Thompson came again in November, 1800, this time with Duncan McGillivray and others of the North West Company, and continued southward to the Highwood River. But if Thompson had visions of a great city, he failed to record them.

Fifty-eight years after Thompson's second journey to the Bow River, the Calgary area was visited by another celebrated explorer, Captain John Palliser, whose name is perpetuated in the Palliser

Triangle on the plains and the Palliser Hotel in Calgary. His instructions from the Imperial Government were to make an assessment of the buffalo country west of Red River, a part of the continent known as Rupert's Land ,and report upon soil, trees, climate, Indians and the possibility of settlement.

After arriving at Fort Garry in July, 1857, Palliser and his staff of scientists zig-zagged their way westward, digging holes in the sod to examine the soil and making pertinent observations about vegetation. The first season's operations terminated at Fort Carlton and the second season's at Fort Edmonton. On September 14, 1858, Palliser was at Bow River, immediately below the mouth of the Elbow and no doubt looking down upon the picture presented by two clear rivers weaving their way from a backdrop of grassy hills and snowcapped mountains.

According to his journal, he "Found a good crossing, then returned to breakfast on a very short allowance of fish . . . Saw buffalo to the east, struck off our course to follow them; ran them and killed three; two of them very good."

The Palliser party's third summer was devoted to exploring "the remainder of as yet unknown country," including the Cypress Hills which served to inspire the travellers. Palliser's colleague, Dr. Hector, returning from the Hills, passed on the south side of the Bow-Elbow confluence and followed the latter stream westward. "The country," he recorded on August 15, 1859, "is exceedingly beautiful, having a rich black soil supporting good pasture . . . It is no exaggeration to say that bands of small deer are as plentiful in this part of the country as in a deer park."

But in a sense, Thompson and Palliser and their associates were transient, uneasy about Blackfoot behaviour and unlikely to pause long for the sake of scenery or to search for visions like that of a city which would someday encompass the river junction. And so, as far as records show, the first white man to distinguish the Calgary site with anything more permanent than a tepee residence was the nimble-fingered trader, Fred Kanouse. His stay was not particularly long either, but his log quarters and his blazing fight against enemies who would have driven him out qualify a claim to the honor of being the first resident on Calgary soil.

Unfortunately, the exact location of the Kanouse building — a combination of house and trading post beside the Elbow — has been lost.

BATTLE-SCARRED KANOUSE LIVED THERE

From his home in the Eastern States Kanouse went west and worked with the American Fur Company, established by John Jacob Astor. The frontier atmosphere in and about Fort Benton suited him like a dark alley suits a cat, and he soon demonstrated that he could accommodate himself to all the vagaries of Montana life. He could be well-behaved or he could be devastatingly rough, as occasion demanded.

Taking time out from more legitimate employment at Fort Benton, Kanouse ventured north to indulge in a sideline of illicit trading with Canadian Indians. With backing from the proprietors of infamous Fort Whoop-Up, Kanouse went overland to the Elbow River, selected a location possessing natural advantages for defence in case of Indian attack, and built a log trading post. It was early in 1871, three years before the Mounted Police came to the prairies, four years before they built Fort Calgary. Although the exact location of the structure is now unknown, there is reason to believe it was about three miles back from the mouth of the river and thus within the present city limits.

But as Fred Kanouse was to discover, it was no place for a person seeking rest or holiday. Before he was in his new residence many days, trouble broke like a storm out of the mountains and the "Elbow Park" district echoed from the gunfire of running battle.

Kanouse had taken four white men and a squaw to his post and one of the men quarrelled with and beat up a Blood Indian. The bruised native rallied his fellow tribesmen to annihilate the traders. As the Indians approached, Kanouse and two of his friends went to meet them, hoping to pacify the warriors. The natives, however, were in an ugly mood and an Indian bullet dropped one of the white men. Kanouse replied with a shot that killed the Indian leader. Then, naturally, the Blood gunfire was directed at the valiant Fred and a bullet penetrated his shoulder. But he and his surviving companion managed to get back to the fort and barricade the door. Now, with three men and one squaw on the inside, preparations were made quickly to resist the major attack which was sure to follow. The squaw loaded the guns and the men fired them, and for three days they kept it up, killing a few Indians and keeping the horde back.

The Bloods retired to prepare another attack and Kanouse seized the opportunity to send a message for help to his friends at Spitzie on the Highwood River. The reinforcements came up promptly and the Indians decided against a continuation of the attack. This marked the end of the "Battle of Elbow Park" and may have explained the presence of human bones seen by the police.

The gunshot wound in the Kanouse shoulder healed; and though his relations with the Indians remained more or less strained, the man was back for the next trading season, still on leave of absence from what Alberta historian Hugh Dempsey has shown was the post of Deputy Sheriff and then Sheriff for Chouteau County, Montana.

While it lasted, the trade at the Elbow post was profitable. In after years the weather-beaten old man told "how he did it" when he was the only permanent or semi-permanent resident within the present bounds of Calgary: "A head wife would come to the post with a party of Indians and dicker for what flour and blankets she wanted, and when she was through, she would hand something to her man and he would buy whiskey. We came to trade and in order to compete, we had to have whiskey." (Cal. Herald. Aug. 6, 1912)

But ill luck seemed to follow Kanouse. On his return to Fort Benton in 1872, he was involved, it seems, in some shooting on the trail and he lost his sheriff's badge. And before the next trading season was in progress, one of Kanouse's helpers, flourishing a gun and demonstrating something that had happened in the battle with the Blood Indians, accidentally pulled the trigger, ignited a supply of gunpowder and blew out one wall of the Elbow River building. Kanouse quit that post and went to build on the Old Man River.

But the coming of the police to build Fort Macleod changed many things — changed Calgary's first resident. Being versatile, however, he had no difficulty in finding another occupation. While the buffalo were still numerous, he drove cattle from Montana and turned them loose at Fort Macleod; he took part in the earliest round-ups; he occupied the oldest building at Fort Macleod and sometimes worried the police about the beverages he was selling; he operated a hotel at Pincher Creek, and when plans were being made for the huge stampede in 1912, the Calgary management brought the old trader and fighter back to build and man a replica of an early trading post.

He had some difficulty in believing that the Calgary he saw in 1912 was the same place at which he had built 41 years before when he was the only resident. He wished he had kept the property on which he squatted.

But except for Brisebois showing commendable French sentiment, the Mounted Police on their arrival were not greatly concerned about who occupied the site in other years. Their immediate interest was in a stout stockade fence and a roof under which to camp. Without delay a rider was directed to Fort Macleod, instructing the I. G. Baker Company to send its men to build the fort according to a pre-arranged undertaking. Even during their short time in the country, the police learned that anybody needing human assistance should not overlook that mercantile company with headquarters at Fort Benton and a trading store at Fort Macleod.

Responsibility for the next step in the creation of a city rested with the Baker Company.

THE BAKER CO.

Two weeks after their arrival at the confluence, police heard the rattle of heavily loaded wagons and the profane shouts of "bull 'drivers." The Baker Company freight was coming in from Fort Macleod, and in due course two ox-drawn outfits forded the Elbow River and stopped in the midst of the police tents.

One wagon outfit carried food, winter clothing and stoves for members of the Force, and the other delivered Baker men and equipment to build the fort. The Company was living up to its reputation of never refusing a business opportunity. As demonstrated repeatedly, Company men would build a fort anywhere, conduct banking at an outpost, deliver a herd of longhorn cattle, buy buffalo hides, trade in groceries, or sell a United States two-cent stamp for a quarter of a dollar with the assurance they'd carry the stamped letter to Fort Benton and mail it there. On at least one occasion, company men undertook to hand-pick a wife in the City of St. Louis and deliver her by freight wagon to a needy bachelor living close to Fort Calgary.

The company was the freest of free enterprisers and served the Mounted Police in dozens of ways in addition to freighting. It was not surprising that the Company was named to be the official representative of the North West Mounted Police in the United States.

Behind the Company was the enterprise of I. G. Baker, who came to lawless Fort Benton in 1865 and almost immediately set himself up to trade with Indians and miners. Supplies came by riverboat from St. Louis — 12½ cents a pound for freight. Boats docking at Benton in the year 1866 numbered 31. From that point on the Missouri River, freight went out over the prairie trails by bull teams, and from 1870 the Baker Company had its own steam boats and its own bull teams to make it the leading transportation institution in the North West.

With the Baker crew arriving to build the fort at the confluence was the Company foreman, D. W. Davis, a man of action who became well known on the frontier. He was a Vermont man who had seen service in the Civil War and came as a trader to the Canadian prairies in 1869 — came with Howell Harris. To the

THE BAKER COMPANY

Indians this earliest builder of Calgary was "the Tall Man," six feet and one inch in height, erect, heavily bearded and imposing. His roles in frontier life were many and varied. When the Mounted Police, after selecting the site for Fort Macleod, returned to check on trading activities at Fort Whoop-Up, the man in charge was D. W. Davis, who received them most cordially and fed them.

With neither delay nor needless formalities, Davis sent the members of his fort-building crew upstream on the Elbow to cut pine and spruce logs of suitable size. A log boom was fixed near the mouth of the river and the building timbers floated down to it.

Before long the fort was taking shape, its low log building roofed with poles and sods, and its stockade fence being constructed by placing 13-foot logs upright in a three-foot trench. The men's quarters and storehouses were no more luxurious than the stables for 50 horses. By means of a whip-saw enough boards were obtained to make the doors; and John Glenn, who was settling at Fish Creek, undertook to construct the stone fire-places. All things considered, the fort was no show-place; but it offered welcome shelter from the chill of oncoming winter.

Having finished the fort, the Baker men turned at once to the construction of a Company store, another low building, about 100 feet long and situated opposite the police barracks, southward. Thus it was on land which, according to a map of 1883, was held in the name of W. G. Conrad. It was a fraction — about 20 acres — of the south west quarter of section 14, on the west side of the Elbow, There, also, the W. G. Conrad house with dirt floors, sod roof and a single window was built, the first home after the police arrived.

For more than a year D. W. Davis remained to direct operations at the Baker store, and in 1877 G. C. King took over the management. Under both men the store was the business and social centre on that side of the river. It attracted travellers, Indians and Indian dogs. Day or night, Indian ponies could be seen tied to hitching posts placed on all four sides of the building. It even attracted mice; and there being no cat in the community, the rodent problem assumed serious proportions until Davis, hearing of a settler who had brought a cat from Ontario, negotiated a deal — traded a horse for the cat and concluded that he made a profitable exchange.

Outside of the police barracks, the Company store was for long considered the best place for a dance. Frequently, at weekends, merchandise was pushed against the walls, fiddlers took places on the store counter, and police, freighters and a few favored Indians, who furnished most of the blanket-clad female companions, danced throughout the night on dirt floors.

They might have termed it a Community Centre. The long shed-like structure, which was a dance-hall on Saturday night, was a church hall on Sunday — available to any denomination wishing to use it. Methodist John McDougall preached Calgary's first Sunday sermon at the Mounted Police barracks late in 1875, but early in the next year he began services at the Baker store. The preacher stood on the counter and members of the congregation sat on barrels or slumped on the floor. The store was open for business seven days a week, but sales were suspended temporarily for the hour or two when a religious service was in progress.

When Reverend Angus Robertson came to Calgary in 1883, he conducted the community's first Presbyterian services there in the Baker store and then made plans which led to the building of Knox Church.

At any time, day or night, the place to meet one's friends was at the Baker Store. Half-breed and other wayfarers came to loiter as well as to buy, but activity reached its peaks after the periodic arrivals of Baker Company bull teams — in from Fort Benton and Fort Macleod with everything from groceries to walking plows and cough medicine. Most of the huge freight wagons on the trails during the '70's and '80's were Baker outfits, wagon units drawn by 14 or 16 oxen and each ox branded on the left shoulder with the Baker "B" and on a horn with the figure "38".

The Company was in the cattle business in other ways. Its employees would buy a settler's cattle at any time. Simultaneously, it also operated the Company herd of breeding cattle and, it may be noted, 30 Baker cowboys were responsible for bringing the big Cochrane herd to its new range west of Calgary in 1881, the biggest herd of ranch cattle to be released on the Canadian range up to that time.

As Calgary grew and the business centre shifted, a Baker store was built on the corner of McTavish and Stephen (Centre and Eighth Ave). The new store at that location was one of the finest in the early city. Later it was renovated to become the Imperial Bank Building.

In 1882 the firm's founder retired and the business was taken over by the Conrads — W. G. and C. E. Conrad — who entered the firm as clerks. And after a few more years the Company retired from the Canadian scene, having sold to the more ancient Hudson's Bay Company, which built its first Calgary store on the east side of the Elbow in 1876.

"Almost everyone will regret that the old reliable firm of I. G. Baker Company has seen fit to go out of business in Alberta," Calgarians read in their newspaper in 1891 (Cal. Tribune, Jan. 28, 1891). "They were in the early days of the country the wholesale merchants, bankers, postmasters, chief traders and general dealers, and they have always been ready to assist every new enterprise."

As for Davis, to whom Calgarians felt a prideful claim, he was the first white person to be naturalized at Fort Macleod and had the greater distinction of sitting in the Canadian House of Commons between 1888 and 1896, the first representative from the ranching country. But this builder of forts and communities couldn't resist the attractions of new country and he died in the Yukon in 1906. It was then that somebody recalled the prophecy of "Tall Man" Davis, father of Ex-Mayor Ryder Davis of Fort Macleod: "We're building a store now but someday there'll be a big city — right here beside the rivers."

A NAME IS CHOSEN

From its beginning as a Mounted Police outpost, Calgary distinctiveness took many forms. Even in the soft, Gaelic name there was romance — and some mystery.

About the meaning of the word Calgary, there was wide difference of opinion. The earliest definition was "clear running water," appropriate, of course. But other interpretations advanced at one time or another by people who professed a knowledge of the lovely Gaelic tongue added confusion. "A Hut In The Thicket," said one authority; and according to others with self-proclaimed qualifications to render judgment, the word could mean "The Willows Beyond The Boundary"; "A Harbour Of The Sea"; "Cabbage Garden"; "Laughing Waves"; or "Den Of The Rough." There is still another theory — that Calgary's name was Scandinavian in its origin and might have been taken to mean "Bay Of Laughing Waters."

But when scholarly opinion differs, Calgarians could ask with Pope: "Who shall decide when doctors disagree?" On one point, however, there was no lack of agreement — that the name was attractive and that the events leading to its choice held more of interest than its derivation.

It was November when the Baker men completed the new fort and the place was still nameless — nameless except that people at Fort Macleod referred to it quite commonly as "The Mouth."

Only Brisebois, it seems, was giving any special thought to the question of a proper name. In this humble post on a magnificent site, he had more secret pride than he was admitting. One police fort, he knew very well, had been named to honor Assistant Commissioner Macleod and another would bear the name of Superintendent Walsh. Why should this new fort beside the Elbow not be given the good French name of Brisebois, especially when it was built over the ruins of what the Inspector still chose to believe were those of the French post la Jonquiere?

That was the way this man with justifiable sentiment for race and name wanted it, and when the Mounties were celebrating

Christmas dinner with roast buffalo hump, prairie chicken and Toronto-made plum pudding brought from Fort Benton by ox-powered freight, the effusive inspector proposed a toast to "Fort Brisebois."

Nobody challenged the proposal until senior officers came that way and displayed some high-ranking displeasure. Two weeks later, when back at Fort Macleod, Major A. G. Irvine, still annoyed about the unauthorized naming of the new fort, penned a Leap Year Day letter to the Deputy Minister of Justice at Ottawa. It was dated, February 29, 1876.

"Sir: As we have now a post or fort at Bow River, it would be well if it was known by some name. I visited the post about a fortnight ago with Col. Macleod and when we were there Inspector Brisebois issued an order without consulting either Col. Macleod or myself stating that all public documents sent out from this fort were to be headed 'Fort Brisebois.' I, of course, cancelled the order at once, as in the first place Inspector Brisebois had no authority to issue such an order, and in the second place the fort was not built by Inspector Brisebois' troop, and neither the troop or the people about there wish the place called Brisebois.

"Col. Macleod has suggested the name Calgary, which I believe, in Scotch means 'clear running water,' a very appropriate name I think.

"Should the minister be pleased to approve of this name, I will issue an order to that effect.

> I have the honor to be, sir,
> Your obedient servant,
> (Signed) A. G. Irvine, Asst. Commr."

The Ottawa people were in agreement with Irvine's suggestion and from Minister of Justice Edward Blake went a memo to his deputy: "Do not interfere with Assistant Commissioner's discretion in choosing the name he mentions. E. B."

And so, in the spring of 1876, the name became "Calgarry," written with two r's. But why did Macleod choose that particular name? Was it because of "Calligarry" on the Isle of Skye, five miles from which his grandfather had a farm? Or was it from memory of Calgarry House on the Isle of Mull? The Assistant Commissioner had ancestral connections on both of those "Misty Islands" and islanders from both places have tried to claim the honor of furnishing the name for a Canadian city.

Skye was the ancestral home of the Macleods and Macdonalds, and Mull the home of Colonel Macleod's mother's people, the Mackenzies. Prior to the formation of the Mounted Police, Macleod visited his uncle, John Hugh Munro Mackenzie, who occupied Calgarry House, a castle-like place overlooking Calgarry Bay on the west coast of Mull — and loved what he saw. Probably it was the impression from that visit which led him to suggest the name for the fort destined to beget a city.

But as though the nice, Gaelic name were not enough, the city acquired descriptive terms of various sorts — mostly complimentary. In 1895 the place was described as "the western edge of civilization"; in 1903 it was the "Sandstone City," and in 1912 "The coming Chicago of Canada." Still later it was dubbed "Sunshine City," and "Stampede City," and "Oil Capital," but not because of any failure to appreciate the attractiveness of the real name.

Any way one looks at it, the community received a good name, one that appealed to song-writers and poets as well as to those who knew something of its origin. And citizens who wrote the word many times a day should have been perfectly satisfied that it was not spelled the way some Gaelic scholars would have done it: "Calgearraidh."

THE DISTRICTS FIRST FARMERS

Two weather-beaten frontiersmen with faces half hidden in whiskers shared the distinction of being Calgary's first farmers. One was Sam Livingstone, who squatted on land later flooded by the Glenmore reservoir; and the other, John Glenn, settled where the Village of Midnapore emerged. Both were from Ireland; both had roamed extensively over the western part of the North American continent hunting for gold, trading in furs and dodging hostile Indians; and both were conducting small-scale farming operations when the Mounted Police rode onto the Valley of the Bow for the purpose of fixing upon a site for a fort.

Sam Livingstone, with great Irish twinkle in his eyes, was ahead of his neighbor farmer in at least two respects — first, by being slightly earlier in settling in the district and, second, in having a family of 14 children. Sam was a "49er" — one of those who had crossed the continent from New York to California to dig for gold in 1849. But adventure had greater attraction than gold; and if he struck wealth he didn't keep it. From California he journeyed to Mexico, then northward to hunt buffalo on the plains, and then farther northward to escape from a band of Indians bent on taking his scalp. It was when being pursued by Indians that he first saw the Canadian Foothills but he didn't stop at that time. There was word of gold on the Fraser River, and Sam Livingstone couldn't resist the attraction of a gold-rush.

When it was time to move again, he went north to the headwaters of the Peace River and canoed down stream, not knowing exactly where the great river would take him. It was a hard journey, as the necessity of eating coyote meat and hawk soup would indicate. But after trading with Indians a while he came out to Fort Edmonton and remained there long enough to raise some pigs, make a few freighting trips to Fort Garry and Fort Benton, and win a wife.

How he obtained the breeding stock furnishing his herd of pigs is not clear, but as the Swine Breeders' Association should recognize, Sam Livingstone was no doubt the pioneer producer in an area now famous for its pork output.

In 1873 Livingstone came south to start a trading post in the Jumping Pound district west of the confluence of Bow and Elbow. But even with the responsibilities of wife and trading post, the man didn't become entirely stationary; when the Mounted Police wanted someone to hunt buffalo or haul freight from Fort Benton, they'd call on Sam. On occasions his brushes with danger were anything but comforting to contemplate. Once on the Montana side, when ruffians might have hung him from a tree, his Irish luck helped him. The story began when Sam encountered a group of six Montana vigilantes conducting a homespun trial of an alleged cattle thief. Three of the vigilantes were in favor of convicting and hanging the accused and the other three were for releasing him. Sam Livingstone was drafted to serve on the "jury" and break the tie. A man's life hung in the balance and Sam considered well. The evidence was against the prisoner but Sam voted mercifully to free him.

C. E. CONRAD, FORT BENTON.   W. G. CONRAD, FORT BENTON.

I. G. BAKER, ST. LOUIS.

Duplicate

Calgary, Alberta, *Aug 1st 1888*

Mr Indian Department

Baker Agency

Bought of I. G. BAKER & CO.,

Wholesale & Retail Merchants.

TERMS: 12 per cent. per annum on all Overdue Accounts.

210 lbs	Baking Powder consigned D's	.35	640
240 "	Beads	...6	1440
457 "	Tobacco	46	21022
7500	Cartridge	W. Oar 24500	47602

THE BAKER COMPANY

On a later freight trip from Fort Benton to Fort Macleod, an outlaw gang with guns drawn swept down upon Sam Livingstone's carts. Robbery or murder would have followed but the gang leader recognized the freighter by his long hair and bright eyes — recognized him as the man who voted to save his life — and shouted: "That's Sam Livingstone; don't anybody harm him."

Next year, when the Mounties rode into the Valley of the Bow with ideas about building a fort, Sam Livingstone was squatting east of the Elbow, considering building a home on the spot the policemen fancied for their fort. For Sam there was a bigger advantage in being on good terms with the police than in having the choicest building site and he withdrew his claim in favor of the law.

Increasingly he was thinking of farming, even though many people considered it folly to cultivate this soil when it was easy to secure food by running buffalo. His first farm residence was on a river flat now flooded by the waters behind Glenmore Dam and his first cultivation was on an island in the Elbow River.

John Glenn, fellow-Irishman with almost parallel experiences, settled on Fish Creek, a few miles south, in 1875. He too had hunted for gold in California and the Cariboo country. When Rev. George Grant, later Principal Grant of Queens University, journeyed across the West with the Sanford Evans party in 1872, he overtook a solitary prospector with two loaded wagons on the route between Fort Edmonton and Kamloops. The traveller was John Glenn, and Rev. Grant was impressed by the man's self-reliance. The minister's parting words were, "God save thee John Glenn and give thee thy reward."

A little later Glenn and another famous early Albertan, Kamoose Taylor, who operated the incongruous frontier hotel at Fort Macleod, made their way through Jasper Pass to Fort Edmonton and ultimately to the Bow River. Hence, Glenn's course was almost identical with that of Livingstone's and 1875 found them living and breaking sod less than six miles apart.

John Glenn died in 1886, the year in which the first fair was held at Calgary, but during his eleven years of residence he had helped to convince skeptics about the suitability of the soil for crop production. Indeed, he demonstrated faith in the community by erecting some of the first buildings in the new town of Calgary.

THE DISTRICTS FIRST FARMERS

Perhaps John Glenn's best claim to a place in agricultural history arises from being the first person in the North West Territories to put irrigation to the test. During his earliest years at Fish Creek, rainfall was light; feed grown was insufficient for his cattle, and in 1878 he took water from the creek and irrigated 20 acres of bottom land beside the present Lacombe Home at Midnapore. It was the first irrigation in the present Alberta which, 80 years after Glenn's trial, has a million acres receiving the benefits of extra water. The Village of Midnapore on Calgary's south side might well have been called Glenville or Glenwater or Glenmore.

Sam Livingstone outlived his pioneer neighbor by eleven years and gained more fame. Now and then the instincts of the old miner got the better of him and he'd sneak away with a pan of work over the gravel in some nearby stream; but otherwise he was serious about farming and ranching. From Fort Benton he brought the first mower and rake to be used in the Calgary district and he introduced the first threshing machine which was driven by horse-power. And his cattle, carrying the Quarter Circle L brand, numbered 300 head.

Were they not cows from Sam Livingstone's herd that furnished the first milk sold on Calgary's streets? The explanation was that Charlie Jackson, with ambition to be a dairyman, borrowed unwilling cows from Livingstone and sold milk for five cents a dipperful.

To further shock the skeptics who clung to the theory that the Calgary country was cold and inhospitable, Trail-Blazer Livingstone planted fruit trees in 1886 and was able, in the following year, to report all alive and thriving. By this time the family residence, west of the spot later marked by Chinook Polo Ground, could boast the only fruit trees for hundreds of miles, proving that soil and climate were not unfriendly.

When Calgary's first Agricultural Society, grandparent of the celebrated Exhibition and Stampede, was organized on August 22, 1884, Sam Livingstone was elected to be a director. The intention was to hold a fair that year; but it was decided, instead, to send exhibits of grain and vegetables to the Toronto Exhibition for the purpose of convincing eastern people and enticing settlers. When one of the first displays was sent to the East, Sam Livingstone accompanied it and proved to be as much an attraction as the heavy heads of oats and big potatoes and long carrots. Inquisitive easterners with an urge to touch his buckskin jacket gathered around him like cows at a salt-lick. They listened to his stories about gold-rush adventures; about fur-trading when the only wheels in the country were on Red River carts; and about farming within sight of the Rockies, where, only a few years before, the soil and climate were considered hostile to agriculture.

Sam Livingstone, with untamed whiskers, long hair draped on his shoulders, and mischief in his Irish eyes, was like something out of a book. John Glenn was heavy-set, with serious determination written on his broad face, and the same Irish accent. Together they were the "trial and error" men in the southern part of a province, which in 1956 had 80,000 farms, over two million cattle and farm production amounting to 694 million dollars.

They were two of a kind — Livingstone and Glenn. They were Calgary's first farmers — first to display a practical faith in the soil around them — and nothing could be more appropriate than that their names should be perpetuated in Calgary's Glenmore Park beside the Elbow River, and the Livingstone Range in the Canadian Rockies where a young daredevil in his flight from killer Indians halted long enough to scratch his name on the stony face of a mountain.

THE SARCEES IN A MURDEROUS MOOD

For several years after Fort Calgary was built and occupied, the shadows of uneasiness and fear were plainly visible across the Indian country of the South West. Buffalo meat, the native's chief source of food, was declining; hunger was a serious prospect, but enforced existence on reservations was no less hateful to contemplate. In the Indian mind were thoughts of murder.

South of the International Boundary, where the rush of gold-seekers and pressures from land-grabbing settlers led to violation of Indian treaties, there were wars and "rumors of wars." When the Sioux and Nez Perce tribes resisted, the force of the United States army was turned against them and there was extensive loss of life on both sides. In the valley of the Little Big Horn, Montana, on June 25, 1876, the Sioux Indians under War Chief Sitting Bull administered resounding defeat to their white enemies, actually annihilating a United States force commanded by General George Custer. Historians called it the Custer Massacre.

It was no secret that the American Sioux had invited the Canadian Blackfeet to cross the border and help destroy the white oppressors there. In return, the Sioux would come north and assist in wiping out the whites on the Canadian side.

Fortunately Assistant Commissioner Macleod, who was elevated to the rank of Commissioner of the North West Mounted Police at about the same time as the Battle of the Little Big Horn, was on good terms with Chief Crowfoot, and that wise Blackfoot rejected the overtures from his hard-pressed American tribesmen. But when Sitting Bull and his refugee followers, fleeing from the crushing force assembled to destroy them, took shelter on Canadian soil, the Canadian Indians became understandably restless and reckless. Mounted Police tasks were multiplied.

It was late in 1878, while Sitting Bull and his half-starved people were still camping near Wood Mountain, that the few people residing at Fort Calgary witnessed Indian temper at its worst, when a single shot into the explosive atmosphere might have led to mass slaughter.

Fortunately that shot wasn't fired, and the incident historians would have recorded with bloody detail didn't take place. The "Calgary Massacre" was averted by what Inspector Cecil Denny described as "bluff and the grace of God."

Everybody knew that the Blackfoot and their allies — Bloods, Piegans and Sarcees — were the most ferocious of the prairie tribes and capable of the same wholesale slaughter which brought notoriety to the Sioux. Indeed, Blackfoot reputation was a major reason for the delayed entry of traders to the South West. White scalps were about the last articles with which the men who indulged in trade wanted to gamble.

It might have been expected that the signing of Blackfoot Treaty No. 7 would have eased the tensions between red men and white, but the effect of hunger had been underestimated. For several years after the buffalo disappeared, starving and rebellious Indians were almost constant sources of worry for law enforcement officers and other white people. With practically no return from the hunt and government rations of beef proving undependable and inadequate, Indian patience was perpetually close to the breaking point. These white intruders, destroyers of the old order, deserved nothing less than slaughter, the natives concluded. And so, as 400 Sarcees shrieked their hatred beside Fort Calgary on that winter day, a reckless trigger-finger might have started a one-sided war.

Following the treaty of 1877, the Sarcees were allotted land on the Bow River, just west of the Blackfoot reservation, but they were satisfied with neither government treatment nor the assigned location. Their traditional hunting ground was along the Elbow River and though they recognized a loose alliance with the Blackfoot, there was jealousy and an urge to move.

Truculent Chief Bull Head sent a message to Major Crozier at Fort Macleod, telling that he and his people were quitting that prairie reserve which offered no wild game; they were going west to Fort Calgary and the Elbow. Crozier, in reply, explained that there could be no government beef at Fort Calgary because there were no cattle at that place. But, he added, "If you will bring your tribe to Fort Macleod, beef will be supplied."

But Bull Head's mind was made up. He and his followers with horses, dogs and tepees broke camp and a few days later presented themselves at the almost defenceless Mounted Police post. Apart from two or three nearby farmers and some transient half-breeds, the human population in the vicinity, according to Inspector Denny, was exactly eight.

Denny had been in command at Fort Calgary until a couple of months earlier when he departed to visit Fort Walsh and Fort Macleod, leaving Sergeant Johnston and three constables at the local barracks. Otherwise, there were only four residents nearby: George King at the Baker store, Angus Fraser at the Hudson's Bay Company store and their two helpers, W. Smith and Walter James. A Calgary population totalling eight faced 400 invading Sarcees and had reason to be alarmed.

Being hungry, the Indians were bold. They surrounded the Baker store, built a threatening fire close to the door and flourished loaded guns. The warlike demonstration continued all night to emphasize their demand for rations. In the morning Trader King produced three bags of flour, but scornfully Bull Head refused such anaemic food. Flour was an insult to meat-eating Sarcees, lovers of buffalo meat. Wieldng a knife, the chief slashed the bags and let the flour be lost on the frozen ground. He and his tribesmen demanded meat and would settle for nothing less.

Meantime a rider carrying a report of Bull Head's war-like actions was galloping toward Fort Macleod. Receiving the message, Inspector Crozier ordered Denny and such other police as could be spared to hasten to the relief of Fort Calgary. According to Denny's story, he was accompanied over the winter trail by Indian Agent Norman Macleod, Sergeant Lauder and eight constables. After two days of hard riding the little group drew up at the barracks beside the Elbow and the tired horses were stabled.

At once Denny sought conference with Bull Head and repeated the offer of beef rations at Fort Macleod, making it clear the Indians would have to go there to get them. The Chief was as sulky as ever. He wanted meat but declared he would not take his people to Fort Macleod. His horses, he argued, were too thin and weak to travel that far; and besides, his Indians didn't want to go.

For three days the Sarcees remained firm in their determination not to travel south. The shrieks of hostility were no less penetrating and the police could not overlook the possibility of violence — perhaps massacre. Nor could the Indians overlook their advantage in numbers — twenty-five to one.

But the Mounted Police were not in the habit of considering numbers when duty was clear; and on the third day Denny resolved to take a firm stand.

"Move before this time tomorrow," he told Bull Head, "or we'll take your tents down and move you."

It was bold talk, but immediately Denny engaged Sam Livingstone to be present with carts and wagons in case they were needed for the move.

As the deadline approached on the fourth day, there was no sign of Sarcees preparing to move. At the appointed hour, Sam Livingstone was there with his carts. Denny walked into the hostile camp with 13 men and ordered them to hold their rifles in readiness. With a display of boldness, he and Sergeant Lauder proceeded to level the tents, starting with that of the Chief. Like angry bees from a molested hive, Indians came out from under tent leathers and made a pretense of fighting it out. Denny and the sergeant paid no attention to threats, simply continued to level the tepees, while the other members of the force stood motionless with rifles held firmly. It was a tense moment. Nobody could have guessed the outcome. But strange as it must have seemed to anyone witnessing it, the Indians, half mesmerized, moved in to help load the flattened tents on Livingstone's wagons.

By noon the entire tribe was on the trail leading to the South, the police following.

Weather turned bitterly cold and there was hardship and suffering on the way, but after a week of travel the Sarcees arrived at Fort Macleod and began drawing rations of beef. There they remained, grumbling throughout the balance of the winter, and in due course they returned to occupy a new reservation on Fish Creek, not far from the Elbow River they loved so much.

Bull Head continued to annoy the police periodically and worry the residents of Calgary; Inspector Denny resigned from the force about a year after the trouble and turned to ranching; and the Sarcees, at one time acknowledged to be the smartest horse thieves in the South West, settled down to raise cattle and live at peace on their reservation, almost at Calgary's back door.

THE FIRST BIG HERD

Late in 1881 residents of the Fort Calgary shack-town saw the first big herd of cattle arrive — three thousand head, many with long horns revealing their Spanish origin and ancestral association with Texas. After fording the Elbow River in the Mission section — about at Father Lacombe's homestead — a halt was called for purpose of an official count and then the cattle were forced across the Bow from a point close to the present Mewata Park.

These were the Cochrane cattle, bought in Montana and being driven to the new ranch headquarters beside Big Hill where the town of Cochrane stands today. In charge of the drive from the International Boundary to the Bow River was the pioneer trading firm of I. G. Baker Company; and the Baker foreman, Frank Strong, was trail boss.

THE FIRST BIG HERD

The president of the new ranching enterprise for which the cattle were being delivered was Hon. H. M. Cochrane of Hillhurst, Quebec, who earlier in the year had appeared on the prairie driving a team of wild native horses and a buckboard. When he met up with frontiersman Kootenai Brown, first settler at Waterton Lakes, he admitted a proposal to start a cattle ranch somewhere in the West. First, however, he wanted to determine if the grass on the British side of the border would support cattle as well as on the Montana side. The tall, lean and brassy Brown, formerly of the Queen's Lifeguards and already 13 years in the foothills country, assured him that buffalo were good judges of grass and they fancied the Territorial grazing as much as anything Montana offered. "Where buffalo thrived, cattle will do the same," he said.

Evidently the man driving the buckboard was convinced and lost no time in confirming the lease of 100,000 acres under a government scheme introduced that year. His next act was to authorize the purchase of cattle and the construction of ranch buildings on a selected foothills site. The cattle were bought in Montana at $16 a head, delivered at the boundary, and I. G. Baker Company was to receive $2.50 a head for taking them from there and turning them over to the ranch manager at the Bow River.

Nestling against a hillside, half a mile west of today's town of Cochrane, is a long, low, log building — first ranch house in Alberta — erected by the Cochrane people in that year of 1881. Long ago its heavy sod roof was replaced by one of boards, but its venerable logs, still pretty sound, are among Alberta's best links with the birth of large-scale cattle operations. And close to it, beside a stream hurrying out of the hills to join the Bow River, is an equally ancient barn with stone foundations and secret memories about big steers, bucking horses and the golden years of ranching.

There, beside Big Hill, right in Calgary's "back pasture," the Cochrane Ranch Company made headquarters and branded with a big "C" on the left hip. From there, too, cowboys — tough, tanned and weatherbeaten — rode to the sprawling settlement built about Fort Calgary and spent their wages on supplies and such entertainment as a community under the watchful gaze of the Mounted Police would afford.

The original herd which riled the Bow water on that October day in 1881 was driven westward, following the river, to the new range. The cattle were thin. The I. G. Baker Company herdsmen were accused of driving too fast, leaving the stock in a run-down state and poor condition to face the winter. As it happened, a snowstorm came down upon the foothills almost immediately after the cattle were delivered and many tired animals drifted and died. Nobody could be sure, however, whether the losses would have been heavier or lighter if the cattle had been driven more slowly over the trails but overtaken by that October storm while still exposed in open country somewhere south of Fort Calgary.

Major James Walker, graduate of Mounted Police ranks and one whose name appears repeatedly in early Calgary history, was the first Cochrane manager, and under his supervision the storm-scattered cattle, many unbranded, were rounded up. In the course of recovery mavericks and cattle owned by settlers may have been taken along and ultimately given the Cochrane brand. The result was warfare between the big company and the settlers. As a consequence many of the unmarked Cochrane cattle not located in the course of the October round-up were later roped and branded by vengeful settlers. In the course of the branding battle the Cochrane outfit lost more cattle than it gained.

But in spite of losses in the first season, the Cochrane directors ordered more stock. Counting calves and the additional cattle driven from Montana, the herd grazing between Calgary and Morley late in 1882 numbered 12,000 head. But troubles were not ended. The second winter was more severe than the first and hundreds of cattle died. The spring count showed a loss exceeding 50 per cent, and company directors decided to move the herd to a range east of Waterton Lakes — between the lakes and Belly River. There the herd was grazing when winter came in 1883, but misfortune was following. That winter, strangely enough, saw open grazing west of Calgary and heavy snow in the South. Hungry Cochrane cattle were snowbound near Waterton Lakes.

Frank Strong, the I. G. Baker Company man at Fort Macleod, saw the predicament and offered, in return for a thousand dollars, to get the cattle out of the snow trap. Strong was resourceful, as cattlemen needed to be, and securing the help of local cowboys, he rounded up 500 Indian horses — cayuses — and chased them through the heavy drifts to make a path for the cattle. The hungry herd was then driven out over the newly-made path — toward Fort Macleod where there was grazing.

By this time some other big herds had been released on Alberta grass. The North-West Cattle Company chose the grass beside the Highwood River; and there were the cattle belonging to the Oxley Ranch, the Winder and the Walrond. But the Cochrane was the real pioneer among the big operators; and although misfortune made the experiment costly for a few years, experience and better methods brought ultimate success. Cochrane cattle were about the first to be shipped from the range to England. The Company was progressive in the selection of improved breeding stock and continued to be a leader until 1906 when cattle and southern rangeland were sold to the Mormon Church.

But what followed at the Cochrane Ranch west of Calgary after the herd was moved in 1883? Activity did not end — not by any means. As the British American Ranch, still a Cochrane ranch, it was to be used for raising horses and sheep. With W. D. Kerfoot as manager, it was the means of introducing sheep on a large scale just as it was with cattle. And the people of early Calgary watched the experiment with as much interest as though they owned the flock.

Kerfoot liked horses — saddle horses, draft horses and even bad horses — and kept a chestnut outlaw in the corral for occasional entertainment, especially for those times when some buckaroo with an exalted opinion of his riding skill came that way.

But sheep appeared especially promising as sources of company dividends; and in 1884 the way was opened because government regulations forbidding sheep in the area south of the Highwood and Bow Rivers left the British American Ranch, north of the Bow, in the territory where sheep were permitted. The Cochrane people, never short of capital and never unwilling to take a gamble, ordered breeding stock in Montana. The first big flock driven from that state arrived at Calgary late in 1884 while residents were awaiting word about incorporation of their community as a town. What the local people saw is best described by a news item which appeared in the Calgary Herald on September 24, 1884: "Mr. Kerfoot of the B. A. Ranche Co. arrived with his band of sheep at the Elbow River on Monday evening. On Tuesday morning they were swam across the river and the novelty of the operation caused a flutter of excitement among the onlookers.

The band, which is composed of Merinos and Shropshires and a cross of the two breeds, numbers about 8,000. They have averaged about six miles per day and came through with scarcely any loss and are as fat as butter. Until Mosquito Creek was reached not one of them was footsore but, having encountered a storm there, a few of them became lame. They will reach the Big Hill this week. We are persuaded that the sheep interest which is just budding will in a few years be the largest and most important in this Territory."

A few weeks later 200 rams arrived from England, and the Calgary district was projected immediately into a position of leadership in British North American sheep circles. The flock didn't escape a share of pioneer trouble, however. Sheep were unpopular with the cattleman, and antagonistic cowboys found numerous ways of making life miserable for shepherds and the stock in their care. Moreover, a part of the flock suffered loss when caught by a prairie fire in the first summer. But the sheep wintered well and in August of 1885 it was reported that the company was shipping 50,000 pounds of wool to Senator Cochrane at Montreal. Spectators were impressed by the magnitude of the operations.

All in all, the Cochrane Ranch of that early period was a fine example in enterprise and Calgary people watched with neighborly interest.

THE MACLEOD TRAIL

Prior to 1883 all traffic to and from Calgary was by trail and most of it moved north and south. The little community beside the Bow was like a coupling-link tying together the 100-mile Macleod Trail extending to the South and the 200-mile Edmonton Trail to the North. The rutted road to Fort Macleod was, in a sense, the northern segment of the 350-mile Whoop-Up Trail terminating at Fort Benton on the Missouri River. But it was Calgary's undisputed lifeline. Most incoming supplies were from the South, the trail to the North being for Edmonton's benefit more than Calgary's.

THE MACLEOD TRAIL

The Macleod Trail started at the I. G. Baker Company store south of today's 9th Avenue East. A southbound traveller's first thrill was in fording the Elbow River not far south of the present 9th Avenue bridge. The original trail deviated slightly from present-day Number 2 Highway, being less direct because bull-team and stage-coach drivers willingly accepted an extra mile or two of distance in order to have high ground and good footing. Immediately south of Calgary the trail forked, one branch adhering approximately to the route of the modern highway and the other bearing eastward to follow a ridge of higher ground. The two branches came together again at a point not far from today's Turner Siding.

Eight miles south the trail crossed Fish Creek. The place wasn't called Midnapore until the early '90's but the homes of two stalwart pioneers were to be seen in 1883; John Glenn had been there for eight years and was prepared to provide beds or meals for travellers, while the Samuel Shaw family — father, mother and nine children from Kent in England —— arrived just a matter of weeks in advance of the railroad in that spring of 1883.

Shaw drove from Swift Current, bringing oxen, breeding cattle, sheep and hens, and leaving it to the new C.P.R. to haul to Calgary the heavy machinery with which he intended to start a woollen mill, the first in the country. John Glenn died in 1886, but Shaw's activities beside the Trail were sources of public interest for many years. His log house was used as the post office about the time the Midnapore name was adopted; his Midnapore Woollen Mill turned out blankets and similar goods until the plant burned down; and just after the turn of the century he had a private telegraph line to Calgary, mainly to permit him to keep in touch with his chess-playing cronies in distant parts of the world.

It was 15 miles from Shaw's place to the crossing at Sheep Creek, and that stream, like others on the route, was capable of making trouble for travellers and news for the press. From the columns of the Calgary Herald of 1885, one may note that "The last Macleod stage, or at least the last half of it, may still be seen in the middle of Sheep Creek where it stuck fast last week. The mails, horses, express and front wheels were saved. The men along the trail speak highly of the way in which Steele the driver got the horses out of the stream after the coach struck. It seems the coach in crossing struck a stone on the lower side, the coach upsetting into deep water. When it upset, the leaders had almost reached the bar and Steele managed to swim to them and set them free. Returning then, he set the other two horses free and managed to lassoo the coach which was floating down stream."

Fifteen miles beyond Sheep Creek the coach horses or freight oxen of 1883 splashed their way across the Highwood River and, rather commonly, were bedded down for the night in the stable of Smith and French whose names are forever associated with trading and ranching in that period. O. H. Smith and Lafayette French, it should be recalled, brought cattle to the upper Highwood in 1883 and founded the OH Ranch.

Next there was Mosquito Creek crossing with stopping accommodations at Trollingers, and the last major stop — still 28 miles from Fort Macleod — was at the Oxley Ranch or Leavings of Willow Creek.

Just before arriving at Fort Macleod there was the Oldman River to be negotiated — certainly not the least hazardous of the crossings. Spills and other accidents were commonplace; sometimes the press would make a report, as the Macleod Gazette did on January 3, 1889: "On Friday evening, while the stage from Calgary was crossing the Old Man River at the ferry, the ice gave way and let the whole outfit into the water. After a great deal of hard work the team was rescued. The driver, Mr. Braden, very narrowly escaped being drowned."

Nobody was likely to ride over that famous stage and freight route strictly for his health or pleasure, but for those who had to travel there was no better or faster way of getting to Fort Macleod than by leaving Calgary on the Royal Mail Line coach at 9 a.m. on a Thursday and arriving at Fort Macleod at 4 p.m. on Saturday. On Monday morning the coach began the return journey and thus it was possible for the resident of Calgary wishing to spend Sunday at Fort Macleod to complete the round trip in one week.

In 1884, however, transportation services were improved. The Calgary Herald reported that Captain Stewart's new Concord coaches had arrived and "are now on the route between Calgary and Macleod. They are nice and comfortable." About the same time, the Royal Mail Line was announcing additional and faster trips over the Trail, leaving Calgary twice a week instead of once and doing the hundred miles to Fort Macleod in two days instead of three.

As for the new coaches being "nice and comfortable," one is entitled to speculate. Each coach, hauled by four horses changed at intervals, accommodated six people on the inside and up to four — depending upon the amount of baggage — on the top. The fare was the same whether a passenger rode outside or in. A seat on the top, though offering the best in scenery and entertainment from the driver, assured the roughest possible ride as the coach body, hung on leather straps, lurched and rolled. After eight or ten hours of travel, a passenger on either an outside or inside seat could expect nothing less than an aching back.

In 1885, when hostilities broke out beside the Saskatchewan River near Duck Lake, and fear of widespread Indian uprising gripped settlers across the West, a still faster means of communication was needed and the Macleod Trail saw the introduction of a system of dispatch riders capable of relaying a message between Calgary and Fort Macleod in a fraction of the usual time.

As related by the Macleod Gazette: "The system for carrying dispatches between here and Calgary is well nigh perfect. Two men are at the Leavings, two at Mosquito Creek, two at High River and two at Sheep Creek. Average time made, 12½ hours. Will probably be reduced to ten."

With fresh horses and riders at approximately 20-mile intervals, good news or bad could be galloped at break-neck speed over the route which freight wagons took a week or ten days to cover.

There was romance, danger and hardship aplenty on that famous frontier lifeline. But its importance and its character changed greatly after that September day in 1892 when "the final rail was laid on the railroad between Calgary and Macleod." Almost at once the stage coaches and the big ox-drawn wagons disappeared from the public gaze. Nobody even thought to bid a nostalgic farewell to those primitive vehicles which served the new communities so well.

The modern maps show it as Number 2 Highway with hard surface and four lanes, but for those people with sentiment for the old days it's still the Macleod Trail. And with its magnificent command of undulating prairie land, billowing foothills and snow-capped mountains, it is still 100 miles of unsurpassed beauty.

BULL TRAINS ON NINTH AVENUE

The first trains in Western Canada and the first to serve Calgary didn't run on rails; they were the cart-trains and the bull-trains, and there were times when the trail which was Calgary's "Main Street" was choked with wagons and oxen.

From Winnipeg long trains of carts consisting of a hundred or two hundred units moved over the 500-mile trail to St. Paul or the 1000-mile trail to Fort Edmonton. Carts of the same Red River type, each hauled by a single horse or ox, cut tortuous ruts in the sod eastward and northward from Calgary. Most of the Red River carts calling at Calgary came off the Edmonton trail, although David McDougall and Sam Livingstone thought nothing of taking carts loaded with furs and buffalo hides to Winnipeg. The two pioneers travelled together in 1876 and made the trip in 60 days, but that time allowed for a few stops to let Livingstone indulge in his lifelong pastime of panning gold on streams they crossed.

But in the country south of Calgary where the ground was usually dry and firm the so-called bull-teams carried most of the freight. Actually, those brutes laboring to move the freight between Calgary, Fort Macleod and Fort Benton were oxen — just ordinary oxen — but their drivers chose to call them "bulls" and students of history should have no hesitation in accepting the term.

A bull-train was as distinctive as pemmican and as slow as the coming of pay day. A traveller passing such a cavalcade might count over a hundred oxen and 24 loaded wagons. But it wasn't a simple case of a wagon being drawn by two or four oxen; custom decreed hooking three wagons together and hitching eight pairs of the animals, tandem fashion, to each three-wagon unit. There was a "bull-whacker" on horseback who was responsible for keeping each three-wagon unit moving. He had to understand the ways of oxen; otherwise, the essential qualifications were a strong voice and some skill in wielding a 16-foot leather whip as he rode alongside the plodding cattle.

Commonly, there were six or eight of the units making up a train. With eight pairs of oxen yoked to each wagon outfit and eight such outfits travelling one after another, it would mean a total of 128 of the big animals per train and they would be spread out for more than a quarter of a mile on the trail. Hence a bull-train was at least as imposing as anything seen on the trails or highways since their time.

As distinctive as the bull-trains were the men who travelled with them — the whackers who handled the bull-whips, the train boss who was like a conductor, the inevitable cook and the night herder or wrangler. For any one of the positions, a man needed an iron constitution and was expected to possess a vocabulary capable of impressing oxen.

As the editor of the Fort Macleod Gazette saw the bull-whacker in 1882, he seemed to be occupied "in composing profanity of startling originality, into which neither iteration nor plagiarism ever creeps. The fully developed bull-whacker never pauses or stutters when he is once roused by surrounding influences to a full play of his powers, but launches forth into a torrent of the fanciest expletives, dressed in colors wonderfully gorgeous and elegant, incandescent and irresistible. His oaths are never microscopic or feeble, but resounding and polysyllabic — they fit into one another with an exactness and a nicety which one never observes except in a piece of exquisite mechanism, and their continuity finds a parallel in the Atlantic cable alone."

The same editor related the instance of an eastern clergyman travelling from Fort Benton to Fort Calgary in company with a bull-train. Having expostulated with one of the drivers because of the extraordinary vigor of his language, the reverend gentleman was handed the blacksnake whip with an invitation to try his hand. Believing that he knew something about cattle, the clergyman accepted the challenge and "began with mild and orthodox language." The attempt was a complete failure for the 16 oxen were in a moment in complete confusion and the heavy loads were about to topple over. The experienced driver rushed to the rescue, snatched the whip from the bewildered amateur, hurled a volley of oaths "nicely chosen to meet the crisis," and at once restored order. Then, turning to his frightened companion, he remarked: 'Taint no use ye see parson; them thare bulls is tew far gone to be jerked up by a sermon, an I guess ye'll find the folks hereabout just as tough. Take advice from an old-timer, parson, and make back tracks, fer nothin'll fetch ony of 'em except a dog-goned good pounding."

At day's end the wagons were drawn up in two half circles to make a corral. As soon as the bulls were released from their yokes, their care was the responsibility of the night-herder who held the least enviable post in the crew. He was required to stay with the cattle all night and, in the morning, drive them into the improvised corral where each whacker had to sort out his own charges and yoke them for the day's operations. Sometimes things went wrong at night. Even the freight bulls were known to stampede in the darkness. In the course of a severe storm at night, an outfit of bulls being herded one day's journey south of Calgary began to drift. In the black of stormy night the herder was helpless but managed to follow the only white beast in the service. When daylight came he discovered that the white was the only animal in sight. It took three days to locate and recover the other members of the teams.

Once the wagons were loaded, work for members of the crews was not usually heavy. One day on the trail was almost like another unless it became necessary to rough-break a new ox or "double up" at river crossings and steep hills like those on the outskirts of Lethbridge. It was something for a stranger to the country to remember when outfits were "doubled" to take wagons across the Highwood or Old Man or Bow River — 32 bulls hauling to take 10,000 pounds of freight through the water, and two or three whackers exercising their experienced lungs and whip-hands.

Even after the advent of ferries, river crossings could be hazardous. As a Calgary-bound wagon was being drawn onto the ferry at the Highwood River in 1885, the brakes failed to hold and the heavy vehicle rolled forward, pushing the unfortunate oxen off at the mid-stream end. But the oxen could swim and they set out for the opposite bank and took the wagons with them.

On an average day a bull-train travelled 12 miles. That meant an eight-day trip from Fort Calgary to Fort Macleod. Size of loads varied, of course, but it was not uncommon for a bull-train to deliver 60 tons of coal or mixed freight. When a Baker bull-train arrived at Lethbridge one day in 1886 with a record 80 tons of hay, the whackers felt as proud as if they had clipped seconds off the Standardbred trotting record, then held by the mare Maud S.

The arrival of a bull-train was the most exciting routine event in the life of early Calgary, partly because of the bustle of new activity and partly because of the presence of men with wages to spend. Usually it was followed by a dance at the long Baker store and it was a guarantee of extra business for Kamoose Taylor who had quit the whiskey trade after a costly experience with the Mounted Police, and had then set up a billiard table with a hut over it, not far from the fort.

Although oxen were the favorites for hauling the Calgary-Fort Macleod freight, a few operators tried horses. For two years Lavasseur and Stedman had a 12-horse outfit on the trail and commanded a good deal of admiration. This was not a freight train in the sense that multiple ox-drawn units made a train; but the 12-horse hitch handling a three-wagon unit was considered pretty smart and "the way Murphy Sullivan manipulates those twelve horses, in and out of intricate alleys and narrow streets, by the aid of a single jerk line operated from a saddle horse on the rear wheel, would put a city coachman with two horses to shame." But even a smart driver could get into trouble on the trails; and when the outfit was leaving Calgary with 10,000 pounds of shingles for Fort Macleod housetops, the rear wagon broke loose, rolled backwards down the grade and into deep water, and came to rest where the river current floated all the shingles away in the direction of Medicine Hat.

Horses were attractive in every generation, but for trail purposes when the Calgary mail still came in by way of Fort Benton, the bulls held most of the advantages, just as they did on many homesteads. The special merit in the bull was his ability to live and work on an all-grass diet — and there was grass everywhere. The horses needed grain as a supplement to hay or grass, and to buy and carry oats was both costly and troublesome. And so the bulls reined supreme on the freight trails between Calgary and Fort Benton, and at the end of a summer season the brutes were simply turned out to rustle their winter feed on one of the ranges in the chinook belt. The I. G. Baker Company had its own winter range on the St. Mary River.

At one time, around 1886, that company had dozens of the big wagons and 320 bulls in the service. Its position in freighting was one of unquestioned supremacy. At the end of the company's first winter at Fort Calgary, the Baker wagons hauled 15,000 buffalo hides to the head of navigation at Fort Benton. Thereafter the shipments consisted mainly of coal, lumber, groceries, kegs of liquid marked "vinegar," and even passengers who were not in a hurry and not upset by bad language. And whackers like M. W. Endsly, Jeff Davis and James Sanford Sims — men who were as much travelled as sailors — became well-known at Calgary.

But the era of bull-train greatness ended abruptly, and grass began to grow in the deep ruts the heavy wheels had made in prairie sod. The construction of the trans-continental Canadian Pacific Railway didn't stop the wagons, but branch lines like the narrow-gauge road of the Alberta Railway and Coal Company and the Calgary-Fort Macleod line completed in 1892, marked the end.

The railroads could offer speedy transportation and the bull-teams couldn't. The heavy wagons were sold to farmers; yokes disappeared; leather harness decayed and the unsociable bulls were turned out to fatten for the butcher. Nothing remained except a few imperfect pictures, a few newspaper clippings about arrivals and departures — and some memories about a colorful chapter in Calgary and Fort Macleod and Lethbridge story.

THE RAILS CAME

Not for two years after the Baker Company built Fort Calgary for the Mounted Police did the West see the first tangible sign of the coming railroad. That evidence, brought to Winnipeg by riverboat, was the wood-burning locomotive. The Countess of Dufferin, now a relic occupying a place of honor in a downtown Winnipeg park. Even then there seemed but small chance that the transcontinental railroad, if ever completed, would touch Calgary. For reasons put forward by those people concerned about the country's defence, an important railroad should be far removed from an international boundary, and the projected route would be well to the North, passing close to Edmonton and through the Rockies by way of the Yellowhead Pass. Even by 1880 when Winnipeg had rail connections with both south and east, the northerly prairie route — 200 miles beyond Calgary — was favored.

But before construction was started westward from Winnipeg in 1881, many plans were changed. The Canadian Pacific Syndicate, undertaking to complete the transcontinental railroad, was attracted by the more direct route across the plains and through the Rockies by way of Kicking Horse Pass instead of Yellowhead.

Accordingly, Fort Calgary was on the path of construction and the few scores of white people living thereabout began to show a juvenile interest. Some had never seen a train or heard a locomotive whistle. But except for a few frontier individualists who resented more than a modicum of civilization, the prospect was an attractive one. By the time the grade was built to Maple Creek the railroad seemed assured, and its week-to-week progress became as much a topic of Fort Calgary conversation as the coming and going of Baker Company bull teams.

The railroad builders, of course, were not escaping interruptions and troubles. Chief Piapot and his disgruntled Crees took a dim view of railroads, were sure the smoking thing called an engine would frighten all game away. Not being familiar with more diplomatic ways of making protest, they simply pulled up all the survey stakes they could find and used them for campfire fuel. Their next act was to pitch camp on the right-of-way, immediately ahead of the grade builders. Construction workers had no desire to use force upon the powerful and ruthless tribesmen and road-building ended until the Mounted Police, with more persuasiveness than the engineers, prevailed upon the Indians to move. Later there was fear of attack from Chief Crowfoot's Blackfoot and in 1883, the year the rails were laid across the Bow River, there was financial crisis.

But in spite of obstacles, construction went forward at a rapid rate, reflecting the driving force of General Manager William Van Horne. Three miles of steel a day was his objective on the prairies — not always achieved. From Medicine Hat westward the new sidings, at 10 mile intervals, were numbered. Strathmore was 16th Siding, and the nine and a fraction miles of track laid from that point in a single day and 20 miles in three days were claimed as construction records by Contractors Langdon and Shephard.

And on August 11, almost exactly eight years after Inspector Brisebois rode into the valley to choose a site for a fort, the rails were laid to the east side of the Elbow River, and the construction train called the "front train" came to a stop in what is now East Calgary. Everybody in the area was a spectator, wondering if this was dream or reality. "What's this country coming to?" a man with many years on the plains remarked. "I didn't think I'd live to see it."

With the influx of railroad workers, Calgary's population more than doubled in one day. New tents appeared like a bumper crop of mushrooms on the east side of the Elbow where the town was expected to remain. The I. G. Baker Company store on the west side of the river and the Hudson's Bay Company store on the east side found the trade with construction workers and others converging to become squatters on the new townsite so great that grocery and clothing shelves were bare by nightfall. And at the Mounted Police barracks, reinforcements showed the authorities were ready to cope with problems to be expected to accompany such influx of population.

Calgary would be 20th Siding, and of course the C.P.R. was expected to build a station — probably on the level ground south of St. George's Island, there on the east side of the Elbow, where most people outside the police post were already living. It was section 14 on the survey. Section 15, west of the Elbow, had been reserved by Order in Council for pasture for Mounted Police horses. There was an immediate rush to secure good locations on the preferred side, and purchasers were trying to guess where the centre of the business section would be.

But the railroad company had its own ideas and was keeping its own counsel. According to charter from the Government of Canada, it had claim to the odd-numbered sections within a certain belt of land; that gave the Company a special interest in Section 15, the section on the side of the police barracks.

The Order-in-Council reserving section 15 for horse pasture was rescinded; the Elbow River was bridged; the grade continued westward; quietly, a new townsite was laid out on section 15, and about midway across, a location was marked for a station.

That produced a shock, especially for those who had bought land or started to build log cabins on the east side. Consternation gripped the community. People squatting in tents had no problem — they could move easily and on short notice — but it was different with the number of settlers who by freeze-up in 1883 had permanent homes.

The settled area was going to be divided, with a river between the two parts. That wasn't good. When James Reilly circulated hand bills calling for a general meeting at the Methodist church in the first week of January, 1884, one of the main purposes was to discuss what action should be taken in the light of the C.P.R. decision to place the station far from the centre of settlement. Protests were heard, Reilly, with something he called a Royal Hotel on the east side, being the loudest objector.

Some residents vowed to remain on the east side, but the majority chose locations on the new townsite which would correspond closely to Calgary's main business section of the present time. Snow made the winter season a good time to move buildings, and before the spring season two churches, a feed store and rather many small structures were skidded to the west side of the river.

When the Canadian North West Land Company, subsidiary of the C.P.R., was ready to sell lots in the present down-town section, the first applicant was Pioneer John Glenn. The parcel of his choice was that on which the Yale Hotel now stands. A buyer could secure the best corner lots on 7th, 8th and 9th Avenues at $450 or less. The Hudson's Bay Company was among those deciding to move, and its selection was the north west corner of what is now Centre Street and Eighth Avenue. And the I. G. Baker Company chose 9th Avenue.

Calgary was now on the railroad and in better position to attract settlers and business people. But the transcontinental line was still far from being finished. The most difficult sections were in the Rockies. Mountain construction was pressed from both east and west ends, however, and on November 7, 1885, the work gangs met and the last spike was driven at Craigellachie. It was to have been a golden or silver spike to signal the completion of the monumental task; but the practical minded William Van Horne, who was destined to become president of the railroad, said, "No. The last spike will be as good an iron spike as there is between Atlantic and Pacific — and anybody who wants to see it driven will have to pay full fare."

On May 25 of the next year Calgary hung out a huge "Welcome" sign in honor of the first transcontinental service. Moreover, Prime Minister Sir John A. Macdonald and Lady Macdonald were passengers on that first train from Montreal, which gave Calgarians a double reason for cheering. With usual good humor the Prime Minister told those gathered at the station platform that if he were younger, he'd buy a location at Calgary and raise grit steers and tory cowboys.

Quite fittingly, that train making railroad history was pulled by the locomotive for which western people have developed special affection, the Countess of Dufferin. And as the "Countess" steamed westward through mountains, it carried at its front end, lashed over the cowcatcher, a special big chair on which Lady Macdonald sat to enjoy the unequalled scenery. It was Sir John's idea.

SILVER AND GOLD

When people meeting at the Baker or Hudson's Bay Company store in 1883 were not talking about the progress of the Canadian Pacific Railway, they were almost certainly discussing J. J. Healy's silver mines a hundred miles to the west.

The country roundabout was good for cattle raising; and Sam Livingstone and John Glenn and now a dozen homesteaders were demonstrating rather convincingly that grains could be grown successfully. But as a means of gaining public recognition and prosperity in a hurry, what could rival a good gold mine or silver mine? Everybody on the frontier possessed the curiosity and hope of a prospector and there were times when gold pans would have outnumbered fishing rods along Bow and Elbow Rivers.

There had been rumors about major discoveries of gold and silver in the foothills and mountains from time to time. Prospectors Lemon and "Blackjack" were supposed to have come upon fabulous gold somewhere south west of the confluence, but disaster always overtook the people who gained the secret of the mine's location. Calgary's Indian-fighter, Fred Kanouse, reported finding gold in the mountains in 1876, but after getting into a violent argument with the local natives and having to shoot a couple of them in self defence, he decided to turn his back upon the gold. And a cow slaughtered by the I. G. Baker Company after she had been grazing in the Porcupine Hills was found to have a handful of gold-dust and nuggets in her reticulum, presumably having licked the stuff up from a stream-bed. It was easy to conclude that somewhere to the west or south west there was gold so abundant that cattle couldn't keep it out of their stomachs.

SILVER AND GOLD

Everybody talked about gold and silver and expected con-stantly to hear of a bonanza discovery. The stage was set for exploit. But no mining stampede developed until J. J. Healy brought samples of rich silver ore from the base of Castle Mountain, just beyond Banff.

Healy, man of many parts — sheriff, prospector, newspaper publisher and whiskey trader — would have been the perfect subject for a frontier novel. In partnership with A. B. Hamilton, also from Montana, he built notorious Fort Whoop-Up in 1869 and now, in 1882, he was returning from prospecting west of Calgary with ore samples so rich in silver and copper that even an amateur could recognize phenomenal wealth in them. With him in promoting a mining rush was "Clinker" Scott, of whom Calgary people were going to hear more.

The railroad being constructed westward from Calgary reached the site of Healy's claims close to the base of that mountain now called Eisenhower, at a most opportune time and the rush was on. A miner's shack town springing up like a mushroom could show two hotels, lots of stores, hundreds of cabins and a peak population of about a thousand. They called it Silver City.

Various mines were promoted and some started. Queen of the Hill was the best known of the mines. It was supposed to have un-limited wealth and the price of its shares soared accordingly.

Calgary, with an uncertain population of little more than 100 including policemen, felt the main impact of the enthusiasm but the mines drew more people away than they brought in. But whether the effect upon Calgary was good or bad, it was brief. Fraud was suspected and Silver City began to fail after a few months of excitement. It was whispered that the silver ore which J. J. Healy had brought to Fort Calgary, Fort Macleod and Fort Benton and used to promote interest in his scheme, had no genuine connection with Castle Mountain — except to have been "planted" there by Healy or his friends. Actually, the samples may have originated in Montana — probably not on the Canadian side of the boundary. No ore quite like it was ever found in the Queen of the Hill mine or any other nearby development.

The miners began to drift away. It was dramatic while it lasted, but as rapidly as it had appeared, Silver City was deserted. Shacks tumbled down and Silver City became nothing more than a memory.

J. J. Healy's life continued to be full of activity and excitement, but a short time later "Clinker" Scott was murdered in his shack on the Bow River 12 miles above Calgary. It was just two days after the Edmonton-Calgary stage was held up and robbed. People wondered about a possible connection.

A NEWSPAPER IS BORN

Calgary didn't have the first newspaper in the North West Territories, but it had one of the first — a modest sheet born just weeks after the rails reached the Elbow and months before there was anything resembling local government.

The first newspaper between the Manitoba boundary and the Rocky Mountains was the Saskatchewan Herald, started at Battleford in 1878, after tall, Aberdeenshire-born Patrick Gammie Laurie carted a primitive printing press over the 650-mile trail from Winnipeg. The next paper was Frank Oliver's Edmonton Bulletin, likewise printed on a press hauled over the twisty trail from Winnipeg.

The miniature pages of the first issue of the Bulletin, dated December 6, 1880, tell that "John Coutts, freighter, arrived today with ten carts loaded with bacon from Carlton;" that "Messrs. Sinclair and McLane have the mail contract from Winnipeg to here, 925 miles, for one year," and that "Sitting Bull is again talking of going south."

The Macleod Gazette, started in the summer of 1882 by C. E. D. Wood and E. T. Saunders — ex-mounted policemen — was the third journalistic adventure in the Territories. A full year before it appeared, D. W. Davis of the I. G. Baker Company talked to Wood and offered to furnish $150 with which to buy a printing press. An order was placed with Miller and Richards of Toronto and the machine was shipped via Duluth and Bismark, to be transported by river boat to Fort Benton, Montana. But the Missouri River was low in the fall and part of the boat's cargo, including the press, had to be unloaded. There on the lonely riverbank the pioneer press was covered with a tarpaulin and left until high water would allow delivery to be completed in the following spring. Winter passed and, sure enough, a Benton-bound boat stopped for the beached freight, and about midsummer the press was delivered by bull-team at Fort Macleod.

Saunders claimed to know something about printing and Wood offered him a half interest in the paper if he would go to work. The first issue, dated July 1 and weighted appropriately with cow-country news, reported that "eight thoroughbred Hereford bulls passed through here enroute to Capt. Stewart's ranche;" also, that a trail herd comprising 800 beef steers arrived to furnish government beef rations for the Indians on the Blood and Piegan reserves. Editor Wood, well known in Calgary, continued to publish the paper for 21 years and ultimately became Judge Wood of the District Court in Saskatchewan.

Calgary was next. With more of optimism than capital investment, A. M. Armour and T. B. Braden, occupying a tent on the east side of the Elbow River, began publishing the paper they chose to call "Calgary Herald — Mining and Ranche Advocate and Advertiser." No doubt the mining excitement at Silver City was a factor in the choice of name. But how the ancient hand press, made by H. Hoe and Company of New York about the year 1845, reached Calgary is not clear. That it came by rail is unlikely because the grade to Fort Calgary was completed only three weeks earlier and no freight service was in effect.

In any case, the Herald was to be a weekly with subscription price of one dollar per year. And in turning out the first issue the publishers had the assistance of a young easterner who happened to be temporarily in the district — none other than Mackenzie Bowell, later prime minister of Canada.

In the initial paper comprising four small pages and dated August 31, 1883, the editor related local news, described a Sarcee Sun Dance he had attended and declared his admiration for the Calgary surroundings: "The above named town which at present is creating so much interest throughout the whole Northwest, Ontario and England, is located upon a beautiful stretch of bottom land about six miles in length and about three miles wide... It is divided into two parts by the Elbow River which, at its confluence with the Bow, forms a number of beautiful islands, well wooded and admirably suited for a park. Both rivers are pure, clear and cold with pebbly beds and beaches, dotted with innumerable trees and capable of supplying a water power for an unlimited number of mills and factories..."

In the weeks and months following, the editor's fine Board of Trade brand of optimism was unshaken, as his words show: "We do not pretend to the role of prophet yet it requires very little foresight to predict that the City of Calgary will be the largest in the North West. We already anticipate another Chicago and can hear the sound of the busy mill and see in our mind's eye, the street cars plying their traffic from the east of section 14 to west of 16, and from river to river in the opposite direction."

Before the Calgary paper was six months old there was talk of converting it from a weekly to a daily. In the issue of January 23, 1884, the editor revealed a combination of lofty ambition and commonplace need for money: "In last week's issue we alluded to the probability of our establishing a daily paper at an early date and on further consideration we concluded that the interests of Calgary and the surrounding country could be better served by carrying out this project at once. With this end in view, Mr. Armour started for Chicago per last train to purchase the presses and plant required for such an undertaking and already the contractors are at work on additional office room. We need not say to our patrons that this involves a large expenditure of ready money and the continuance of our daily will depend on the support it receives. To meet the outlay, we are going to ask the citizens of Calgary for 100 subscriptions at $6 per annum, payable in advance, and for this we will give them a 16-column daily... We also take this opportunity to remind those of our subscribers both at home and at a distance, who have not yet paid their subscriptions and also those whose accounts are due, that we shall need every cent of money we can place our hands on."

Calgary was still without a banking and loaning institution and there was no alternative to the rule, "Pay as you go." Hence the appeal.

The regular dollar subscriptions came in at an encouraging rate but not the ones at six dollars. Eleven weeks after the announcement the editor reported having received 80 of the high-priced contracts. But on August 27, as he closed Volume One of the paper, and did some justifiable anniversary boastings, the total number of regular subscribers stood at "close upon one thousand." It was more than anybody would have expected in a new community where 25 percent of the citizens were unable to read.

By this time, however, the pioneer paper had competition, the Nor' Wester having made its appearance about midsummer. Between the two papers there was the most bitter of rivalry and the senior editor denounced "the bombast, egotism and literary bravado characteristic of that paper." But the Nor' Wester had but a short life; and on September 16, 1885, still another newspaper was started — this time the Calgary Tribune, which survived for ten years.

On July 2, 1885 the Herald hope was realized and subscribers read: "Today notes the first issue of a daily paper in Calgary. Slight as the proportions of the first paper are, they are not much less than those of Winnipeg's first daily and it is hoped that presently they will be enlarged as the Winnipeg Daily Free Press was enlarged."

In time other papers with Calgary datelines made appearances — the Albertan, which was to serve the city and district for many years; the Eye Opener with a spectacular reputation, and so on — each a chronicler of frontier character and history. None, however, could encompass such time and story as the Herald, from among whose countless recorded items of local history one may learn that:

"Dutch Al who worked around town last winter and Buckley the cowboy who played the bad western man have been treated to a hempen necktie for horse stealing in the neighborhood of Mussel Shell River." (Sept. 3, 1884)

"Mr. F. W. Haultain arrived in town last Wednesday, enroute to Fort Macleod where he will enter partnership with Mr. McCaul. Mr. Haultain is a rising young man and we feel sure he will make his mark in his new home." (Sept. 24, 1884)

"On Tuesday, the first train load of western cattle was shipped by the Northwest Cattle Company to the Old Country markets. The cattle range from three to five years of age and will weigh about 1500 pounds each." (Oct. 7, 1887)

"Mr. A. Blair collected and shipped twenty carloads of buffalo bones." (July 10, 1894)

"Chief Bull Head of the Sarcees was arrested and lodged in the barracks Monday for being drunk. This morning he was fined $2 and costs... Mrs. Bull Head gave an 'at home' and a lawn party on Centre Street Tuesday noon which was well attended by representatives of all the first families. Music and a little social hop were the entertainments." (Oct. 23, 1895)

Indeed, some of the best accounts of western development lie almost unnoticed in the columns of the early newspapers whose pages are now yellow and brittle from age. The pioneer editors were observant fellows who captured effectively the incidents, character and humor of the frontier. Unfortunately many copies of the pioneer papers failed to survive, but a few priceless files gather library dust and invite inquisitive souls to explore among their venerable pages.

Calgary's next adventure was local government. In this the newspaper played a leading part, even to the point of a fearless editor going to jail because of his stand on civic issues.

THE BEGINNING OF CIVIC GOVERNMENT

The Fort Calgary community was eight years old when the first steps were taken to provide local government. For that many years citizens lived secure from taxes, politics and progress, but 1884 promised from its beginning to be a year of change. In his New Year message the editor of the infant Calgary Herald noted that all the natural advantages enjoyed by the flourishing City of Denver were conspicuous locally. The Colorado centre — just like Calgary — had good water, opportunities in ranching and proximity to the mountains. And Calgary, the editor pointed out, had the added advantage of being close to "mineral fields." He was thinking about the mines at Silver City.

Before the end of the first week in the new year James Reilly, owner and manager of the incompleted Royal Hotel on the east side of the Elbow, circulated 200 hand bills announcing a "Public Meeting Tonight at 7.30 in the Methodist Church, To Consider Location of the Townsite, Bridges, and Other Local Matters. All are Cordially Invited."

Anything in the way of a public meeting was considered good entertainment at that period and church pews were full. Invited to state his reasons for calling the meeting, Mr. Reilly mentioned the need for a bridge across the Elbow and a civic committee to watch over the interests of the public until the place could be incorporated and provided with a proper Council. The ideas were well received and when the meeting reconvened the following evening it was agreed that a committee of seven citizens would be elected by ballot on the next Monday.

It was Calgary's first election and neither pony race on the main avenue nor Sarcee war dance at the riverbank could have aroused more interest. Twenty-four candidates were nominated — ten percent of the adult male population. In the balloting that followed every eligible voter voted and not more than a few voted twice. Enthusiasm ran high and Major James Walker, retired officer from the original force of Mounted Police, topped the poll with 88 votes. Other elected members of the seven-man committee were Dr. Henderson, G. C. King, Thomas Swan, George Murdoch, J. D. Moulton and Captain Stewart.

The committee's first formal business consisted of naming Major Walker as chairman and agreeing to take no bold action on other matters until a conference was held with Lieutenant-Governor Dewdney to discuss four issues of immediate importance: an allowance for a school, an increase from $300 to $1,000 as grant toward erection of a bridge, incorporation as a town and, finally, Calgary district representation in the Council of the North West Territories.

Meeting a few days later, the committee reported success "in getting $200 added to the grant for the bridge over the Elbow." It wasn't as much as hoped for but they'd be foolish committeemen if they wouldn't accept a gift of $200. At the same time, encouragement about incorporation was reported and a committee was named to take the census, a necessary preliminary to incorporation.

The census when completed showed 428 residents, but zealous organizers wanted at least 500 and by some means or another the population of 1884 went into the official records at 506.

But the path of progress is not without pitfalls; and at this point Calgary's civic committee experienced its first financial crisis — a bill for $17.40 from the Hudson's Bay Company for "powder and flannel used in firing the mid-day gun" — and had no funds with which to pay anybody. When Committeeman

George Murdoch called on Col. Steele of the Mounted Police and asked that one of the cannons at the fort be fired every day at noon as a service to people who didn't have clocks, he hadn't anticipated the embarrassment of a bill for ammunition; but there it was — $17.40. The committee agreed the bill should be paid as soon as that much money accumulated and then, with traditional civic wisdom, decided to ask the government to furnish the gunpowder thereafter.

But the committee had another financial worry — a hundred dollars to be submitted with the application for incorporation as a town. The local press, still less than a year old, furnished an editorial "pep-talk" about Calgary's future, however, making it less difficult to collect the necessary number of dimes, quarters and 50-cent pieces and on April 15 the full amount of $100 was on hand and ordered sent to the seat of Territorial Government at Regina.

While awaiting the pleasure of the Lieutenant-Governor on the matter of incorporation, the committee concerned itself with many things — a fire guard to protect buildings and tents in the community, a public meeting to discuss "the advisability of organizing some fire protection," and other timely matters.

The Lieutenant-Governor's reply was delayed and members of the Committee became impatient. Some unpleasant words were used in discussing the Territorial administration, still dictatorial more than democratic. But on November 12, 1884, it was announced through the press that "The booming of Mr. Murdoch's gun on Monday afternoon ... proclaimed ... receipt of the telegram from Regina notifying the citizens of the issue on Friday last of the proclamation creating sections 14, 15 and 16, a town."

Progress was now on the march — no doubt about it — and it called for a local election, a real one. This time the Town would elect a mayor and four councillors and do it constitutionally.

Again there was no shortage of candidates. A properly constituted election was a new experience for many people and one man, by his admission, believed he had to be a candidate in order to have a vote.

The principal interest was in the contest for mayor; and when the ballots were counted on the evening of election day (Dec. 3, 1884), George Murdoch with 202 votes in his favor was far ahead of his opposition. Hence, that Scot who had driven from Maple Creek to Calgary in the previous year became the Town's first mayor. Elected with him were Councillors S. J. Clarke, N. J. Lindsay, J. H. Millward and S. J. Hogg.

On the day following the election the new Town Council met twice, once in the morning and once in the evening — meeting on each occasion in the rear part of Clarke's saloon. The first business consisted of appointing a Town Clerk and then steps were taken to draft bylaws to govern the conduct of the Council. At that time, too, the first official mention of the disagreeable word "taxes" echoed ominously above the clink of glassware in the adjacent room and the rattle of wagon wheels on the stony street outside.

Of that first civic year everybody said "a good one," and in December energetic George Murdoch was elected for a second term. By this time, however, unforeseen troubles were crowding in upon him. One of his councillors was in jail, having been sentenced to six months of hard labor by a newcomer magistrate who had already made himself very unpopular. Most citizens were on the side of the mayor and members of council who were visibly incensed by the magistrate's actions in pronouncing such a severe sentence for allegedly assaulting a mounted policeman and threatening him with a bottle held over his head. Something close to a state of warfare seemed to exist. All sections of the community writhed with anger and excitement.

It had begun about the time of the December election. Late at night two men in civilian clothes entered Clarke's saloon, stating that they were there to conduct a search. The councillor demanded to see their search warrant and when they failed to produce such, he ordered them out and may have applied some pressure, even in the face of a drawn revolver. Soon after, the ejected men returned with a posse of police and the fighting councillor was arrested for resisting.

At the hearing before Magistrate Travis, the weight of evidence seemed to be in Clarke's favor and the Mayor testified to the accused's good character. But the judgment showed small regard for the evidence and a storm of public indignation followed. A protest meeting was held and following it, with no diminution of belligerency, the magistrate warned the town lawyer who had spoken publicly about the case that he too might be sent to jail.

Another public meeting was called at Boynton's Hall and

speaker after speaker denounced conviction or the severity of sentence or both. It was decided that a deputation should proceed at once to Ottawa to plead for Clarke's release. And though it took weeks in the previous year to collect $100 needed to accompany the application for town incorporation, the people present at the indignation meeting subscribed $200 to help pay the delegation's travelling expenses, in a matter of minutes. Next day the sum was raised to $500.

And the Town Council, for purpose of the record, passed a resolution: "That this Council views with regret the decision of Stipendiary Travis in so far as he has passed a very severe and arbitrary sentence on one of our citizens who is a member of this council board. Our reason for knowing as we do that he acted on principle as a Councillor of this municipality and considered it his duty to take a stand so as to make a test case of the matter and have a final decision as to whether or not mounted policemen have the power to force their way into private houses and business places of citizens of this town without a search warrant or even their badge of office, which is their uniform. It is therefore resolved that in the opinion of this Council the sentence passed is very unjust, considering the fact the assault was simply a technical one and purely to test the law."

The mayor was one of those named to go to Ottawa to protest this judicial autocracy, but when he returned on December 20, 1885,he faced more trouble than ever. "Things in great muddle in civic affairs," he wrote in his diary. The magistrate, with more of zeal than judgment, was proceeding to unseat and disqualify the mayor and councillors of the town, just days after their re-election, for having, in supposed fulfillment of their duty, added names to the voters' list.

By this time, the editor of the Herald was in court trouble too. Having written editorial comment about the Clarke case, unfavorable to the magistrate, he was charged and ordered to apologize publicly and pay $100 costs.

Even the most moderate people agreed with an eastern magazine's comment that "The magistrate may be within his rights but it looks as if there is not room enough in one town for him and the people of Calgary."

Calgary's first civic year ended on a sour note. Indignation and confusion were noticeable everywhere. It might have helped some

THE BEGINNING OF CIVIC GOVERNMENT

if the well-meaning but worried councillors could have seen into the future, observed that 10 years later their Town of Calgary would become the City of Calgary, and 75 years hence their community, which they knew to have a population of 428 — by honest count — and civic debt of $17.40, would have a population exceeding 200,000.

AND THEN THE EDITOR WENT TO JAIL

The editor's name was Cayley — Hugh St. Quentin Cayley — and in one way or another he accounted for a lot of Calgary history during the late '80's.

Before a year elapsed Armour and Bredin, who started the Calgary Herald, were joined by Toronto-born Cayley. He was a graduate of the University of Toronto, and after working as a city reporter for the New York Tribune he practised law at fabulous Silver City in the Rockies. Although small in stature, this Cayley was mighty in oratory and vigorous in his views about justice.

In May of 1885 the three-man Herald partnership was disolved, the business to be carried on thereafter "under the name of H. S. Cayley who assumes all the liabilities of the late firm and to whom all debts owing the late firm are to be paid."

Late in 1885 George Murdoch was re-elected for a second term as mayor, with a big majority over James Reilly. Murdoch's good leadership, it seemed, was commanding appropriate recognition. But as men in public life are sure to discover, political climate can change like Calgary weather. As Murdoch celebrated the New Year in 1886, there wasn't much to warrant cheer. One of his aldermen was still in jail; his friend Editor Cayley was on his way to jail; the town solicitor was being warned that he might land in jail; the Mayor and Council were facing disqualification, and citizens generally were hopping mad. Events had become steadily more tempestuous since that November day when popular Councillor Clarke was sentenced to six months imprisonment with hard labor for evicting men in civilian clothes when they entered his premises to search for contraband whiskey. The main criticism was at Travis — Stipendiary Magistrate Jeremiah Travis — for what some people were calling "judicial tyranny."

Months earlier Editor Cayley had expressed a reasonable hope that the magistrate to be assigned to Calgary would be a westerner with an understanding of the Territories, instead of some stranger from the remote East. As it turned out, the appointee was a Nova

Scotian, a stranger to western ways, and Cayley found good reason to criticize in clear and caustic terms.

But Travis struck back, dismissed Cayley from the position of Clerk of District Court and charged him with contempt of court. The magistrate then ruled that Cayley must apologize to the Court, publish the apology in his paper, present the Court with 25 copies and pay $100 in costs of the trial "before Tuesday morning."

But Cayley, like Clarke, believed it was his right and duty to resist injustices and was in no mood for apologies. Came Tuesday and at eleven o'clock "His Honor stated that as Mr. Cayley of the Herald has not appeared to make apology, the period over which the mercy of the Court extended has now closed." The vengeful magistrate's judgment was a fine of $500 or, in default, a jail term of three months and a fine of $200.

On January 5 Cayley went to jail. And while his case was on everybody's tongue, a small faction led by James Reilly laid complaint about the recent civic election, charging that the Court of Revision had, with authority of Mayor and Council, added names of non-property-owners to the voters' list. The petition prayed that George Murdoch should be declared ineligible to take his seat as Mayor and Reilly declared elected by certificate of the court.

As the case proceeded it became clear that Murdoch wasn't even in town when the offending names were added to the original voters' list and his associates swore he did not in any way influence their actions which they believed to be proper procedure. But the magistrate seemed determined to ruin certain leading citizens and run the Town. He ruled to amend the returning officer's official statement, declared "James Reilly duly elected as Mayor and Soules, Bannerman, Grant and Davidson as Councillors." And while unseating the elected representatives, the magistrate, for good measure, imposed a fine of $100 on each of the Councillors and $200 on the Mayor and disqualified all from holding public office for two years.

Calgary people were mad before. Now they were almost ready for rebellion — the very idea, a magistrate attempting to "rule the town by means of a family compact." The police were prepared for violence but there wasn't much of that, except that the rivals, Murdoch and Reilly, met one evening on a secluded path. Angry words were followed by a private punching match but, as far as anybody could learn, it ended in the same sort of deadlock as was stifling the Town's administration at that time.

The Herald, on February 6, 1886, stated that "The auction sale of Mr. Murdoch's goods by the sheriff to pay the fine Mr. Murdoch refuses to pay, has been postponed for two weeks." The same issue reported the most recent mass meeting of angry citizens. Boynton's Hall was "jammed from end to end." It was the biggest meeting that Calgary had seen up to that time.

But the temper of the meeting mellowed somewhat by a message from the Minister of Justice ordering Cayley's release from jail, with remission of fines. At once the assembled crowd authorized the chairman to send a telegram to the Minister: "At a mass meeting held at Calgary tonight it was unanimously resolved to tender you the thanks of the citizens and residents of Calgary for the prompt release of Mr. Cayley and the recognition thereby on the part of the Government of the liberties for which the people in this distant part of the Dominion are struggling."

There were three cheers for the Minister of Justice, cheers for George Murdoch, cheers for Cayley.

"It is surely a grave thing," said an editorial, "to reflect on the bitter feeling that has crept into the heart of the town, gathering strength week after week since Travis came among us, until now it has reached the point of jesting at his efforts to enforce the decisions."

At the beginning of April it was announced that Judge Taylor of Winnipeg had been appointed to look into the differences between the Stipendiary Magistrate and the people of Calgary. In due course Clarke was released from jail and about the same time there was rumor, received with joy, that Travis would be replaced be Judge Roulean from Battleford.

Travis was as unrepentant as he was unpopular. The investigation dragged on while business in Calgary came almost to a standstill. Moreover, the town was virtually without government. In a sense there were two Mayors and two Councils — one elected and the other appointed — but neither faction could muster a quorum and hence no constituted meeting was held between December 23 and April 3, just over three months. It was an unfortunate year for local government, but recovery was rapid.

Weeks after the editor was released from jail there was a Territorial election and Hugh St. Quentin Cayley was one of two elected to represent Calgary on the Council of the North West Territories. The stigma of jail might have been seen as a political handicap but it wasn't. People voted for him because he was a man of principle. In each of 1887, '88 and '91 he was re-elected and, ultimately, he was elevated to the bench.

As the year 1886 was drawing to a close the Council of the North West Territories got around to authorizing a special civic election to end the paralyzing deadlock in Calgary. New names were submitted to the electors. G. C. King who had been part of the Calgary community from its beginning, defeated John Lineham for the office of Mayor, the vote being 195 to 172. With a new Council, civic administration returned to normal. A budget was drawn up and Major James Walker was awarded a contract to construct some plank sidewalks.

"It was a terrible year," an old timer said with a chuckle. "It was a wonder there weren't more black eyes. But we soon forgot — even forgave Travis after a while."

THE DARK DAYS OF '85

It was Sunday evening at the end of March, 1885, and, as anyone sitting in the congregation at Calgary's little Methodist church would sense, fear gripped the community. Rev. Joshua Dyke was more grave than usual. He was trying to hide his anxiety but it wasn't possible. He announced the source of his text: "Are not two sparrows sold for a farthing, yet not one of them falleth to the ground without your Heavenly Father's notice. Fear not, therefore, are ye not of more value than many sparrows?"

Everybody knew that Louis Riel, who had led the half-breed insurrection at Red River 15 years before, was back among his own people on the South Saskatchewan and unrest was growing to hostility. The Mounted Police were aware of the dangerous situation. As to the consequences of an uprising at that time, much would depend upon the attitude of the Indians. If they decided to take to the war-path in sympathy with their half-breed relations, they could annihilate the white population in places like Calgary, Medicine Hat and Lethbridge.

After the first clash between the Mounted Police under Major Crozier and the half-breeds under Gabriel Dumont near Duck Lake on March 26, the alarm travelled rapidly. The Ottawa Government, with the murder of Thomas Scott at Fort Garry fresh in memory, acted promptly. Before many days, General Middleton and an impressive field force were on the way west, prepared to shoot it out with any group threatening the peace of the frontier.

Superintendent Herchmer was in charge of the Mounted Police garrison at Calgary, but when he was ordered to accompany Commissioner Irvine to Prince Albert, Calgary people had a terrifying feeling of defencelessness. There were the Blackfoot Indians not far to the East, Stoneys to the West and Sarcees almost on the town's outskirts. Why wouldn't the Indians, forced to accept a restricted reservation life they hated, seize such an opportunity to rid themselves of the white interlopers? It was known that Riel's scouts and runners bearing gifts of tobacco visited the prairie tribesmen as far west as the foothills urging them to the warpath.

Who could judge the possible result? People attending the church service knew that George Murdoch, the town's mayor, had called a special meeting to discuss the danger, then taken immediate steps to count the rifles available. But at best, the small preparations townsfolk could make would be sadly inadequate if the nearby Indians decided to rise. Everybody in Joshua Dyke's congregation knew it.

Senator Richard Hardisty, with high forehead, bushy eyebrows and penetrating gaze, was sitting with his wife immediately in front of the pulpit. Also in the pews were James Lougheed (later Senator Lougheed), H. B. Douglas, W. H. Cushing, Andrew Armour and wife, a few mounted policemen who were off duty, and some members of ranch families who had moved to town for reasons of better safety. And standing at the door was T. B. Braden, a founder of the first newspaper.

Midway through the sermon, Mr. Grant of the hardware store appeared in the doorway, whispered something to Mr. Braden who immediately walked up the aisle and whispered the message to Senator Hardistry. The Senator seized his hat and walked out. In a few minutes, 20 or 30 men did the same. The congregation throbbed with inquisitive unrest and the preacher had no less trouble in keeping his mind on the sermon.

As Rev. Dyke recalled it years later (Cal. Herald, July 16, 1902), he folded his notes and said, "Dear friends, there is no need for excitement or fear. I know that reports have reached us that bands of Blackfeet have been seen making towards Calgary today. I do not believe the report. There are two missionaries on the Blackfoot reserve and no Blackfeet with hostile intent could leave in any numbers without their knowledge. They would warn us."

The minister, having tried, unconvincingly, to set those who remained in the church at ease, resumed the sermon. But it was of no use and abruptly he pronounced the benediction. When he and others walked from the church to the hardware store, they saw men arming themselves with revolvers and guns. At the same moment, Mayor George Murdoch and Old Soldier and Ex-Policeman James Walker were swearing in 14 special constables and directing them to patrol the outskirts of the town, day and night. The mayor would take his turn at night duty.

Yes, there were valid reasons for fearing a Blackfoot attack, and if it happened it would be a bloody thing indeed. Better to be ready to offer all the resistance possible, the men were saying. It was a fear-filled night, and men and women went to bed or went to patrol assignments wondering what might happen before morning.

But the night passed without incident. Tensions were only a little relaxed next day and steps were taken to organize a Home Guard unit under the command of Major Walker. Mayor Murdoch, in his diary, mentioned swearing in 104 men for the Home Guard in one day.

Major-General Strange, retired soldier turned rancher and operating the Military Colonization Ranch downstream on the Bow River, was called back into service. Arriving at Calgary, he found "quite an excitement" caused by the rumors of a Blackfoot raid. Strange, authorized to act for the government, went immediately to the nearby reserves and made arrangements for increased beef rations, hoping that red meat would make the Indians forget their hostility.

But the news from the North was not reassuring. On April 2, Big Bear's Crees attacked at Frog Lake, killing nine men and taking the women prisoners. It was reported, moreover, that a thousand Indians were ready to attack Edmonton. Calgarians shuddered, knowing the danger was constant and an army from the East could not arrive for days.

The Indians were scarcely impressed by the stories of a white man's army. It was not overlooked, however, that the native people might listen to their friends, and Father Lacombe and Rev. John McDougall were urged to use their influence. The Methodist missionary went among the Crees, and the "black-robed voyageur" to Chief Crowfoot of the Blackfeet. The result was good. Crowfoot promised the priest that his people would not rise and would not join with Riel. The residents at frontier Calgary breathed more easily.

At mid-April the army from Eastern Canada arrived. The general plan called for one of its columns under General Middleton marching northward from Qu'Appelle; a second under General Otter leaving the railroad at Swift Current and marching to Battleford; and the third under General Strange going from Calgary to Edmonton and eastward.

At Calgary, tents whitened the landscape. The town looked more like a military camp than the centre of a peaceful ranching community. The 65th Battalion from Montreal was being joined by various western units and a detachment of Mounted Police from Fort Macleod.

On April 20 Calgary saw General Strange start north with the right wing of his Alberta Field Force; and a few days later, Major Perry with the left wing. Citizens were sorry to see them go. While the soldiers were camping at the town, Calgarians felt secure. When the imported soldiers departed, however, and with them many of the able-bodied residents who volunteered for army service or hired to do transport duty, people remaining were understandably uneasy. Anybody with a team and wagon or anybody who could drive a team of horses had opportunity of earning better wages in the transport service than he had ever received before.

Though a skeleton force of Mounted Police remained and there was still a depleted Home Guard, Calgary had some of the characteristics of a deserted village and was again exposed to danger if Indians decided to rid their country of intruders.

General Strange's force made the journey to Edmonton in 11 days and continued eastward toward Frog Lake to capture or engage the perpetrators of the massacre at that point. Big Bear's Indians made a stand at Frenchman's Butte and Strange's army attacked. But the natives had the advantage of strength and better positions and the white army withdrew for reinforcements.

In the meantime, Middleton's soldiers met the half-breeds at Fish Creek and later gained a clear cut victory at Batoche beside the South Saskatchewan River. A few days after Batoche, Louis Riel was captured and taken as a prisoner to Regina. The back of the so-called rebellion was broken and settlers at Calgary and elsewhere relaxed, knowing the insurgents had been chastened and the danger of Indian attack had passed.

In due course Chiefs Poundmaker and Big Bear were captured. Louis Riel was tried in Regina and sentenced to be hanged. The Calgary men marched home in triumph. On September 8 the sentence of hanging was carried out, and what Canadians called the rebellion became history. Many people in Calgary and elsewhere agreed, however, that Riel's neglected half-breeds had legitimate grievances; that if the Indians had risen in sympathy with their part-Indian relations the bloodshed might have been terrible; and that the general strategy in directing military operations wasn't good. Many observers contended that if the militia had been placed under Mounted Police command instead of the police being placed under the unpopular and strongly imperialistic General Middleton, the trouble would have ended more quickly.

Anyway, the Home Guard was disbanded; General Strange returned to his ranch on the Bow River; Major Walker turned his attention to lumbering and other private interests; Cappie Smart reported back for volunteer fire brigade duty; and Rev. Joshua Dyke conducted a thanksgiving service, completely free from interruptions and worries.

COMMANDER OF THE HOME GUARD

There wasn't much to bring cheer in those dark days of '85 when the spectre of Indian uprising hung like a black cloud over Calgary. But, at least, local people felt more secure when they knew that Ex-mountie James Walker, who understood Indians and knew all about military tactics, was organizing local defence.

Unhesitatingly he had taken charge, recruited a group of 109 special constables, instructed them on handling rifles, and announced that he would be responsible for patrolling the area between the Highwood and Red Deer Rivers. Sitting in a saddle as though he were welded to it, he rode night and day during the period of greatest danger.

"When are you going to stop to eat a real meal?" George Murdoch asked him; and the reply was, "When the Blackfeet and Sarcees have washed the war paint off their faces."

If Calgary's people had been called to name a "Man of the Hour," the honor, unquestionably, would have gone to the ramrod-straight Mounted Policeman who had turned to business and then back to public safety.

Calgary people knew him intimately from 1881, and in the years following they were to know him as a man whose fingers were in nearly everything. At one time or another this member of the first detachment of Mounted Police to come to Fort Macleod was a soldier, rancher, lumberman, homesteader and contractor. He built Calgary's first sidewalks, built bridges and hotels. When Calgary's first Civic Committee was elected prior to the town's incorporation, Major Walker was the person chosen to be chairman. When Calgary had its first fair in 1886, the same man was president. It was he who selected the site for the Exhibition Grounds; he was the first immigration agent at Calgary; and when the Southern Alberta Old Timers' and Pioneers' Association was organized in 1920, Walker, quite appropriately, became its first president. The ex-Mountie was a good man for his community.

When James Walker became a Westerner, he became a good one. For 50 years following his arrival, nothing could draw him away except a war. But when fighting started the Major just had to go. He saw service in several theatres of war, and although he was 68 years of age when the First Great War broke, he was annoyed because authorities refused him permission to raise a regiment and take it to France. When his plan was blocked he accepted a compromise and went overseas as a captain in the Forestry Corps, returning at war's end at age 73. His soldiering record prompted General Sir Arthur Currie to remark that "Walker is a man who breaks out every 50 years and goes to war."

He was born in Wentworth County in Ontario in 1846. At 20 years of age he entered Military School in Toronto and when there was threat of Fenian raids he volunteered for duty and served in the Niagara Peninsula. In 1873 he was at Royal Military College at Kingston, attending Gunnery School under the direction of Colonel G. A. French. It marked the beginning of an important association between teacher and pupil because French was about to be appointed to take command of the North West Mounted Police being created for service in the far West where whiskey trading was profitable and law and order were practically unknown.

Walker applied and on March 30, 1874, he was appointed to be a superintendent and sub-inspector with special duties in recruiting and organizing. Selection of horses for the force was in his hands, also.

In June of that year two special trains carrying the rookie policemen and their horses and equipment left Toronto. Walker was still in charge of the horses. Travel was by way of Chicago to Fargo in North Dakota. At the latter point the Mounties and horses left the railroad and took to the 150-mile trail leading to Fort Dufferin, just inside the Manitoba border. The horses were green and so were the men. And with belligerent Sioux Indians lurking in the region, the newcomers found their sleep a bit disturbed as they made night camps along the way.

At Fort Dufferin the force from the East was joined by a group from Fort Garry and plans were drawn for the great adventure — the march across nearly a thousand miles of uninhabited prairie. One of the first tests of the Walker fibre came with a mad stampede of police horses before the cavalcade left Dufferin. Two hundred and forty-two horses were corralled in a ring of covered wagons when a midnight storm broke over the camp. Sir Cecil Denny recorded that it was one of the worst storms he had experienced anywhere. With violent wind and canvasses flapping from wagons, pandemonium broke loose and so did the frantic animals. Horses dashed through the barriers of ropes and carts and wrecked the police tents. A few men were injured.

Walker had not retired for the night, and as the horses galloped over tent-ropes he managed to catch one of the despairing creatures. Saddling that horse and mounting, he followed the galloping brutes through darkness broken now and then by flashes of lightning. There were no fences to worry about, fortunately, and the terrified band dashed south in the general direction of Pembina. The wild ride continued mile after mile and took Walker nearly as far as Grand Forks in North Dakota, almost 60 miles from Fort Dufferin, before he could begin gathering horses for the return drive. Before getting back to camp, 24 hours after the storm struck, he had ridden five different mounts and travelled an estimated 120 miles in wet clothes. But he returned with all the police horses except one, which never was located.

Walker's experiences while in the Force were many and varied. Almost singlehanded he faced truculent Chief Beardie and his painted followers and instructed them to retreat or he'd shoot. Such was the Walker courage. He had no qualms about riding out alongside Lieutenant-Governor Dewdney with a hundred thousand dollars in one-dollar bills to pay treaty money one year.

On February 1, 1881, Walker resigned from the Mounted Police to devote himself to ranching — to become manager of the newly formed Cochrane Ranch west of Calgary, first big outfit to invade the grasslands east of the Rockies. In his new position he received the initial Cochrane herd of 3,000 cattle driven from Montana. Pioneers tell that Walker, about this time, inaugurated a new mail service between Fort Macleod and Calgary. Riding in from Montana he stopped at Fort Macleod to enquire for mail and was informed that it had been sent on to Fort Calgary by ox-powered freight wagon some ten days before. Overtaking the bull train plodding along close to the Highwood River, he made up his mind that Calgary needed something better than this and his efforts led, almost immediately, to a service with two deliveries a month and a mailman called Hugill.

After two years with the Cochrane Ranch, Walker resigned this time to work for himself. Quickly he became the best known figure in and about early Calgary, as his elevation to the post resembling that of reeve or mayor in Calgary's first civic committee would indicate.

In 1881 he took a homestead on the Bow River in the present East Calgary and there he was making his home when the troubled community handed him the task of directing home defence as the Riel trouble broke. One of his main interests at that time was his saw-mill, started to furnish lumber for homes and the advancing C.P.R. The operation of that mill beside the Elbow River gave him another Calgary distinction, that of being the first to embark upon any form of manufacturing enterprise.

And two years before the "dark days" Community Builder Walker called a meeting of citizens from which came Calgary's first public school. For the next 18 years he was a member of the School Board. The little frame school made from lumber cut in Walker's mill was situated on Atlantic Avenue; and, unfortunately, nothing now marks the place.

When danger was passed in 1885, the tall, dignified and friendly man whose black hair was parted down the centre of his well-formed pate, continued to be one of the Town's most conspicuous citizens. When the Militia Act was extended to include the Province of Alberta, Walker organized the 15th Light Horse Regiment and commanded it for the next five years. After the First Great War he was made Colonel of the regiment and about the same time his Indian friends made him "Chief Eagle That Protects." People, generally, called him the "Grand Old Man of the Defence Forces," and well they might because his was the longest military and police record anybody could remember. He had joined a defence unit in Ontario at the age of 18, and he was connected one way or another with soldiering for the next 70 years.

Colonel Walker died in 1936. He was 90 years of age. Had he lived another three years and seen World War II spreading itself across Europe, he'd have wanted to go and there would have been trouble explaining why a 93-year-old shouldn't.

Perhaps the full significance of that name which he received with the honorary Indian Chieftainship was not fully appreciated by members of a younger generation. Certainly, residents of Calgary in the early part of 1885 would have understood — and appreciated — "Chief Eagle That Protects."

THE FATHER OF A CITY

After those two trying years highlighted by political crisis and fear of Indian attack, black-whiskered George Murdoch left the office of mayor to give full time to private business. He was still a community builder, however, and Calgary people acknowledged his right to be hailed the "Father of a City."

When he unhitched his tired team at Fort Calgary on May 13, 1883, he was 33 years of age and his trade was harness-making. Coming to this shapeless community straddling the Elbow was pure speculation and he wasn't sure he'd stay. At once, however, there was a compelling attraction. After pitching a dilapidated tent close enough to the police post to provide a feeling of safety, he wrote in his diary: "The finest natural townsite I ever saw."

Arriving three months ahead of the railroad, Murdoch found 200 people living within the shadow of the Mounted Police fort and deriving their livings from freighting, trading and herding cattle. Nobody had more than a little money but such a lack seemed of small importance. If a man couldn't pay cash for groceries the I. G. Baker store would accept furs, potatoes or a second hand rifle. And a man needing lumber could work for a few days in Major Walker's mill and take boards as settlement.

Murdoch's immediate enthusiasm for Calgary was that of a man who had already seem many parts of the world. He was born at Paisley, Scotland, and came to Canada with his parents when four years old. From St. John, New Brunswick, he went at the age of 18 to big and bustling Chicago, then considered "Western America." There he learned saddle and harness-making; there the young Scot had his own harness shop — until that fateful day when Mrs. O'Leary's cow kicked over a lantern and started a fire that left a hundred thousand people homeless. The Murdoch harness shop was in the path of the flames and the young proprietor, ruined financially, went back to New Brunswick.

After a few years he was travelling again, this time to seek fortune in Manitoba or somewhere beyond. Winnipeg wasn't attractive so he bought a team and wagon, loaded them on a freight and billed to the end of the railroad in the North West Territories. Regina, he observed, was "quite a town, with five harness shops." Moose Jaw's leading industry was shipping buffalo bones and Maple Creek marked the end of the rails.

On the morning of May 4, 1883, Murdoch unloaded his wagon and team and started westward from Maple Creek — drove 30 miles the first day. On the second day of wagon travel he was at Medicine Hat and crossed the river on a scow. After eight more days on the trail and eight nights beside it, he sighted Fort Calgary and camped for the night on the river bank, opposite the Fort. Next morning he forded the Bow River, tethered his horses beside the Fort and set about to get acquainted.

From that day until February 2, 1910, when the local paper reported that the "first mayor of Calgary died today at the residence of his son-in-law, Mr. Frank Collicutt," George Murdoch was one of the most devoted community builders.

Throughout the settlement Murdoch was greeted like a friend rather than a stranger, and the very next day he bought boards and scantlings at Major Walker's mill, put up a shanty 12 feet square and wrote in his diary: "The view of the Rockies is beautiful tonight. They seem about 10 miles off but are 45." And on the third day beside the Elbow enterprising George Murdoch placed a sign in the window of his shanty, announcing his trade: "HARNESS-MAKER."

Like other newcomers he gazed with admiration at the Mounted Police whose bright uniforms and unchallenged authority were constantly in evidence. But they, too, had their reverses, he noted in his diary. On the day he hung his shingle in the shack window, the Mounties answered a call from the Sarcee Indian Reservation and rode out proudly to make the necessary arrest. Humiliated,

Address

To Lt. Col. Amyot, Commanding at Fort Calgary and the Officers, Non-commissioned Officers, and Men of the Volunteer Force now in Garrison at Calgary

We, the Citizens of Calgary would be lacking in our duty if we did not attempt to show, in some way, our appreciation of your services to our Country———

You are not hired soldiers but citizens who have left peaceable occupations in your far-off homes, and have donned the caparison of war, to uphold law and order in this part of our Country. You have left your homes and have undergone the fatigue of some thousands of miles of travel over difficult roads and have submitted to every inconvenience and all the hardships incident to so long a journey without a murmur in order to reach here and protect us from the savage who surrounds us———

Some of you have forgotten kindred blood and as true patriots have listened alone to the call of your Country and the voice of duty.———

The people of Calgary wish you all success, and hope that you and comrades who have gone before you will soon return, crowned with the laurels of victory, and that our Canadian Nationality will be more firmly established than ever before through the noble and patriotic efforts on behalf of your Country of you and fellow-volunteers.

May 8th. 1885.

Signed on behalf of the Citizens

[signature]

Mayor of Calgary

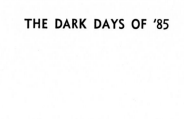

THE DARK DAYS OF '85

they returned without their prisoners. In apprehending the offending Indian braves the police were entirely successful, but at this point the squaws interfered and made it so hot for the police that the prisoners had to be released. It was woman's first major triumph in the new country.

Apart from police activities, the coming and going of freight wagons furnished most in public interest in that first summer. One day there was a bull-train of 63 oxen and 11 wagons arriving; another day, 80 oxen and 26 horses brought freight for G. C. King, and then the pattern was varied by arrival of a mule-train — six wagons and 24 mules.

But that was soon to change. Five weeks after Murdoch's arrival a Fort Walsh freighter drove in reporting that railroad builders were only a few miles out and creeping closer every hour. At once the harness-maker wrote to his wife in St. John to prepare to come to Calgary where they'd build the family home.

The grade and steel rails reached the east side of the Elbow and a construction train crawled uneasily to river's edge in what is now East Calgary. All except the men who lived by freighting were happy. The railroad promised to transform George Murdoch's adopted community. "Imagine," said George Clift King of the Baker store, "travelling to Winnipeg in three days by rail instead of a month by the trail."

Murdoch's first Christmas in the country was a quiet affair, his family being three thousand miles away. But he made the best of the situation, shared Christmas dinner with some of the other lonely males about him and served boiled tongue, plum pudding and a snifter of brandy.

Soon after the beginning of 1884 he was projected into civic politics. But both town planning and harness making ended abruptly on the evening of February 8 when word went from one cabin to another that a murder had been committed — a popular young fellow, James Adams, was murdered in McKelvie's store close to the west bank of the Elbow. It was Sunday night and cold, but excitement soared to fever pitch. Every able-bodied man turned out, eager to help catch the suspect, Jesse Williams. They found him after hours of hunting and tracking in the snow, caught up with him in a half-breed's shack at Shaganappi Point. Hot-heads were for lynching there and then, but George Murdoch was among those whose voice was clear: "No, there'll be no lynching; there'll be a fair trial."

There was a fair trial, there was a conviction, and finally a hanging. It was the first experience of that kind in the community, and until it was over there wasn't much enthusiasm for town incorporation.

As soon as people were willing to talk and think about other matters, George Murdoch undertook to get signatures on the petition to be sent to the Lieutenant-Governor. The names came easily and the list bore some familiar signatures — those of James A. Lougheed, James Walker, R. Hardisty, A. Carney, James Reilly, Thomas Burns, W. H. Cushing, G. C. King, W. B. McNeill, James Smart, John vfln Wart, Wm. Bredin, Archibald McNeill, and so on.

Undertaking to raise the necessary $100 in cash required to accompany the petition took more nerve, and time after time Murdoch heard, "You'll never get it." But the determined fellow didn't stop pestering people until he had the full amount. Actually, he was in almost everything. When the Agricultural Association was organized, he was a director; when there was a meeting to form a St. Andrew's Society, Scotty Murdoch emerged as president.

Incorporation having been granted, Calgary had its first constitutional election and George Murdoch was elected to be the first mayor. It was a lively election with more election fights than election speeches. But on election night there was a torch-light parade with the Mayor-elect carried shoulder high through the avenues. There being no such thing as an organization to support a candidate, election was in all respects a personal triumph.

When Murdoch's family arrived from the East there was a new log house awaiting. It was at the corner of today's 7th Avenue and 2nd Street East — across from where the City Hall now stands. To that home the friendly citizens turned out in a crowd to serenade the Mayor's wife and children with band music and fill the Valley of the Bow with welcome. Incidently, Mrs. Murdoch brought a means of music with her — the family piano — first of its kind in Calgary.

There the family home remained until 1892 when the Murdochs went to live on their homestead a mile north of where the Union Packing Plant stood later.

Like every Mayor, Murdoch hoped his years in office would be peaceful. Actually, they were not peaceful. The period of half-breed unrest south of Prince Albert imposed serious problems of local defence, and at one point even the Mayor was getting his rifle in shape "in case of emergency," and taking his turn as a sentry for night duty. It was a grim chapter in the life of the young town but the danger passed without bloodshed in the district. For the balance of that summer he was helping to organize one pioneer project after another. On April 11 he was swearing in Calgary's first school trustees; on April 24, swearing in G. C. King as first postmaster; on August 25, organizing a volunteer Fire Brigade, and so on. And periodically he was on the Chief Magistrate's bench listening to charges of reckless driving with buggies or the age-old mistake of imbibing too freely.

Moreover, the harness business flourished. Every settler needed horse collars and tugs and bridles. Murdoch erected an imposing building on Atlantic Avenue, and in 1889 saw it destroyed by fire. But he built again. George Murdoch was by nature a builder.

In his later years he suffered from paralysis. Activities were curtailed but he continued to drive down Stephen Avenue in the family phaeton to be greeted by all who saw him. To the Indians he was the "Leather Man," to most Calgarians he was "George." To historians he will be the "Father of a City."

THEY HELD A FAIR

Many of the people who came from Ontario regarded a Fall Fair as a mark of high achievement and community maturity. It was highly desirable, therefore, that such an event be held as early as possible.

Calgary's first fair occupied two bright October days in 1886 and offered competitions for everything from pure bred bulls to cinnamon bear skins and human babies of any shade. Five hundred people attended, which meant that just about everybody in the town and some from outside were present. Society President James Walker and the directors who had talked about such a venture for two years felt the thrill of triumph and resolved to make the Calgary Fair an annual event.

The parent organization was practically the same age as the incorporated Town of Calgary. Just months after the railroad reached the Bow River the Weekly Herald proposed that "farmers, cattlemen and merchants join hands" in forming an Agricultural Society. Such an organization, it was pointed out, could hold an exhibition to put an end to the annoying misrepresentations about Calgary's climate, soil and productivity. "No amount of writing can convince as readily as the exhibition of our produce," the editor added.

The idea was to exhibit farm products locally and then send them for display at Toronto to demonstrate for the benefit of Eastern Canada's hardened sceptics that this was not a "land of ice and snow."

Everybody agreed with the proposal; and on August 16, 1884, Boynton Hall, which was located across the Avenue northward from the present Queen's Hotel, was the scene of a meeting called to decide a course of action. If opposition was present it melted quickly after an announcement to the effect that agricultural societies could qualify for grants of $200 from the Council of the North West Territories. That was a lot of money — enough to buy all the lumber for a house. Earlier in the year it had taken nearly a month to collect the $100 needed to accompany Calgary's application for incorporation as a Town.

J. G. Fitzgerald was on his feet instantly to move "That it is desirable to organize an Agricultural Society for this district." Thomas Burns seconded the motion and everybody was in favor. Just as quickly it was agreed that another meeting would be held six days hence for the purpose of "enrolling members and electing directors." Before the meeting broke up, however, the acting secretary had another cheerful message — J. D. Geddes, who represented Calgary in the Territorial Assembly, would contribute $20; and James Reilly, George Murdoch and the Calgary Herald would each give $10 if a society were organized. That settled it; a society would certainly be formed.

Nobody with an ordinary mortal's limitation of vision could sense it at the time, but there and then the seeds were being planted for an Exhibition and Stampede having international interest and appeal.

At the organization meeting in the following week, 50 memberships were received — one dollar each — and officers and directors of the Calgary Agricultural Society were elected. Augustus Carney, who homesteaded the land which became Union Cemetery, was elected president and the list of directors included familiar names like John Glenn, J. G. Fitzgerald, T. B. Braden, Charles Geddes, James Reilly, Leo Gaetz, George Murdoch and Sam Livingstone.

Directors talked about holding a fair in the autumn, but decided for the first year to limit their program to a shipment of agricultural products for display at the Toronto Exhibition. Secretary J. G. Fitzgerald accompanied the exhibit and estimated that 150,000 eastern people saw it. Some hard-to-convince Ontario spectators enquired if the long straw seen in the sheaves of oats was genuine or if short straws had been spliced together to give the effect.

Although there was no fair in the first year of the organization, strange circumstances led to negotiations for a fair ground. A. M. Burgess, Deputy Minister of the Interior, was inspecting federal property at Fish Creek when he had the misfortune to fall off a playful horse and break a collar bone. As though the hand of fate was playing a leading part, Major James Walker, with strong views about the need for an agricultural fair and place to hold it, drove that way with team and wagon and rescued the injured civil servant and took him home.

While the man from Ottawa was in the poorest possible position to resist a benefactor's request, Walker mentioned the Agricultural Society's need for a place to hold fairs and pointed to Dominion Government land on section 10, beside the Elbow River, known today as Victoria Park. Being so far from the centre of the Town, Walker opined, it would never have any other value except for farming.

Before leaving Calgary Mr. Burgess and Major Walker inspected the land together and the government man promised to do what he could to make it available at small cost. The result was a triumph for Major Walker; the Agricultural Society bought the 94 acres at $2.50 an acre — a total of $235 for 94 acres now in the heart of the city.

It wasn't completely overlooked that the horse responsible for the Deputy Minister's fall and detention in Calgary deserved some of the credit. The Herald proposed editorially that the bronco, having performed such a fine service to the community, should be nominated for a seat in the Territorial Assembly at Regina.

The next was Rebellion Year in the North West and it was again Society policy to limit activity to a display for Eastern Canada. But in 1886, with Major Walker bringing characteristic drive to the office of president, plans were made to hold a fair with a $900 prize list. The dates would be October 19 and 20. Claxton's Star Rink was secured for the inside exhibits and the adjoining field for livestock and machinery, the new grounds on the Elbow not being available until later.

Came the day of the show. Livestock entries were light because of wet roads but quality was declared better than anybody expected to see. Major Walker and Leo Gaetz were the principal winners with grains and vegetables; and the Massey Manufacturing Company won the award for the best collection of implements suitable for the North West. The Mounted Police band furnished the trophy-winning music and President James Walker made a speech. Nothing was missing except a fence around the ground to keep non-paying visitors out.

Clearly, no useful home-grown products were overlooked by those who planned the first fair, and even the babies had their show. The baby class was called on the morning of the second day and though there were only a few entries — all boy babies — the judging problem proved more perplexing than any corresponding tasks encountered in the horse and cattle departments. When the contestants were summoned to the ring, the terrified judges tried to remain in hiding but finally were forced to face their duties. What happened next is best told by the Calgary Herald of October 23, 1886:

"After some futile attempts to ascertain the weight and age of the exhibits, the judges withdrew to the back of the stage, out of pistol shot range and came to the conclusion that the only way to avoid bloodshed was to award a prize to each competitor."

Directors co-operated, showing fine appreciation for the gravity of the situation. There being no entries in the sheep classes, extra prizes were transferred from sheep to babies. The result was a triumph for frontier resourcefulness. Every baby received a first prize; every parent was satisfied that justice had been carried out, and there was no shooting.

The fair ended at four o'clock on that second day because the building was booked for a political meeting. But with the general result everybody was satisfied.

For the next few years the annual fair grew steadily bigger but growth didn't ensure against financial difficulties. The growing debt turned out to be the grimmest chapter in society history.

To meet demands for improvements the directors borrowed $400, then $600 and $1000. By midsummer of 1889 the debt secured by mortgage on the property stood at $3000. Three years later the old mortgage was paid off with money raised with a new one for $4000 but the mounting liability was the forerunner of downfall. Unable to meet payments, the directors, in August, 1896, saw their creditors taking steps to sell the fair ground property. Foreclosure was completed on October 19, 1896, ten years to the day after the first fair was held.

To all appearances the Calgary Fair, notwithstanding its noble beginning, had about as much future as that of a rooster with its head cut off. If the Society couldn't succeed when it had a good ground for its use, how could it hope to operate without such? Only the optimists believed it would be revived.

CHINOOKS AND THE WINTER WITHOUT THEM

Nothing in the memory of early Calgarians stood out more vividly than the "bad winter" of 1886-87. The suffering and losses of that season couldn't be forgotten.

A succession of mild winters had given a false sense of security and ranchers and others were not prepared for the long spell of cold weather and heavy snows. To cattlemen who had come to consider it unnecessary to stockpile winter feed, it was the "winter without chinooks."

The mushroom-shaped rise in evening clouds over the southwestern horizon was one weather sign local people had come to recognize with familiarity and confidence. It was the "chinook arch," foretelling the coming of warm winds from that direction. Summer chinooks commanded but little attention; but when snow blanketed the countryside, folks seeing the arch proclaimed with joy, "Tomorrow we'll get a break." When the oncoming chinook followed a common pattern, temperature might rise 50 degrees in a few hours and a winter night give place to a spring-like morning with melting snow.

A newcomer to the country told about stepping outside on a cold winter morning. Suddenly a chinook struck. "I hadn't been out more than two minutes," he said, "when puff, puff, came the wind from the south-west, just like a fellow's best girl blowing red hot kisses at him through a stovepipe, and in less than five minutes jewhillaken — down she came, a regular howling, snorting, ring-tailer from away back, blowing like sixty. Well sir, I hadn't time to get off the platform before my feet were wet and in two hours our snow had entirely disappeared. The whole country was dry by noon and we had a prairie fire that evening."

It was a case of Pacific air moving inland, cooling, expanding and depositing moisture as it rose to pass the mountains, then becoming warmer as it descended along the eastern slopes of the Rockies. But the academic explanation was dull compared with the legends left by Indians and stories told by the Fort Macleod and Fort Calgary pioneers who tried to outshine each other.

An oft-told Indian tale begins with the native maiden, Chinook by name, and beautiful as all legendary maidens should be. It was winter time and, wandering alone in the mountains, she became lost. A weakness in the story is that one so beautiful and young would not be expected to travel "alone," not even in Indian society. Anyway, when Chinook failed to return to camp, all the young braves and many who were not so young turned out to search the mountain passes for her.

The hunt was of no avail; but as it ended, a warm and kindly breeze blew in from the snow-covered mountains to change winter into summer, and Indians, still sorrowing for the lost beauty, said, "Ah, 'tis the breath of our dear Chinook." And through the intervening years, Miss Chinook with unpredictability typical of a beautiful woman, continued to breathe her charm and warmth upon foothills and plains of Southern Alberta.

David One Spot, wise old man of the Sarcees, had a different explanation and it should be authentic because his grandfather travelled extensively in the Rockies and knew all the mountain secrets. According to the One Spot theory, the warm chinook winds originate as the breath of a monster wedged in a mountain cavern, with head toward the East.

To Indians of an earlier generation the big creature was the "Wind Maker." His ears were longer than the tallest spruce trees on the Sarcee Reservation, and when he was asleep, as he was most of the time, breathing was quiet and ears lay motionless along his back. But when the mountain monster was awakened, he would fan and beat with his ears so violently that the hot breath from his nostrils was driven across foothills and plains to send temperature upward. There was just one trouble — the big thing would go to sleep again and then the ears would cease to drive the warmth eastward and a chinook ended as suddenly as it came.

Less mystic but no less dramatic were the chinook stories from the pioneer years of settlement. Some of the favorites were attributed to that prince of story-tellers, Dave McDougall, Morley trader, who was the first man to take a cart on a straight line from Calgary to Winnipeg. He was supposed to have told about Stoney Indians attending a meeting at the Morley Church. Because snow was extremely deep the only object to which they could tie their horses was the church spire. But while the meeting was in progress, the chinook wind came up and melted the snow. When Indians came to get their horses for the drive home they found the unfortunate animals hanging by the tie-ropes from the church spire — horses and sleighs dangling in mid-air like plumb-bobs swinging from a rafter. If it can be proven that the old Morley church had no spire, then it must have been a flag-pole from which the horses were suspended when the snow disappeared.

Some exaggeration in the description of chinooks should be pardonable. Often the warm winds seemed too good to be true, especially to people who were exposed to the talk about the West being a "land of ice and snow." Chinooks gave the South-West a double attraction for cattlemen because they not only moderated the cold seasons but extended the periods when winter grazing was possible. Nobody could fully appreciate the sense of relief that a chinook arch brought to stockmen who saw their ranges blanketed with snow and feed reserves dwindling dangerously.

Ranching on the plains and foothills was still in its infancy when that memorable winter of 1886-87 struck so disastrously. It was all very well to tell fantastic stories about the maiden Chinook and about Dave McDougall's famous race with a Calgary chinook, in the course of which he could barely keep the front runners of his sleigh on snow while rear runners were stirring up dust all the way. But not much romancing about chinooks came out of that grim winter.

As autumn was yielding to winter the amateur weather prophets — present in all generations — were assuring settlers of good weather ahead. Even Father Lacombe allowed his forecast of a mild winter to get into the records. But to confound the prognosticators the weather turned severely cold in November and heavy snows fell in December. By mid-January, with no effective chinooks, fuel and feed supplies were dwindling alarmingly.

The Bow River was reported to be frozen to the bottom and stage coaches from Fort Macleod and Edmonton were coming in from one to two days behind schedule. Nobody envied the drivers whose noses seemed to be frozen perpetually.

One of Mayor King's chief worries was the threat of fuel shortage in the town. All available men with teams were encouraged to haul wood for stoves. But with hay supplies getting low and no oats, many of the horses became too thin and weak to haul loads of wood. Only a few residents made it a practice to use coal for heating but the available stock was quickly bought up. Everything possible was done to conserve fuel in the face of threatening crisis — even to closing the school for a few weeks.

The cattlemen, however, were in the most serious position. Every citizen of the town shared concern because there was a sense of nearness to the expanding ranching industry. The price of hay soared to $16 a ton and by mid-February — still no chinook of any account — the stacks were about exhausted. Cattle — their ribs protruding pitifully and their bony backs humped — drifted aimlessly. Some, with nothing to eat except the twigs from trees along the rivers, wandered into the town. Some of the poor, anaemic creatures died or froze right on Calgary streets. Even a few half-starved white-tail deer, having lost the usual fear of humans, drifted into the community looking for feed and shelter.

It was a grim chapter but it ended and ranchers counted their losses. Around Calgary the death loss in cattle was placed at 25 percent, somewhat lower than at Fort Macleod. For some cattlemen it was crippling; for all it was a lesson about hoping for the best and preparing for the worst. The chinook had lost none of its charm and welcome but nobody could really depend upon it.

That there was an occasional bad winter nobody could deny, but foothills weather — varied and uncertain — gave Calgarians some reason to brag, and even from the early years the answer to the critic, always with a smile, was: "If you don't like the weather, just wait a few minutes and it may be different."

TRAILS AND RAILS TO THE NORTH

Progress and all its civilizing changes were on the march and on July 21, 1890, Calgary was the scene of an epic sod turning. Two thousand eager citizens, a brass band, the local fire brigade and a highlander with bagpipes were present for the moment when Hon. Edgar Dewdney, Minister of the Interior, lifted the first sod in the construction of the Calgary-Edmonton railroad.

After the shovelful of soil was duly turned and somebody expressed well chosen words about coming prosperity, the Calgary people and their guests turned their attention to a carcass of ox, roasted whole, and waiting to be consumed. Big appetites were then the rule and no part of the ox remained except bones and a few sinews. As far as a student can judge, the only discordant note in an otherwise happy program was a public objection from one, Thomas Smith of Edmonton, to a remark that the Calgary area was equal to the best. It wasn't, the man from the North insisted; Edmonton's soil was superior and so were the products grown there. But the Calgary crowd was in a benevolent mood that day and there was no violence.

What should not have been overlooked, however, was that the events of the day signalled the end of the historic Calgary-Edmonton Trail — a rutted lifeline of 200 miles which had witnessed freight and transportation vehicles of almost every conceivable size and shape. Every adult munching barbecued beef on that midsummer day knew something about the romance and hardships associated with the "North Trail."

The Edmonton-bound trail traffic differed distinctly from that going south. For one thing, Red River carts — those two-wheeled, all-wood contraptions with dry axles screaming to be heard for miles — were quite conspicuous. The Calgary Herald might note in a commonplace manner that a freight train "composed of 16 carts went north to Edmonton today," and just as often, the Edmonton Bulletin would report something of the kind: "Seventeen carts of Ad McPherson's in charge of J. Westway arrived on the south side on Sunday, nineteen days out from Calgary. The roads are very bad for cattle, wearing their feet out rapidly and making quick travel impossible."

With a freight rate of eight to ten cents a pound, operators on the Calgary-Edmonton route found their business fairly attractive and the more progressive ones were seeking ways of enlarging their carrying capacity. The carts were inherited from the older trails, but bigger freight wagons began to gain popularity — two-horse wagons, four-horse wagons and six-horse outfits. Edmonton people were said to be rejoicing when, in December, 1884, "Two four-horse and two six-horse teams belonging to Ad McPherson" were expected to arrive in good time "with loads of green apples, fresh oysters, whiskey and other Christmas groceries" for the festive season.

The trail south of Calgary was famous for its huge ox-drawn freight wagons or bull-team outfits, but only a very few of those went over the softer ground northward. The first of their kind seen on the northerly route arrived at Edmonton in June, 1885, an I. G. Baker Company outfit comprising nine units. Each unit carried 7000 pounds of freight on two wagons hooked together and was drawn by 12 oxen. Thus, there were 108 oxen furnishing power for this particular "freight train." Seeing such a freight-moving outfit was a new experience for the people of Edmonton, but for the owners the result was not entirely satisfactory; owing to the soft ground the time was slow and the experts concluded that the Red River carts and small wagons were still best for this particular trail.

One of the mongrel outfits adding distinction to the trail went out of Calgary at the first of September, 1886, propelled by "three teams of horses, five pairs of oxen and one span of mules on the lead," all hitched together and all working like one big unhappy family.

The one-way trip to Edmonton with freight took anywhere from two to three weeks, although the stage coaches carrying passengers and mail did it in five days. In the mid-'80's the travelling

public enjoyed the convenience of a weekly service on the route
— two Concord coaches drawn by four-horse teams. One would
leave Calgary and the other leave Edmonton at the same time, pass
at the crossing two or three miles above the present City of Red
Deer and arrive at their respective destinations at the same time
— if they were fortunate. Each coach could accommodate four
passengers in the back part and one riding with the driver.

While Calgary was still without a newspaper, the Edmonton
Bulletin carried the stage coach schedule: "Edmonton and Calgary stage making weekly trips between said points leaves Jasper
House, Edmonton, Monday at nine, and the steamboat dock at
9.30, stopping at Peace Hills, Battle River, Red Deer Crossing
and Willow Creek, arriving at Calgary on Friday. Returning leaves
Calgary Monday, stopping at same places and arrives Edmonton
on Friday. Fare each way, $25.00. 100 pounds of baggage allowed.
Express matter 10 cents per pound."

Strangely enough, the two regular drivers over the route,
although unrelated, had exactly the same names; both were Pete
Campbell. For purposes of convenience one was "Little Pete" and
the other "Big Pete"; or one was "Northbound Pete," and the
other "Southbound Pete."

They were courageous drivers and often they were on time.
Delays could be expected, however, and sometimes mishaps.
Storms resulted in loss of time and occasionally there were accidents. Indeed, anything could happen along that 200-mile route
and over the years nearly everything did happen — broken wheels,
upsets, sick horses and even highway robbery on a story-book
scale.

The encounter with brigands occurred in the summer of 1886,
just four years before the sod was turned for the new railway. The
stage coach, with full complement of passengers and "Little Pete"
Campbell driving, was 18 miles out of Calgary when two bandits
stepped out on the trail and took complete command. The men
were armed with carbines and revolvers and wore masks made
from a Union Jack flag. They had been hiding in the long grass
close to the roadside and sprang up suddenly when the stage
horses were within ten or twelve feet from them. The stage stopped at once.

Driver and passengers were rudely ordered to come down and
march to a coulee. In the sheltered spot chosen by the gunmen the

victims were searched and their money taken. A newspaper report told that "The driver, P. Campbell, lost $200; J. Burns, Jr., travelling for Ashdown of Winnipeg, $70 but another seventy he had on him was overlooked; J. Clockey, representing the Massey Manufacturing Co., $30, and Mr. Gautier who had been working all last winter for Lamoureux Bros., $125."

Any way one viewed it, the total represented a tidy haul. After pocketing the money the robbers returned to the stage and went through the mail bags and luggage. Evidently they got nothing of value in the baggage and, somehow, overlooked the sacks of registered mail.

After completing their searches they unhitched the horses, mounted them and rode away, leaving driver and penniless passengers stranded helplessly on the prairie, somewhere north of where Balzac stands today.

The two highwaymen, with pockets bulging and good horses under them, rode north while within view of their victims and probably reversed the direction of flight as soon as they considered it safe to do so. As for Campbell and his stage passengers, they started southward toward Calgary on foot, dejected and totally unimpressed by the bit of glamour added that day to the story of the Calgary-Edmonton Trail.

Passenger Burns was the first to make his way to Calgary where he reported the costly experience. Mounted Police took to the trail at once. Fresh in their memories was a recent robbery on the Elbow River, and they suspected a connection between the two crimes. At the scene of the hold-up the police picked up the tracks of the fleeing robbers and followed until they came upon parts of the flag used for masks.

The police net was extended in all directions but not with much encouragement. No suspects were encountered — unless there had been reason to be suspicious of two strangers seen at "Clinker" Scott's cabin beside the Bow, west of Calgary. But Scott, who figured prominently in the Silver City mining debacle, assured the police the two strangers were his friends and had been there for days.

A day or two later, however, "Clinker" Scott was murdered in his cabin and the two strangers had disappeared. Speculation was rife. Was it that Scott couldn't be trusted with the secret of a hold-up on the Calgary-Edmonton Trail or was there a quarrel about the division of the loot? In any case, police pursuit continued as far as Denver, Colorado, but without success.

But the interruption to passenger transportation on the Trail was brief. On the morning after the robbery "Little Pete" was hitching for the journey to Edmonton — just 24 hours late.

Over the same twisty route went soldiers ordered to suppress rebellion in the year 1885; land-seekers like Stephan Gudmundsson Stephansson who became the great Icelandic poet of Markerville; nation-builders like Reverend Leo Gaetz who stopped at the Red Deer River in 1884; and people bound for the far north country like Sheridan Lawrence's family making the 900-mile trip to Fort Vermilion in 1886. The cart and wagon wheels turned slowly and perchance monotonously, but for nearly two decades that north-south trail was "Highway Number One" to the people living and travelling between the Bow and North Saskatchewan Rivers.

Now, things were changing. A month after the ceremonial sod was turned, a railroad grade being built by use of wheelbarrows and horse-drawn scrapers reached a point 40 miles north of Calgary. And in the meantime, railroad construction was bringing its boom-type prosperity to the community beside the Bow River. Men who chose to be tracklayers commanded $1.75 a day and those who could qualify as "spikers," $2.00 a day.

Until August, 1891, when the railroad was completed for operation, the Calgary-Edmonton Trail lost none of its lifeline character; but then, abruptly, most of the carts and wagons were abandoned at one end or the other — many to remain in obscure places until they rotted. Too late it was realized that the creaking carts and heavy wagons held sentiment and memories and some of them should have been preserved.

For the eyes of any who might be able to peer into the future Calgary and Edmonton felt the advantages immediately. For the cart and wagon drivers, however, those hardy and distinctive men who liked to sleep in their blankets beside the trail, the adjustments were difficult. Many of the men were half-breeds with French names and no other form of livelihood invited them. As the rails advanced they became displaced persons, in many cases going into semi-retirement in northern settlements where they would feel only a minimum of irritation from advancing civilization.

For the eyes of any who migh tbe able to peer into the future there were still bigger changes to be made along "The Trail". Not only would engineers produce a railroad, but they'd build a graded highway and then a super-highway for speeding traffic — right where cart and wagon wheels cut their deepest ruts. And if such were not enough, planes would fly back and forth many times daily to add to the story.

Perhaps Hon. Edgar Dewdney had a vision that day in 1890. He said it was not an ordinary sod-turning and insisted upon filling a big wheelbarrow with sods. Or perhaps he was just working up an appetite for the barbecued beef.

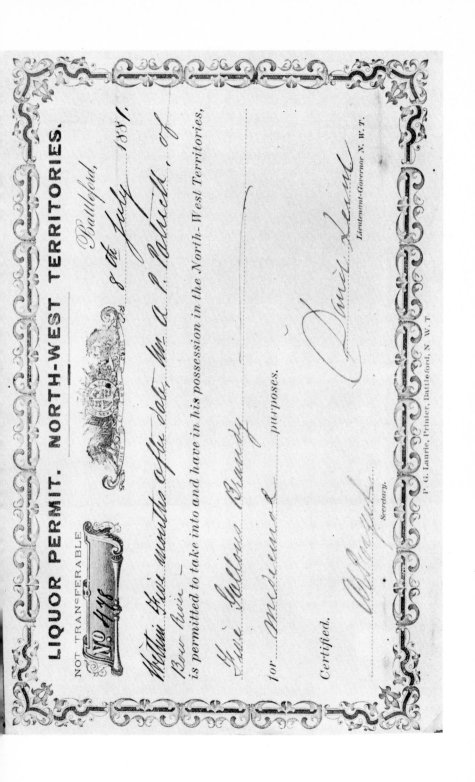

LIQUOR PERMIT. NORTH-WEST TERRITORIES.

NOT TRANSFERABLE

No. 146

Battleford,

_8th_ July 1881.

Within three months after date, Mr. A. P. Patrick, of

Beaw Rivei —

is permitted to take into and have in his possession in the North-West Territories,

Five Gallons Brandy

for _medicine_ purposes.

Certified.

_____ Secretary.

_____
Lieutenant-Governor N. W. T.

P. G. Laurie, Printer, Battleford, N. W. T.

THE BOOZE PROBLEM

THE BOOZE PROBLEM

Until 1891 — when James Reilly became Mayor and the railroad to the North began to operate — Calgary shared with other parts of the North West Territories the problems arising from hopelessly unenforceable liquor laws. One year before the Fort was built Ottawa had decreed that intoxicants could not be manufactured in or brought to the Territories except for medicinal purposes and by permission of the Lieutenant-Governor.

Calgarians, it was noted, were needing a lot of "medicine." The licenses to bring liquor in for medical use were a farce. "There is enough liquor brought into Calgary alone," an editor wrote, "to supply all Canada for medicinal purposes." When asked if there had been any haunted houses in Calgary, Bob Edwards of the Eye Opener replied that half the houses were formerly full of spirits, "their habitat being the cellar."

Whiskey and white men came to the South West almost simultaneously and the Indians were the unfortunate victims. Indeed, the demoralizing effect of trade liquor upon the susceptible natives was one of the primary reasons for organizing the North West Mounted Police. Many of the traders were ruthless fellows working out of Fort Benton, Montana, and the very first wrongdoer to fall into the police net was a whiskey pedlar, a dark skinned fellow named Bond, caught with the goods.

Chief Three Bulls reported exchanging two horses for two gallons of whiskey and a detail of policemen sent out to investigate returned with Bond and four other men, 16 horses and two wagons loaded with buffalo skins and liquor. Following charges the men were convicted and fined or jailed, the buffalo robes confiscated and the whiskey dumped on the snow.

What the Indians bought at a price of one buffalo hide for two cups of the stuff bore small resemblance to real whiskey. Always it was well diluted and sometimes its composition reflected ingenuity more than logic. A gallon of rum or alcohol, a couple of pounds of chewing tobacco, unstated amounts of red peppers or ginger, and some odds and ends like red ink or painkiller could be boiled and diluted with water to make five or ten gallons of trade liquor well deserving the name "firewater."

Rather quickly the police put a stop to the wholesale peddling among the Indians but complete prohibition was extremely difficult, if not impossible, to enforce. The new regulations were conceived with the best of moral intentions but neither prohibition law nor the presence of enforcement officers could remove men's desire for liquor and one degree or another of smuggling and illicit trading continued.

By far the biggest percentage of cases coming before Justice of the Peace George Murdoch grew out of drunkenness. And evidently it happened in the "best circles." "It is bad enough," wrote one of the editors, "for a civilian to get drunk and whoop about the streets but it is much worse for a policeman. We trust we shall not be obliged to speak of a similar occurrence again. But really, this blazing away with a pistol whenever a man gets drunk, whether it is in the hands of a policeman or a citizen is getting monotonous."

Some of the contraband was made in well-hidden stills in sheltered spots west and south west of Calgary but much of it came by freight train, marked "kerosene," "varnish," and "barn paint," or it might be concealed in barrels of oatmeal. Senator Lougheed told about a feed merchant bringing in a carload of bagged oats with a small keg of whiskey concealed in each sack. Another consignment, according to the Senator, consisted of iron safes with doors securely closed and the safe combinations known only to consignees who made enough from the sale of the liquid contents to pay for the safes.

In any case, the imported stuff sold for $5 a bottle and proof that the volume was large is furnished by a news item appearing in 1889, reporting that there were "16,000 empty bottles in the carload recently shipped to Winnipeg by Mr. McLeod."

It meant that the bootlegger was a pioneer in the area and every now and again in early years local interest was enlivened by some big haul made by the police. One of the first trains to arrive in 1883 brought about "40 gallons of whiskey and two dozen bottles of brandy, all nicely concealed in barrels of oatmeal. After it had been watched for about two days without anyone appearing to claim it, it was destroyed. At the rates usually charged this haul would have retailed for $2,000."

Weeks later there was a bigger seizure and Calgarians read that, "On January 2nd word was received at Police Barracks that the freight train which arrived the previous night had brought a number of suspicious looking barrels which had been left a short distance east of the Bow. Accordingly, Sergeant Dann accompanied by Constables Cudlip, Bell, Morgan and McCarty were dispatched to overhaul the barrels and if found to contain liquor to bring them in. After a ride of about nine miles they reached the Nineteenth Siding and found what to all appearances were eight barrels of pork lying on the prairie. On opening one of the barrels, the contents were found not to be pork but 144 bottles of liquor. A fresh trail was observable and following this a short distance, the police found three more barrels cached in the bush; pursuing the trail still further they came upon a log hut, well hidden by trees on the bank of the river. Here two cans of alcohol, three rifles and a quantity of ammunition were found, but no person was visible. The articles were appropriated and the police returned to the siding, loaded their spoil and started for the barracks which they reached after midnight. Each barrel contained twelve dozen bottles of very fair liquor, superior to any that has yet been captured. Had the persons for whom it was intended secured the liquor, the snug little sum of $8,000 would have been made, at $5 a bottle."

But in spite of the newspaper reports, some Calgary people doubted that the big consignment of illegal liquor was really destroyed. In acknowledging the high quality of the whiskey and pronouncing its superiority to that of other seizures, the newspaper man was ignoring the fact that he, in the ordinary course of events should not be in the position of sampler or judge. Story had it that many of the male members of the community joined in the searching effort to establish identity of the bottled liquid and by the time all concerned were ready to admit that, beyond all reasonable doubt, the bottled fluid was in fact whiskey, there was nothing left to destroy.

In later months when Calgary's Town Council was in existence, according to one pioneer with a good memory, the responsibility for testing seized bottled goods was sometimes referred to the Councillors, who found it necessary to retire behind closed doors to conduct the appropriate investigations.

By almost any standard the permit system was faulty, and the Mounted Police who had the responsibility of enforcement were among those who disliked it immensely. After Joseph Royal became Lieutenant-Governor in 1888, the Territories were granted a slight concession in the form of a mild beer — alcohol content under four percent — but it failed to silence the critics.

The elected members of the Legislative Assembly understood the weaknesses and unpopularity of sale by permit and called for substantial change. The change came in 1891 when amendments to the British North America Act gave the Assembly authority to deal with liquor questions. Steps were taken to abolish the permits and allow hotels to have licensed saloons, except where electors declared for prohibition.

Thereafter, Calgary had its bars — lots of them — some famous like the 125-foot bar at the Alberta Hotel, acknowledged to be the longest west of Winnipeg. The bars flourished until voters in the provincial plebiscite of July 21, 1915, declared in favor of a "dry" province, except for the sale of liquor on prescription from a medical doctor. It worked well for the bootleggers.

But as passing years were to show, there was no such thing as a "satisfactory" liquor law, and legislative change followed change —— sale by government vendors, beer parlours, and ultimately, a demand by plebiscite for still further outlets.

In 1891 they thought they had found the answer — but they hadn't.

"SANDSTONE CITY"

Calgary's first buildings — the fort, the I. G. Baker Company store, the Hudson's Bay Company store and some homes — were of log construction. That was perfectly logical, there being good building logs a short distance up the Elbow River. Not until 1881 when Major James Walker set up a saw mill on that stream was there any real change in structural methods. But logs and sawed lumber had one shortcoming in common: both were vulnerable to fire, a fact made brutally clear by the tragedy on November 7, 1886.

Like Chicago, London and St. John, the infant Calgary had its "great fire." It was Sunday morning and the fire started in a log structure on the north side of Atlantic Avenue and spread mercilessly from one tinder-dry wooden building to the next.

The town's volunteer "bucket brigade" bustled about with little effect while fire consumed 14 buildings including four stores, three warehouses, three hotels, a tinsmith shop and a saloon. Nor would the flames have stopped there had the citizens not pulled down George Murdoch's harness shop to create a fireguard. They tried at first to dynamite the Murdoch building but without success and then went at it with axes and ropes and dragged it away piece by piece.

Two lessons were clear — the need for better fire-fighting equipment and the benefit of stone or some other building material possessing more fire resistance than wood. Brick would have to be brought a great distance and would be expensive, but as already discovered, there were huge quantities of sandstone underlying much of the surrounding country. Immediately there were jobs for stone masons, and within the next year several quarries were opened, one of them by Thomas Edworthy in the big coulee on Shaganappi Ranch, west of the present Wildwood. Entering the same business were W. F. Orr, J. G. McCallum, William Oliver and others.

Sandstone was durable as well as fireproof. It had everything in its favor, it seemed, and stone masons working long hours were available at $1.50 a day. The prospective builder could buy stones cut and ready for use at $20. a cord. Sandstone popularity soared like a rocket and the Town Council considered a proposal to restrict all new buildings on the main avenues to sandstone construction.

The first big building to be constructed with the native stone was Knox Presbyterian Church. Started under the direction of Rev. Angus Robertson, who had arrived at Calgary a couple of months in advance of the railroad, it was completed in 1887. It was at the corner of the present Seventh Avenue and Centre Street.

Among the first sandstone buildings to emerge was the Court House, to serve the Judicial District of Calgary. Bearing date of 1888, it was the pride of McIntyre Avenue and 70 years later when there was decision to proceed with demolition, it was the architectural patriarch of Calgary's streets. It was the last place at which Judge James Farquharson Macleod held court before his death on September 5, 1894; it was the scene of many famous legal contests. If its stone walls and iron bars could speak, they'd have told about the widely publicized Ernest Cashel and Jumbo Fisk murder trials, and about the performances of some of Canada's greatest lawyers: the reasoned pleadings of Frederick Haultain, who became premier of the North West Territories; the sparkling wit of Paddy Nolan; the gentlemanly demeanour of Senator James Lougheed; and the oratory of R. B. Bennett, who became Prime Minister of Canada.

It is said that men calling themselves stone masons were so numerous in 1889, they might have elected a mayor and council of their own choosing. The centre of activity was at Stephen Avenue and Scarth Street (8th Avenue and 1st Street West, today) where construction operations resulted in almost complete traffic obstruction. Three of the four corners of that intersection received handsome sandstone buildings during the year — the Alexander Block on the northwest corner, the Bank of Montreal with its castle-like turrets on the northeast corner, and the famous Alberta Hotel on the southeast.

But structures which rate high in elegance today may be considered ugly and inadequate in the rush of tomorrow, and two of the three beauties built in 1889 were ultimately leveled to make way for bigger business operations. Only the hotel building survived although its use changed with the times. The old hotel which saw horses in the bar-room, John L. Sullivan shadow boxing in the lobby, Mother Fulham calling regularly at the kitchen door, R. B. Bennett coming daily for lunch and a few gunmen taking liberties in various places, closed its doors in 1916 when prohibition became law in the province. Thereafter, its space was occupied by stores and offices; but to many older people it was still "The Alberta," still the hotel with a name recalling the longest bar in the country west of Winnipeg.

For 20 years after the Alberta Hotel — "finest in the Territories" — was built, sandstone retained its popularity and the people operating quarries were busy. Among typical buildings erected at that period and still standing are the Thomson Block, Neilson Block, Imperial Bank Building, James Short School, Cathedral Church of the Redeemer, Calgary Grain Exchange Building, City Hall and some other landmarks.

When the Province of Alberta was created in 1905, one reason advanced in support of Calgary's bid for the Capital was the solidarity of buildings in the down-town area. "Our people have built for eternity," Mayor John Emerson boasted at that time.

Building methods were to change, however, and the glory of the native stone was to depart. Nevertheless, the old buildings, reminiscent of years when Calgary was the "Sandstone City, retained a proud character in their stout walls — the character of the "gay '90's."

SIR JAMES HAD FAITH

When Calgary graduated to the rank of City in 1893, Mayor Thomas Underwood could boast about waterworks, sewers, electric lights and a population approximately 4,000.

But by this time the country was feeling the grip of economic depression and building operations with the native sandstone were slackening alarmingly. Calgary's growth had slackened. The people who had contracted to build a street railway system were asking permission to postpone and many property owners were inclined to "unload," even though the cost of holding real estate was so low that some absentee owners of single lots found it convenient to remit tax money in the form of postage stamps.

Significantly, however, the citizen who was already paying more local taxes than any other — indicating that he owned more real estate than any other — was not "unloading;" he was steadily buying more property. It was an expression of his faith in Calgary — a faith that never failed — and there came a day when he was paying about half of all the taxes in the Corporation.

He was Calgary's first lawyer, first Senator and the first Alberta resident to be knighted. He was James Lougheed, whose vision of Calgary greatness led him to buy property in the present down-town section — all he could finance — right from the time when the price of lots was about $200 each.

Following his death on November 2, 1925, when Calgary's Anglican Church came far short in accommodating all who wanted to pay tributes of respect to an outstanding figure in the public life of Canada, it was said convincingly that, "No other individual played as large a part in the actual building of this city."

James Lougheed was born at Brampton, Ontario, on September 1, 1854. His father was a building contractor and the young fellow, starting to work as a carpenter, was following paternal footsteps — until a friend said, "Jimmie, you've got a good head on those shoulders. Why don't you take up law?"

The lad resumed his studies, matriculated from Western High School and attended Osgoode Hall. He was called to the bar in 1881 and practiced briefly in Toronto. Then, in company with his brother, Sam, he journeyed to Winnipeg. That was in 1882, but still more westerly horizons were beckoning and he moved on to Medicine Hat and, in 1883, to Calgary — on foot.

As Calgary's first lawyer he knew all about the frontier's rough processes of law, especially as they applied to charges of smuggling whiskey, stealing horses and rustling cattle. With intimate knowledge he recalled the celebrated and confused case of Michael Oxarat who in 1884 drove 175 head of Montana horses into Calgary with the purpose of selling them to settlers. At Fort Macleod he made declaration to the customs officers and paid duty on a stated value of $35 per head. While at Fort Macleod the man purchased an additional hundred head brought from the United States at an earlier date by the I. G. Baker Company.

On arrival at Calgary where Oxarat intended to sell the horses, Customs Officer Bannerman observed more horses than the number on which the Frenchman had paid duty, concluded there had been smuggling, and seized the whole band. The customs officer from Fort Macleod and D. W. Davis of the Baker Company were obliged to drive over the hundred-mile trail to Calgary in order to vouch for Oxarat's ownership. The horses were then released but again seized because of alleged under-valuation for purposes of import duty. After more delay, this charge was dropped and the horses were ordered released again. But by this time, half the horses had disappeared and Oxarat vowed he would hold the federal authorities responsible for their disappearance. The customs official was being called to deliver horses whose care he had assumed by seizure and had good reason to be worried. But suspecting that Oxarat knew where the lost animals were, he charged the owner with theft of his own horses and again seized the ones remaining. Ultimately the lost horses were located, Oxarat was tried and acquitted and, anxious to get out of Calgary as quickly as possible, he sold some of the troublesome brutes and took the rest to Brandon.

In that same year, 1884, James Lougheed married Belle Hardisty, daughter of William Hardisty and niece of both Richard Hardisty and Lord Strathcona. She had come to Calgary to visit her Uncle Richard, who, as Chief Factor with the Hudson's Bay Company, was in Calgary to supervise operations at the Company's store. The young couple took up residence in a small building situated on the Stephen Avenue site later occupied by Ashdown Hardware.

The young man was anxious to make the renovated house as attractive as possible for his bride and had an ultra-modern bay window built at the front. It was the first of its kind in Calgary and brought pride to the occupants of the home until a run-away horse veered off Stephen Avenue, plunged through the lovely window and landed in the middle of Mrs. Lougheed's parlour.

There is a story about Lougheed having a dream in which he saw Ottawa being abandoned as the national capital and Calgary being fixed upon to take its place. Whether or not there was such a dream is unimportant; certainly, of the man's confidence in Calgary's growth and ultimate importance there could be no doubt. Soon after his arrival he bought 30 lots from the townsite company — selected them where later demand for business locations made them soar in value.

SIR JAMES HAD FAITH

The first lots on the new townsite west of the Elbow River were made available in December, 1883. W. T. Ramsay was in charge of the sales and customers drew lots from a hat to determine the order of choice. Nobody was sure where the centre of the business section would be and guessing was popular. John Glenn of Fish Creek drew the first choice and selected the north west corner of the present 9th Avenue and Centre Street, also the north east corner of 8th Avenue and 2nd Street West — both excellent selections, but John Glenn didn't live long enough to realize the benefit of his good judgment. James Lougheed acquired as much as he could finance on 7th and 8th Avenues, so much that some spectators wondered if the man was completely sane.

Moreover, Calgary, at the time of his arrival, needed a lawyer. Over the years which followed he formed various law partnerships, the one having the greatest historic significance being with the young Maritimer, Richard B. Bennett, who was practically "hand picked" for the personal qualities Lougheed demanded. His ideals were high and in the country-wide search for a partner, the Calgarian was looking for a young man, scholarly, of good habits and a Conservative. The search terminated in New Brunswick, and the firm of Lougheed and Bennett was formed.

When Senator Hardisty, Mrs. Lougheed's uncle, died in 1889 following an accident when travelling from Prince Albert to Qu'Appelle by wagon, James Lougheed was appointed to succeed him in the Canadian Senate. The new Senator was only 35 years of age, and when he took his seat in the Upper House he was the most youthful of its members. The frontier Town of Calgary rocked with surprise and enthusiasm in the realization of having a real and living Senator — still Jimmie Lougheed to most residents. He was the last Senator to be appointed by Sir John A. Macdonald.

For 36 years this Calgarian sat in the Canadian Senate, and for the last 19 years of his life he was the Conservative leader in the Upper House, having followed Sir Mackenzie Bowell in the position of leader in 1906.

The Senate, he believed, had a real and vital part to play in the life of Canada, in spite of what critics might say. Democracy is fine, but it has its weaknesses; and the Calgary Senator saw the unspectacular Upper House as a "bulwark against the clamour and caprice of the mob."

Not only was he Conservative leader in the Senate for nearly 20 years, but when Robert Borden came to power in 1911, Senator Lougheed was brought into the cabinet as Minister Without Portfolio. Later, in Prime Minister Arthur Meighen's cabinet of 1920, Senator Lougheed was Minister of the Interior. It was said many times in his latter years that he would have been Prime Minister had he been in the House of Commons instead of the Senate.

In 1917 the charming and cultured Calgary pioneer was knighted, and because Canada soon after that declared against knighthoods, Sir James was the first and last among residents of the Province of Alberta to be so distinguished.

In the business world he was a big man, as he was big in everything he undertook. History will pronounce him a great Canadian; but Calgarians recalling his leadership — especially in the '90's when the City seemed to be at the "awkward age," — will insist upon a prior claim to him.

Senator James Lougheed, Calgary pioneer and party leader in the Senate to the end of his life, died four days after the general election in October 1925. He was 71 years of age. At the time of his passing there was uncertainty about who would form the next federal government, no party having a clear majority. But a Calgary constituency had returned with a big majority his one-time partner, R. B. Bennett, and the Conservatives were sure of the largest block of seats. It appeared that the people of Canada were returning to the political party for which Pioneer Lougheed had worked long and conscientiously — the party closest to his heart.

The Lougheed Block in the downtown section of the City and the big Lougheed House on 13th Avenue West became Calgary landmarks. It was fitting, also, that a western mountain, a Calgary school and an Alberta town should bear the name of the man who, through good times and bad, backed his faith in Calgary with investment dollars.

CAPPY SMART'S FIRE BRIGADE

Everything about Calgary in the '90's seemed to revolve around the Fire Brigade. The citizens' pride and joy, it was sort of service club, social order, pressure group and fire-fighting body, all rolled into one organization. The fire station was even a good place at which to borrow a ladder if a citizen had to cope with storm windows. When the Brigade was called to a big fire in early 1892, all the ladders were out on loan, which prompted the Town Council to rule: "No more loaning of ladders."

The inimitable James Smart became Captain of the Brigade in 1891. Thereafter he was "Cappy" and the fire-fighters' program of activities broadened. For many years the firemen staged an annual 24th of May sports day, a St. Patrick's Day social and that gala event of the year, the Firemens' Ball. They had a brass band, and on at least two occasions won the highest honors for the entire North West Territories. Records show that wise directors seeking the best musical entertainment for the Calgary Exhibition of 1900 hired the Fire Brigade Band to play for four days. The reward was $100.

Moreover, a candidate for Town Council in one of the early years acknowledged that he couldn't be elected because the Fire Brigade members refused to support him. Such was the community influence of the volunteer fire-fighters.

It began in midsummer of 1885 when a committee recommended the purchase of ladder-cart, ladders, hooks and buckets — also ropes and pails for use at the town wells — it being the intention of the committee to call at once "for volunteers to enroll as members of a Hook, Ladder and Bucket Company." The Town Council approved, and on August 25 the volunteers were formally initiated and informed of payment of 75 cents per man for each fire they fought.

Now there was the problem of a place to store the new equipment. With commendable pride in their hook-and-ladder push-cart, the Town fathers decided to delay painting the new Town Hall, just completed at a cost of $1694, and use the $125 appropriated for painting it to build a fire hall alongside. And so, late in the year, Calgary acquired a $125 fire hall with a big room in which firemen could spend leisure hours.

Proud of the room in the Fire Hall, aldermen saw it as a good place in which to hold Council meetings. It was more spacious than the office in the Town Hall and the chairs were more comfortable. But the volunteer firemen resented the intrusion and resigned in protest. Even at that the Mayor and Councillors were reluctant to relinguish the cozy meeting place and hit upon a bright idea — the Mayor and Councillors would become the volunteer fire-fighters and then there would be no doubt about their rights and privileges in the hall they coveted.

At a subsequent meeting the Council adopted a motion to instruct former volunteers to surrender their keys to the Fire Hall. Although not recorded, story has it that Mayor and Aldermen acting as a bucket brigade at the first fire thereafter made a dismal showing and citizens demanded that the former volunteers be reinstated.

Peace settled once again upon civic circles, but the Town Council did not relinguish its guardianship over the Fire Hall quarters and the records show that zealous aldermen refused to rent the room to Dr. Campbell for such a worthy purpose as a lecture on Robert Burns — not even at a fee of $10 which Dr. Campbell was prepared to pay.

At Calgary's first big fire in November, 1886, the buckets were totally inadequate. Fire had broken out in a feed store opposite the present C.P.R. Depot, and before the volunteers arrived the flames were out of control. With loss amounting to a hundred thousand dollars, the need for better equipment was very apparent. The new technique embraced water tanks situated at strategic points in the town, reels of hose on two-wheel push carts, and a Ronald steam engine for pumping.

A team of horses was required to pull the engine, and because it was neither economical nor practical for the Town to maintain its own horses for that purpose, a payment of five dollars was offered to the teamster who was first to reach the engine and haul it to the point where it was needed when an alarm was sounded.

More horse-drawn equipment was added and horses were acquired and trained to be equine specialists. Thanks largely to Fire Chief Cappy Smart, Calgary had some of the best trained horses in the business. Citizens watched with quiet admiration when, at the proper signal, understanding horses dashed from their stalls to take places below suspended harness, and in fewer seconds than it takes to tell it, raced away at a gallop. The special favorite among the animals quartered at the Fire Hall at 6th Avenue and 1st Street East was an old grey mare — White Wings — the one that hauled the two-wheel chemical cart. The mare understood her part about as well as firemen knew theirs, and when on one occasion the driver fell from the cart as it was drawing away from the station, White Wings dashed off as she had been trained to do and didn't stop until she was at the scene of the fire, along with the other horses.

In 1908 when Calgary had the Dominion Exhibition, Chief Cappy Smart directed a demonstration that thrilled thousands of grandstand spectators. Two of the experienced horses from Calgary's Fire Hall were released on the infield in front of the grandstand and a fire-wagon with harness suspended in front of it was placed on the race track. An alarm was sounded; the two horses raised their heads, paused momentarily to locate the wagon and then, abandoning grass and freedom, galloped away to stand in front of the vehicle long enough for harness to be dropped and fastened. Then, away they ran, rounding the race track for a cheering audience and obviously annoyed that it was just another "false alarm."

The man who imparted the special character to the early fire department was indeed James Smart. His 54-year association with firefighting began the day Calgary's volunteer Hook and Ladder Corps was organized in 1885 and ended when he died in 1939, leaving behind a highly efficient and completely mechanized department. For 35 years he was Calgary's Fire Chief. Actually, he was retired from the post of Chief in 1933 when, at the age of 69, he had nearly half a century of service with the Calgary Fire Department behind him. But it wasn't complete retirement because he was appointed Fire Prevention Officer so that he might extend his associations to the full 50 years.

Cappy, with round face, loud voice, convincing vocabulary and a big heart, was born in Scotland. His father, a ship's captain, was lost at sea and in 1883 mother and children came to Canada and ended their journey at Calgary. The lad tried various types of work including carpentry, and when the fighting started around

Duck Lake, Jimmie Smart hired as an army transport driver and packed a loaded gun as he travelled.

When hostilities ceased Smart returned to Calgary and began work with an uncle — Yarlett by name — the Town's first undertaker with premises on Stephen Avenue, east of Centre Street. Although hardly anybody died in that period, young Smart believed there would be enough work for two undertakers sooner or later and he started in business for himself. But he was never so busy that he couldn't drop everything when a fire alarm sounded.

In 1898, seven years after being appointed Captain, Smart became Chief of what was still a volunteer brigade. It was a popular appointment because Cappy was already an institution in Calgary. He was a showman as well as a fire-fighter. At a fire he would take a conspicuous position and roar his commands, about as much for the benefit of spectators as for his own men. Smoke made him swear, he admitted, and sometimes his language was about as hot as the flames he was trying to combat. He liked spectators, but when they crowded too close he issued just one warning. If that wasn't heeded, he ordered his men to "turn the water on them."

Boastful as Cappy Smart might be at times, he lacked nothing in courage and willingness. When, in 1906, word was received that fire was threatening the Town of High River, Cappy ordered a special train, loaded his equipment and arrived in time to help quell the blazes.

He was too old to be a soldier in World War I, but if things in Europe became any worse than they appeared in 1915, he figured he might have to take his Calgary fire-fighters over there "to capture the Kaiser."

For as many years as Cappy Smart was Fire Chief and Captain, he was the official starter for Calgary road races, referee for boxing matches, marshal for parades and sometimes a source of consternation for prohibition workers. Several times he was dismissed for departing from the ways of sobriety, but on each occasion the public demand was for his re-instatement. There was no more generous man in Calgary, and when Christmas was passed Cappy was usually penniless, having spent all he had on Christmas charity.

As one of his colleagues recalled: "Cappy was always ready for either fire or fun." If he was incapacitated, it was never for long. There was that day when he had all his teeth extracted. In the light of dental methods of the time, he should have been laid up for a week. Instead, he fortified himself with a favorite brand of "medicine," and about midnight the toothless Fire Chief was seen getting himself dressed to go out to make some "social calls."

By his personality he fitted most appropriately into the Calgary of the '90's; nevertheless, he must be seen and remembered as the principal link between a modern fire department with one of Canada's finest records based on per capita fire losses, and that primitive brigade manned by volunteers paid 75 cents per fire.

1900

Calgary entered the 20th century with a population of 5,000. Male members of the community outnumbered females by three to one and most were young and unmarried. Adventuresome fellows were returning from the Klondike gold fields — richer only in experience — and some were volunteering for service in the South African War. But despite masculine restlessness, eligible women would find no better hunting ground and, with the idea of attracting homemakers, the fact was being publicized in Toronto.

W. H. Cushing was Mayor and the City was extending its ownership of public utilities by buying the Calgary Gas and Water Works Company. A proposal to adopt numbers instead of names for streets and avenues was under consideration and loaded with controversy. And City Council was trying desperately to attract industry. Free sites and ten-year exemptions from taxes were some of the inducements held out for men who might start a cigar factory or woolen mill. Why shouldn't Calgary have a cigar factory, it was being asked, when the amount of $20,000 a year was being sent to Montreal and elsewhere to buy cigars for the local trade?

Entertainment was mainly of the outdoor kind, although Calgarians had their first opportunity to see moving pictures in that year. The first public shows were in a tent. For the hunter there was game in abundance and every stream seemed to be full of fish

No. 26

$700.

Municipal Debenture

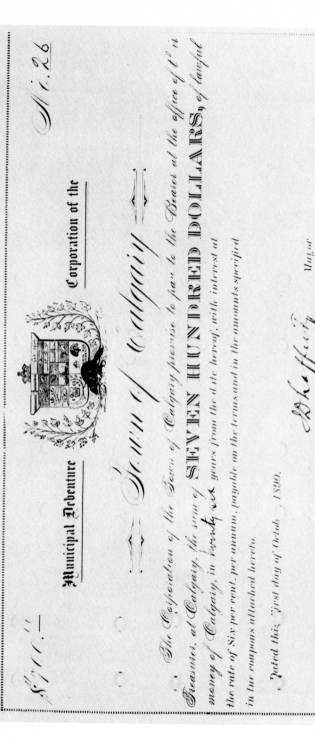

Corporation of the

=== Town of Calgary ===

The Corporation of the Town of Calgary promise to pay to the Bearer at the office of t' e Treasurer, at Calgary, the sum of **SEVEN HUNDRED DOLLARS**, of lawful money of Calgary, in twenty six years from the date hereof, with interest at the rate of Six per cent. per annum, payable on the terms and in the amounts specified in the coupons attached hereto.

Dated this First day of Octob , 1890.

Shaffner Mayor

Orr Clerk

"SANDSTONE CITY"

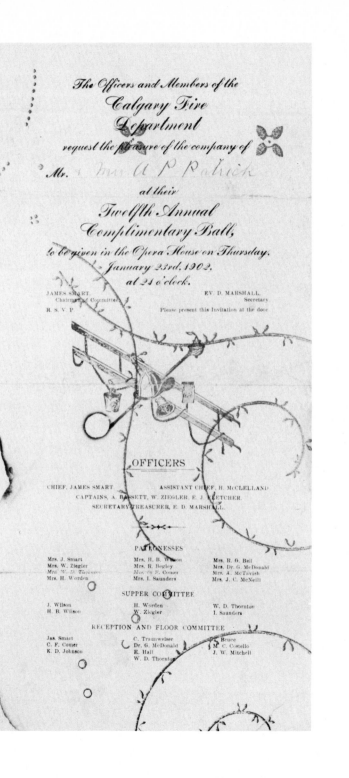

The Officers and Members of the

Calgary Fire Department

request the pleasure of the company of

Mr. *Mr & Mrs A P Patrick*

at their

Twelfth Annual Complimentary Ball,

to be given in the Opera House on Thursday,
January 23rd, 1902,
at 24 o'clock.

JAMES SMART,
Chairman of Committee

EV. D. MARSHALL,
Secretary

R. S. V. P.

Please present this Invitation at the door

OFFICERS

CHIEF, JAMES SMART   ASSISTANT CHIEF, H. McCLELLAND
CAPTAINS, A. BASSETT, W. ZIEGLER, E. J. FLETCHER.
SECRETARY-TREASURER, E. D. MARSHALL.

PATRONESSES

Mrs. J. Smart	Mrs. H. B. Wilson	Mrs. R. G. Bell
Mrs. W. Ziegler	Mrs. R. Begley	Mrs. Dr. G. McDonald
Mrs. W. D. Thornton	Mrs. by F. Comer	Mrs. A. McTavish
Mrs. H. Worden	Mrs. I. Saunders	Mrs. J. C. McNeill

SUPPER COMMITTEE

J. Wilson	H. Worden	W. D. Thornton
H. B. Wilson	W. Ziegler	I. Saunders

RECEPTION AND FLOOR COMMITTEE

Jas. Smart	C. Traunweiser	T. Bruce
C. F. Comer	Dr. G. McDonald	M. C. Costello
K. D. Johnson	E. Hall	J. W. Mitchell
	W. D. Thornton	

CAPPY SMART'S FIRE BRIGADE

— and other things, if one accepts the report that "a gentleman fishing at the Bow Marsh bridge hooked a sea serpent yesterday."

Nobody had much money but nobody needed much. The Criterian Restaurant was offering business men's lunches at 20 cents and featuring chicken dinners on Sundays at 25 cents.

A few people loitering on the plank sidewalks wore bowler hats, wing collars and checked suits, but the Calgary character was more like that of a carelessly dressed cowboy who had work to do. No man was judged harshly because of the clothes he wore — unless they were very good.

In point of influence upon city residents, farming and ranching in the country round-about far overshadowed that of the limited urban industry. People were strikingly conscious of nearness to the soil. The conversations of men meeting at R. C. Thomas' Frontier Stable or the Alberta Hotel were essentially agrarian. The troubles and successes of settlers and ranchers were the troubles and successes of the citizens of Calgary.

Western soil was emerging from the experimental stage. Two and one-half million mid-western acres seeded to wheat in that year produced a return of 23½ million bushels. It wasn't a good crop year; nevertheless, confidence was growing and millions of unbroken acres were waiting for homesteaders.

Prairie land, an advertising appeal explained, could be broken for $2 an acre, disked and cultivated for $1.50 an acre, provided with seed for $1 and harvested and threshed for $2. From a total outlay of $6.50 on an acre of homestead land a person could anticipate 15 bushels of wheat worth 88 cents a bushel. The investment money would be doubled. That sort of figuring was sure to stimulate immigration and land settlement.

But Frontier Stable discussions were about ranching, round-ups and the price of cattle more than wheat. It was big news when, a short time later, George Lane, with backing from Gordon, Ironside and Fares, bought the Bar U Ranch along with the 5,000 cattle and 1,000 horses on it. Everybody knew George Lane, the raw-boned and amiable rancher who came to the foothills in 1884. His range was west of High River, but frequently he was registered at the Alberta Hotel and just about as often he was visiting with his friends who met at the Frontier Stable.

And of course the livery stable fraternity would find enjoyment in Bob Edwards' account of an alleged incident in Lane's activities about that time. The big, lean rancher, it seems, was a train passenger going to High River but there was locomotive trouble near De Winton. "Mr. Lane," according to Edwards' reporting, "thought this delay would afford an excellent opportunity for shooting a few ducks. This particular vicinity is usually all water. If one drop of rain falls it immediately expands and widens into a great lake, making it hard on the railway men but all right for the duck hunters. So out George sallies, bent on belting Okotoks out of forty or fifty mallards and blue wings.

"The genial Lane approached a pond — it was a pond — and espied a couple of beauties. The unfortunate birds made an awful bluff at getting away, doing the splutter-flutter act; but bang-bang went the trusty blunderbuss. Down they came. The next thing that came down was a very indignant lady who wanted to know why he was shooting her tame ducks.

" 'Tame ducks!' stammered George. 'Whatthehellbill! Very sorry madam, but were those ducks really tame — I mean well broke?'

" 'Yes sir.'

" 'Well, in that case, here is a five spot. You probably have heard of me. I'm Dr. Ings of Calgary.'

" 'Oh yes, I've heard of Dr. Ings often enough and have heard that he often has a treat of wild ducks up at Calgary. But doctor, if you can't kill 'em up there, it is no reason why you should come down and shoot 'em on my property.'

" 'That is so, Madam, and anything I can do to mend the mistake, will, I assure, be done on the spot.'

" 'Well, there's a neighbor's wife up here who is about to become —'

" 'Hullo, by gun, there goes my train. Good bye and God bless you. Here's another V.'

" 'Good bye Dr. Ings,' said the mollified lady. 'Call again.'

"When Mr. Lane got back to the train he was asked what he had.

" 'Had a close call,' said he with a dark smile."

But nothing about the opening year of the 20th century bore more significance than the emergence of a new sense of pride in Calgary — a new concern for the appearance of boulevards and fences and front yards. A citizen was fined 75 cents for having a stack of hay on the street; Central Park was laid out for horticultural development and tree planting was being encouraged as never before. Aldermen and citizens had a vision of a city beautiful.

From the Caldwell Company of Virden, Manitoba, the City ordered a carload of young trees — mostly Manitoba maples and ash — and followed with a supplementary order for 2,000 seedlings and 1,000 cuttings of Russian poplar, to be sent express. Many of the trees were planted on boulevards and in parks and many more were sold to private property-owners at cost — about ten cents per tree.

By their tree-planting activities in the year 1900, Calgarians were declaring a new devotion, building for the future.

But who was principally behind the drive to obtain more trees? Who was the man pestering City Council to plant trees on boulevards and the islands in the Bow River, nagging at citizens to plant trees in their yards? Who was that benefactor for whom many of Calgary's older trees are memorials? The answer: William Pearce, of whom more must be told.

THE COMMANDING WILLIAM PEARCE

Calgarians with long memories have vivid mental pictures of the commanding figure of William Pearce — six feet tall, robust in build, well provided with whiskers, and wearing an expression of severity that almost hid his kindly nature. That dignified gentleman, pronounced the father of irrigation development in Southern Alberta and most ardent advocate of tree planting half a century ago, attracted attention wherever he went.

Many people whose memories will not embrace the man and his authority will at least remember the famous William Pearce house beside the Bow River in East Calgary — a huge sandstone edifice built to endure like the pyramids but demolished in 1957 after standing nearly 70 years. For some time after its completion in 1889, that house was the architectural pride of Calgary, and in 1891 was publicly proclaimed the finest home between Winnipeg and Vancouver.

THE COMMANDING WILLIAM PEARCE

Of those who saw Pearce coming and going — walking at his long practiced land-surveyor's stride of 2,000 paces per mile — not many knew him intimately. But everybody recognized him as a human power-house and one of the most influential public workers in the West — "Czar of the Prairies," William Toole called him.

Moreover, he was a devoted conservationist at a time when too little thought was being given to management of natural resources. He was for saving soil and planting trees. Some of Calgary's big spruce on what was the Pearce Estate and elsewhere were set out by him, and if he had had his way, Prince's Island and other islands in the Bow would today be supporting small forests of evergreens.

In training, Pearce was an engineer; by instinct, a scientist. It was as a member of the Dominion Land Survey facing the task of laying out the western country in sections and townships that he made his first big contribution. From his home on the north shore of Lake Erie where he learned resourcefulness and love of soil, the young fellow went to University of Toronto. As a trained engineer, his first professional employment was in his native province, but as everybody knew, the biggest tasks confronting men who could run a transit were in the West where in 1869 the Hudson's Bay Company relinguished its territorial claims and made way for farming.

A proper survey was a prerequisite to settlement. The long, narrow river lots as Peter Fidler laid them out in Lord Selkirk's colony beside the Red River were appropriate as long as the few settlers in the country wanted to live close together and use the river as their highway. But when settlement promised to extend back from the river, another form of survey was needed.

The new township survey with square sections containing 640 acres each as units was just well started when Pearce accepted a position with the Dominion Land Survey in 1874. The International Boundary had to be confirmed. Then from a point near Pembina, the first meridian line was projected northward and township lines worked east and west from the meridian.

For the next few years — winter as well as summer — Pearce travelled about the unsettled parts of Manitoba and the North West Territories. In summer the main part of his day-to-day diet was wild meat, and in winter, hardtack, tea and pemmican. In the winter of 1889-90 he was working north of the settled portion of Manitoba and travelling by dog-team. Life was primitive and only a man with powerful physique and endurance could survive it. With not even a tent for shelter, Pearce put himself to bed by crawling into a buffalo-robe sleeping bag placed in the snow and inviting his sleigh-dogs to sleep on top or around him.

There were hardships but life was not dull. To one with the mind and observation of a scientist, an abundance of wild life proved absorbing. If hostility would furnish interest, there it was: the continuing objection to the new survey, stemming from the half-breed population whose members under Louis Riel had once already shown willingness to fight for the old system. One day he could record in his journal that Sioux Indians were camping nearby; and another day, that 300 Red River carts passed, hauling freight to Fort Edmonton.

Surveying with the meticulous care that characterized the man led to bigger responsibilities. In 1882 he was appointed inspector of Dominion Land Agencies and a member of the Dominion Land Board charged with initiating policy recommendations bearing on all natural resources in the West — lands, trees, minerals and water. Nobody knew more about the country's resources and nobody had more concern.

Superintendent of Mines for the North West Territories was the next appointment, and in that position Pearce took the office to Calgary in 1887 and became a resident of the foothills community where he had visited and acquired land at least four years before. A map dated 1883 shows Pearce as the owner of the south west quarter of section 13, township 24, range 1, west of 5. There, in what was later called East Calgary, the big house was started in 1887. Bow Bend Shack, some people called it, and what a shack! Fifteen rooms including a billiard room in the basement, bathroom with running water and toilet when such conveniences were almost unknown, three fireplaces, enduring sandstone masonry, the finest hardwood floors, wall panelling of elder, and black walnut pillars from trees on his father's Ontario farm.

Calgary pioneers looked with admiration and envy. And as soon as the house was ready for occupation, Pearce began a long program of planting trees and caring for them the way one would tend a young Thoroughbred. He wrote to Calgary's mayor and aldermen insisting that trees would do well on local soil and urging that plans be drawn to make Calgary the Forest City of Canada. When planes began scheduled flights, pilots admitted that Pearce's patch of dark-colored evergreens was one of their landmarks by day or night.

From Calgary, Pearce continued to travel back and forth across the West. He cultivated acquaintances with Indians and settlers, mapped coal deposits, raised optimistic questions about oil long before any worth while discovery, and furnished advice for the Department of Interior. For good reason, the government people looked upon him as a sort of walking and breathing guide-book. On matters of resources, nobody either east or west argued with Pearce.

But it was his aggressive proposals about irrigation that gave him the most secure place in the West's history. John Glenn took irrigation water from Fish Creek in 1878 and others conducted small scale operations, but Pearce was the first resident of the West to recognize practical possibilities in large scale irrigation and the first to proclaim the importance of conserving water because the need for irrigation would one day go far beyond the supply of water.

In 1881 he visited Utah and studied irrigation in that State. Four years later, in an official government report, he made bold to advocate extensive irrigation in what is now Southern Alberta, and was laughed at. Many government and railroad officials, anxious to attract settlers, considered it a mistake to admit the necessity of irrigation. Others said the idea was impractical. When first submitted to directors of the C.P.R., Pearce's scheme was voted down, but Sir William Van Horne was impressed and gave encouragement.

By way of public example, Pearce, in 1894 took water from the Elbow near Bragg Creek, conducted it to his Calgary property and grew grains and vegetables such as local people had never seen before.

The big irrigation projects undertaken later by the C.P.R. had their origin in the difficulties encountered in finding water for the steam locomotives, Pearce declared, and told about going over the line with William Whyte and William Cross, who were perplexed at the necessity of pumping water long distances from the Bow River to the railroad. Pearce pointed out that by building a dam where the Bassano dam arose later, "We could get water for all the eastern area," for locomotives, for irrigation and for stock watering purposes. "We could change the face of the country," he argued.

Recognizing that an Irrigation Act was a basic need in a program of development, Pearce went to Ottawa and requested it. But, as he discovered, some members of parliament didn't know what he was talking about. "Some people asked me what irrigation was," he reported. "I told them to look out of the Parliament Building windows and see the lawns being sprinkled with water."

During the early '90s the country was especially dry. In looking back Pearce said, "I think 50 percent of the settlers in that tract between Calgary and High River abandoned their farms and many took the barbed wire off their fences and sold it." Coinciding with this period of drought, the North West Irrigation Act was passed and some large irrigation companies were organized, among them the Calgary Irrigation Company in which Pearce and members of his family were the largest stockholders. In that undertaking to use water from the Bow, irrigation was a success, but the business of operating it was not and Pearce lost heavily.

His pet project, to become known as the William Pearce Scheme, embraced millions of acres of land between the North and South Saskatchewan Rivers, and extending into both Saskatchewan and Alberta. The water was to come from the North Saskatchewan. Pearce began advocating it in 1898, and throughout the balance of his life insisted the idea was practical. Surveys have been made and people have talked about it, but coupled with some alleged engineering difficulties, its size was frightening and no serious steps were taken to develop it.

The much-talked-about irrigation scheme was, like the William Pearce house, imposing in its plan, a symbol of faith in the future and designed to give protection indefinitely. Pearce was thinking constantly about the needs of the next generation as much as about his own. William Pearce, the tree-planter and irrigationist who died in his beloved Calgary at age 82 in 1930, was essentially a conservationist, and therefore a good Canadian.

THE DAY THE LEGISLATORS CAME TO CALGARY

The most memorable occasions of celebration in early Calgary were the arrival of the first train in 1883; incorporation of the town in 1884; and the special visit from the Lieutenant-Governor, Premier and members of the Territorial Legislature in 1901. The idea of inviting the entire governing body to Calgary was born in the Board of Trade. City Council backed it enthusiastically — and for good reason. Many members of the Legislature had never seen the Sandstone City of the Foothills and, officially, promotion of understanding was the purpose of the invitation. But there were other reasons: Calgary needed a new bridge, needed bigger grants for schools, and needed support for poorly disguised convictions that here was the only logical site for a capital — Territorial Capital or Provincial Capital.

Calgarians had long claimed that Regina had a poor claim to the Territorial Capital; and years before, the Town Council had proposed to the Government at Ottawa that meetings of the Legislative Assembly should at least be alternated between Regina, which had been an early choice, and Calgary, which would have been a better one. Moreover, if two provinces were to be carved out of the Territories, a second capital would be needed, and it would be well for Calgary to have friends in government.

The invitation to be Calgary's guests for two days was extended through the city's two members of the legislature, R. B. Bennett and A. E. Cross, and the august body moved to accept it. It was the signal for a thorough Calgary clean-up. Store owners placed special orders for flags, and the mayor instructed that loose stones be picked off the main avenues and family cows which normally enjoyed freedom of the city be tied up. The Lieutenant-Governor and the Premier and all the governing big-shots were coming and Calgary must be clean and tidy.

Home owners who could afford such extravagance painted their houses, and people with less means painted the front sides only. Even at that, paint supplies on store shelves were quickly exhausted. It was the most complete transformation the young city had experienced, and on the eve of the big day the city looked clean and orderly like a brand new wagon.

The train bearing the government party was late; it arrived at 3 a.m. to find the reception committee completely disorganized. Representatives of the Board of Trade were on hand but not the Mayor and Aldermen. But Lieutenant-Governor Forget was charming, despite the hour. Clever French lawyer, he came originally to the West as clerk when Mr. Laid occupied Government House at Battleford. He was taken to the Alberta Hotel for the remainder of the night; and Premier Haultain, who was no stranger in Calgary, to the home of Mr. Morris, president of the Board of Trade.

Friday, May 24th, was bright and clear — looked like an answer to the Methodist minister's public prayer for good weather. The program was to begin with an official breakfast at the Alberta Hotel; but Mayor Mackie, who had been asleep when the 3 a.m. train arrived, insisted that the entire party return, first of all, to the C.P.R. depot, at which place the order of events said he was to deliver the formal civic welcome. After hours of preparation the mayor was not going to be denied the privilege of delivering a speech, even though he was its only admirer.

Planned as the highlight of the program was the street parade beginning at 10 o'clock, just like a Monday morning Stampede Parade of a later year. Even the parade route was similar, west on Stephen Avenue and back on Atlantic — or, using present-day terms, west on 8th Avenue and back on 9th.

To anyone who has studied Calgary's early history, it will be no surprise that the Fire Brigade dominated the parade, even to the point of Fire Chief "Cappy" Smart riding in a more prominent position than the Lieutenant-Governor. Somebody suggested that, after the Volunteer Fire Brigade of that time, City Council and Board of Trade rated as the most influential bodies in the community. And so the Fire Brigade band led the parade, followed by Fire Chief Smart in a fine buggy, then the balance of the fire brigade personnel.

Mayor, aldermen and other city officials followed the fire-fighters and then the Lieutenant-Governor, Premier and Honorable Members of the Assembly, all crowded into the cleanest buggies in the community. But there was much more to the parade — four other bands, 50 cavalrymen back from the South

THE DAY THE LEGISLATORS CAME TO CALGARY

African War, floats entered by the Hudson's Bay Company, Hull Brothers, the brewery, Great West Saddlery and others. And comic floats? There were lots of them. Most of Calgary's population of 5,000 stood or sat on the plank sidewalks and agreed it was their city's proudest hour.

After the parade there was a banquet in Hull's Opera House, with Members of the Legislature and the South African returned men as guests of honor. It was a man's party. Hand-picked Calgary girls waited on tables, but otherwise, Calgary ladies were permitted only to sit in the balcony and watch their noble men devour the best food the community could provide. Women didn't vote at that period and they didn't always share the best banquets.

But it was a big party, and 400 well-fed men listened to Lieutenant-Governor Forget's speech in which he devoted more time to admiration of the waitresses and the women in the balcony than to the city he was supposed to praise. At the psychological moment, however, Paddy Nolan, Calgary's prize after-dinner speaker, made it very clear to all assembled that a city of brave men and beautiful women would make the best possible capital for either a province or a nation.

For the afternoon there was a huge sports program, organized, of course, by the Fire Brigade — football games, rifle shooting, lacrosse, Indian pony races, bicycle races, field events and a band contest which the Fire Brigade band won.

There was still another day of activities. The planners were determined to impress the visitors, and two days of entertainment should achieve more than one in realizing a dream of a capital building rising on the banks of the Bow. At 9 a.m. on Saturday the city's finest horses, carriages and buggies were lined up in front of the Alberta Hotel. In the foremost carriage, drawn by the Mounted Police four-horse team, rode the Lieutenant-Governor, the Premier, Speaker Eakin, the president of the Board of Trade and Inspector Wilson.

The day's tour was planned with care, first stop being the brewery where a full hour was required to "see" the institution. The unfortunate horsemen who were obliged to remain outside became restless and annoyed as they thought of all they were missing. But somebody had to stay with the horses. That the great men from Regina were properly impressed with the brewery there could be no question, and their conclusion, as recorded in the press was — "A product as good as any lager in the world, not excepting the beer that made Milwaukee famous." Evidently the legislators considered themselves qualified to render judgement.

The party overstayed at the brewery, but through the use of buggy whips arrived at the P. Burns abattoir only a little behind schedule. Then there was a drive south to the ranch of W. R. Hull. The Macleod Trail scenery on that clear day was enough to make the visitors forget everything except their trip to the brewery, and they were at the beautiful Bow Valley Ranch for lunch at 12.30.

Following lunch there were more toasts, of course, and with Mayor Mackie in the chair, members of the legislature heard for the fourth time the chorus: "For They Are Jolly Good Fellows." It was then for Premier Haultain, in responding, to touch upon the right note, saying that during the trip from Regina 16 places were mentioned as sites for a Capital; but after two days at Calgary he had "narrowed his views," and if the people of this city could offer a site midway between Hull's Ranch and the brewery, he was sure every member of the Assembly would be ready to vote approval at that moment. Such a splendid suggestion called for singing "They Are Jolly Good Fellows," for the fifth time. The party then boarded the buggies for the drive back to the city to see Calgary beat Millarville at polo — score 5 to 4.

Next day the men who ruled the Territories waved farewell after some extravagant proposals about new bridges across Bow and Elbow and the best riverside spot for a Capital Building. They really liked the place, which one member more scholarly than others described as "That poem set in stone and writ in running water — the City of Calgary."

The local people returned to their work, the Fire Brigade Band took a holiday, and family cows temporarily denied their freedom were released to graze where they chose. Members of City Council congratulated themselves on their efforts and wondered how long it would be until the scheme began to bear fruit in terms of bridges and capital buildings.

In other towns and cities there was evidence of jealousy. The incomparable Bob Edwards, then editing the Wetaskiwin Breeze, wrote: "I know what is in store for His Royal Highness the Duke of Cornwall when he visits Calgary. He will be shown over the brewery, given a Fire Brigade run and a drive out to Hull's

Ranch." But however others might regard them, May 24 and 25 in that year of 1901 were gala days in the early life of the city and residents talked about them for a long time.

QUEEN OF GARBAGE ROW

Nearly every city of half a century ago had a truculent old woman who chased the boys, infuriated the neighbors and gave the temperance forces a bad time. Calgary had Mrs. Caroline Fulham, better known as Mother Fulham. And though her conduct left much to be desired, she gained about as much local prominence and immortality as contemporaries like Mayor Ramsay and Senator Lougheed.

The plumpish lady with uncombed hair and a good bit of Ireland clinging tenaciously to her tongue, could neither read nor write. Lack of education, however, imposed no apparent handicap when she chose to express herself. Her voice was loud and her vocabulary outrageous, especially at those times when she departed from the path of sobriety. And if more were needed to attract attention, a scandalous manner of dress would furnish it.

For 15 years after 1889 her residence was on 6th Avenue, a short distance west of the present site of Knox United Church. If one could call it a profession, she was a keeper of pigs, for which she hauled kitchen waste from Calgary's best hotels and restaurants — Alberta, Royal, Queen's, Windsor, Criterion and New Brunswick.

As regularly as restaurant potatoes were peeled, Mother Fulham, sitting squarely in the middle of her democrat, garbage barrel at her back, drove an emaciated horse through the streets and lanes to gather feed for her swine. "Hurray for Ireland," somebody would call from the sidewalk, and immediately get a reply that could be heard for half a block: "Ye'd like to be Irish, too, ye pur fool."

Cleanliness was not one of the lady's characteristics and Calgary's primitive facilities for bathing didn't worry her in the least. And so it happened that Dr. H. G. Mackid, who came to Calgary in 1889, met Mrs. Fulham on Stephen Avenue and, noticing a limp, enquired sympathetically if she was having some trouble. Informed that she had a sore ankle, the kindly doctor said: "Come into Templeton's Drug Store and I'll examine it." Inside the store, Mother Fulham removed a stocking, and the doctor, reeling from what he saw, exclaimed: "By George, I'll bet a dollar there's not another leg in Calgary as dirty as that one."

"Put up your money, Doctor," the woman shouted with Irish impulse. "I'll bet it's not and here's me dollar." Before the doctor could retract, she pulled down her other stocking to expose "another leg" that was obviously as dirty as the first, and held out her hand to collect the bet.

Young fellows looking for fun turned to tease the celebrated Queen of the Garbage Trade. They put itching powder on her horse and watched the poor brute stride with unusual speed down the lane. On one occasion while the lady was quenching her thirst at the Alberta Hotel, boys separated horse and democrat, and after pushing the shafts through the woven wire fence at the railroad right-of-way, re-hitched with the democrat on one side of the wire and horse on the other. Mrs. Fulham, with spirits stimulated, came out to drive home, mounted the vehicle as usual, klucked at her horse to move on and then, as she discovered the impossible position of horse and democrat, she seized the dilapidated whip and looked about angrily to find somebody on whom to use it.

From the Herald of September 1, 1903, Calgarians read: "Mrs. Fulham last night was awakened by hearing some men moving around her yard and saw them running away. This morning she got in her buckboard and the wheels came off after the horse had gone a few yards, so she knew the men had taken the nuts. She thinks she knows who the men were."

Often she was in trouble with neighbors, and when police action was necessary, it would take Chief English and his entire force of two constables to bring her in. When she was to appear before magistrate, she'd have none but Paddy Nolan to plead her case; and with such a combination in court, all of Calgary's residents wanted to be present to enjoy the entertainment. Nolan was able and witty, and Mother Fulham found it impossible to hold her tongue, even in the court.

Usually she was the defendant, but in April of 1890 she was charging a Chinese with assault. According to the Calgary Tribune, "When His Worship took his place the hall was crowded to its

115

utmost capacity with a crowd which evidently expected some fun."
As the charge was explained to the court, Mrs. Fulham had reason
to believe the Chinese employee at the Alberta Hotel was stealing
her garbage. Sure and she had found him bent over the barrel
and the conclusion was natural. An argument followed, and according to Mrs. Fulham, John struck her. But the evidence was
contradictory. The most plausible explanation was that the Chinese
had stolen a dressed chicken from the hotel kitchen and was
merely trying to hide it in the garbage barrel when Mrs. Fulham
came along. Anyway, the case was dismissed.

In at least one other court appearance she was the plaintiff
— this time charging her neighbor, Rev. Mr. Jacques, with in-
sulting her. J. A. Lougheed acted for the defence and Paddy Nolan
as usual, for the Fulham woman. Testimony was that she had
threatened to kill the minister's hens if they wandered her way
and he called her a "blackguard." She admitted she didn't know
what the word meant but she didn't like it anyway. Her lawyer
said there was a "Fulham Extermination Society" in Calgary and
that it was time a stand was taken to protect this female citizen.
Lougheed, in support of his client, called the woman "a notorious
nuisance" and pointed out that property in her neighborhood had
depreciated in value because "of her residence there." Mrs. Fulham
heckled until she was ordered removed from the court, but the
reverend gentleman was fined a dollar.

Time didn't change things very much. Ten years later she
was still making periodic visits to the police station, still paying
fines for disorderly conduct or abusive language, still making it
difficult for those whose duty it was to lock her up now and then.

On October 21, 1901, she walked into the Herald office, announcing her arrival with: "Good morning to you young man! An'
it's an ill-used woman I am this day." In response to a question about
her troubles, she placed a large parcel on the table and removed the
wrappings to display a pile of iron grey hair. Taking off her old hat
and pointing to her tangled locks, she said: "The bastes of policemen tore that from me head."

A few days later when Calgary's City Council met in regular
session, Mrs. Fulham was present with the same parcel of hair,
strode forward, uninvited, and submitted a letter of protest, explaining that while she was sitting in the kitchen of the New
Brunswick Cafe on a recent night, Constables Fraser and Waldon

entered, seized her, managed to place her in the police wagon and locked her in a cell. Next morning, she was charged, and according to her statement, was obliged to pay the customary "fee" for being arrested.

The Mayor promised to look into the complaint and called for the next item of business. But the lady was still talking: "Sure, an' isn't it mesiff that knows the wickedness of them both. Those policemen are bad men. Sure, gintlemen, this is my hair thim bastes pulled out."

The other side of the story was that Mrs. Fulham had celebrated and refused to be arrested without a fight. And there was still some doubt about who pulled out the hair.

But though frequently in trouble, the woman enjoyed a certain amount of frontier affection. An unvarnished nature is refreshing at any time. She was granted almost unlimited freedom on March 17th each year. It was her day and she dressed in bright green and poured drinks for any she considered her friends.

When a C.P.R. train killed her milk cow, Nellie, she laid claim for damages. It was brought out at the hearing that "No Trespassing" signs were posted and neither cows nor people were supposed to be on the track.

"Ye pur fools," the old lady interjected, "what makes ye think me pur old cow could read?"

Not satisfied with the judgment, she boldly broached the president of the railroad in his private car when he came to Calgary, and brazenly placed the blame for her loss on him. With some sympathy for the woman, the president promised to get her another cow, but even that didn't set her entirely at ease and she challenged him: "Where in the world can ye git another cow as gude as my old Nellie?"

Anyone as vigorous as Mrs. Fulham was bound to be influential, either for good or evil; and at least some of her influence was useful. She was constant entertainment and she was good hearted. A settler who lost three horses from glanders and had no money with which to replace them, saw the old lady roll down a stocking and remove a roll of money, then press $40 in his hand, saying, "That'll help ye buy another horse."

And there is documented reason for believing that the city's most unconventional citizen was the means of Calgary getting its first building restrictions. Senator Lougheed, addressing city aldermen, said, "Look here... I believe the city council of Calgary should have some building restrictions... I, for instance, have a number of lots in the vicinity of Mrs. Fulham's place, and certainly no one would buy them when her pig ranch is taken into consideration... Indeed, I had a sale balked just on that account."

Calgary got its building restrictions, but about the same time the city's Lady Keeper of Pigs departed. On September 12, 1904, the Herald announced: "Mrs. Fulham, who has been a noted character in Calgary for many years, has sold out her business and property and gone to Vancouver to live."

The last news item to be found concerning the woman was in the Herald six months later: "Mrs. Fulham, who was without doubt the best known woman in Calgary, passed through the city on Monday night. She informed some of those at the station that she was coming back to live here in about six weeks. This news will be received with mingled feelings."

The plan to return wasn't carried out but the memory of Mother Fulham lingered. For some of the pioneers the ghost of the Garbage Queen continued to hover about 6th Avenue West.

IN THE MATTER OF THE

Execution of Ernest Cashel

On the 2nd of February, 1904, at the North West Mounted Police
Barracks, Calgary.

Certificate of Execution of Judgment of Death.

*I, E. H. Rouleau, Surgeon of the North West Mounted Police
Guard Room at Calgary, in the North West Territories of Canada,
hereby certify that I, this day, examined the body of ERNEST
CASHEL, on whom judgment of death was this day executed in the
said prison; and that on such examination I found that the said
ERNEST CASHEL was dead.*

E. H. ROULEAU, M. D.

Dated this 2nd day of February in the year A.D., 1904.

DECLARATION.

We the undersigned hereby declare that judgment
of death was this day executed on ERNEST CASHEL
in the jail yard at the North West Mounted Police Barracks, Calgary, in the North West Territories.

Dated this 2nd day of February, 1904.

P. W. KING, Sheriff.
R. S. KNIGHT, J. P., in and for the N. W. T.
G. E. SAUNDERS, Jailor.
G. W. KERBY, Clergyman.
M. ROGERS. Guard.
C. W. CAPREY, Guard.
H. DES BARRES, Sergt. Provo.

INQUISITION.

CANADA:
NORTH WEST TERRITORIES,
DISTRICT OF ALBERTA.

An inquisition taken for His Majesty King Edward VII, at the Barracks of
the North West Mounted Police, in the District of Alberta, on the 2nd day of
February, 1904, in the fourth year of the reign of His Majesty King Edward
VII, before H. Goodsir Mackid, one of the Coroners of our said His Majesty for
the said district of Alberta, on view of the body of ERNEST CASHEL, then and there lying dead, upon the oath of Robt.
Jno. Hutchings, Jas. Findlay, Jno. Thos. Macdonald, Wendell McLean, W. H. Heald and Jas. Campbell Linton, good
and lawful men of the said District, duly chosen, and who being then and there duly sworn and charged to inquire for our
said His Majesty, when, where, how, and by what means the said ERNEST CASHEL came to his death, do, upon their
oath, say:— That the evidence placed before us, we find that ERNEST CASHEL came to his death on February 2nd, 1904,
by hanging by the neck until he was dead in accordance with the LAW, and that the execution was properly conducted.

In witness whereof as well as the said Coroner as the Jurors aforesaid, have hereunto set and subscribed their hands and
seals the day and year first above written.

H. G. MACKID,
Coroner, N. W. T.

[SEAL] R. J. HUTCHINGS, Foreman.
[SEAL] JAS. FINDLAY.
[SEAL] JAS. T. MACDONALD.
[SEAL] WENDELL MACLEAN.
[SEAL] W. HERBERT HEALD.
[SEAL] J. C. LINTON.

HERALD PRINT.

CALGARY'S MOST NOTORIOUS CRIMINAL

CALGARY'S MOST NOTORIOUS CRIMINAL

Ernest Cashel, it seemed, was born to notoriety. Trouble was, he chose the wrong ways to achieve it. From the time his name first appeared in local papers in October, 1902, until he was hanged at the Mounted Police Barracks at Calgary on February 2, 1904, Cashel was one of the most publicized people in the North West Territories.

At times the cunning fellow appeared to be "playing tag" with the police and outmanoeuvering them. Paddy Nolan, who was constantly in the role of counsel for the defence, said, "The boy is smart; he'd have made a clever lawyer." After his second escape from custody, Cashel became a man of mystery for whom many people held acknowledged fears, and perchance some secret admiration. Men meeting on Stephen Avenue speculated about where the elusive Ernest would appear next, and women, over cups of tea, confessed hopes it wouldn't be in their backyards or woodsheds. But folks came to expect something dramatic and skilful, and didn't discount the possibility that the accused man's next trick would be performed right beneath Calgary noses.

The good-looking Cashel, medium in height, dark in complexion and about 20 years of age, was not strictly an amateur in crime when he came to live at Ponoka.

Calgarians reading their daily papers on October 18, 1902, learned about a prisoner making a daring escape from Chief English — "the first person the chief ever lost." It was this way: Two days earlier, the Calgary chief of police went north with a warrant for the arrest of a young fellow charged with forging two cheques in the name of John Phalen and cashing them in Calgary. Nine miles east of Ponoka Chief English found his man at work, made the arrest, placed leg-irons on him and brought him back to the railway station by wagon.

The prisoner proved most co-operative and the first part of the train journey southward was uneventful. At Red Deer the train made a scheduled stop for dinner, and to enable the accused man to accompany the chief to a restaurant, the leg-irons were removed and a "twister or come-along" chain attached to his wrist.

But Cashel had no appetite for food and very soon the two men — one appearing dejected, the other, proud and domineering — were back on the train and speeding toward Calgary.

After leaving Red Deer, Cashel made a perfectly natural request for permission to visit the washroom. Nodding consent, the chief accompanied him to the end of the coach and remained outside when Cashel entered the washroom and closed the door. Minutes passed, and when the accused man didn't come out the chief became suspicious and forced open the door. Cashel was not there but the washroom window was open. The man had jumped, "though the train was going about 20 miles an hour."

From the next station a search was organized but with no success. The chief, humiliated by failure, returned to Calgary and passed the task of finding Cashel to the Mounted Police. In the days that followed, the escaped man was seen by various people. A sectionman on the railroad saw a coatless stranger walking with a limp. Near Lacombe, Rancher Amassy Diggs was visited by a young man reporting that his pony got away, taking his coat and all belongings. Impressed by the fellow's misfortune, Diggs loaned him a horse and saddle so he might hunt for his own property, the understanding being that the borrowed horse would be returned next day. But the rancher's horse was not returned.

The next report was that Ernest Cashel was seen near Calgary but the police discounted it, saying the suspect was another fellow — one called Nick Carter. Three months after the escape, a Springbank farmer living close to the city reported the theft of a horse and laid a charge against a Bert Ellsworth who came that way telling a hard-luck tale about his own pony having strayed away. Again, the stranger was accommodated with horse and saddle so he might more effectively search for his own animal.

The borrowed horse was not returned, but when the police overtook this Bert Ellsworth they discovered he was both Ernest Cashel and Nick Carter.

As related at the trial for horse stealing, the Springbank farmer located his horse on the Stoney Reservation and Stoney Indian George McLean told the court how it happened to be there. The accused man, riding through the reserve, stopped to talk with McLean and explained that he was hunting for a lost pony. McLean fancied the animal on which Cashel was riding and offered to do some trading. After lengthy negotiations, a trade was made, Cashel's horse for the Indian's horse and a rifle and box of bullets. Cashel then rode on, but three or four days later Indian George McLean found the horse he had traded, abandoned on the reserve.

When Cashel came before the court in May, 1903, he faced two charges of theft, one involving the horse and the other, a diamond ring stolen at Kananaskis. To both he pleaded guilty and went back to jail.

When spring weather melted the ice on lakes and rivers, some of Cashel's other misdeeds began catching up with him. The decomposed body of a bachelor farmer, Isaac Rufus Belt, was discovered floating at the mouth of Tail Creek on the Red Deer River. A deformed toe indentified the man, and from the coroner's inquest came the report that Belt "came to his death from murder . . . and in our opinion by the hand of one Cashel, now in Stony Mountain penitentiary."

Red Deer neighbors, who had noticed the sudden autumn disappearance of Belt, recalled that a young man by name of Ellsworth had been staying with him. The young fellow was supposed to be buying cattle to stock his ranch. It was also recalled that Ellsworth, Belt and Belt's buckskin horse disappeared at the same time.

In September, 1903, Cashel was brought back to Calgary to face a charge of murder, and again Paddy Nolan was retained for the defence. After the preliminary hearing, the young man came for trial before Chief Justice Sifton and jury. After days of evidence which Calgary people followed with special interest, the jury, out 35 minutes, returned with a verdict of "guilty" and the misguided fellow was sentenced to be hanged on December 15, 1903. That chapter, people remarked, was about to end. But Cashel was unpredictable and the most exciting part of the drama was yet to be enacted.

A news item in the evening paper of November 10, 1903, told that "Ernest Cashel, the prisoner under death-sentence, has received word that his brother who is a game warden in Wyoming will visit him soon." Well, Brother John arrived about two weeks before the date set for the execution — just as Paddy Nolan was seen catching an east-bound train. Although he told reporters he was "just going down the road for a few days," Nolan was on his way to Ottawa to interview the Minister of Justice about a new trial for his client. At the capital, the great defence lawyer received no encouragement but refused to leave while there was even a slight hope of reconsideration.

Back at the Mounted Police Barracks in Calgary, a scaffold for the hanging was being completed when, on the afternoon of December 10, John Cashel, wearing a heavy overcoat, visited his doomed brother and talked with him through the bars of his cell. As Ernest was being given his supper, immediately after the brother's departure, he confronted his guards with two cocked revolvers, quietly herded three of them into his own cell, locked the door and walked out into the night.

Late that same night, a young man needing shelter and food called at the farm house of C. W. Rigby, six miles west of Calgary. He was given a bed and next morning he talked freely about Ernest Cashel and, with no show of emotion, watched a detachment of police gallop past the house. With no evidence of hurry he went on his way, but returned later to steal a complete change of clothing and leave a note saying he'd call back in six months and signing it, "Ernest Cashel."

The news of the daring escape spread like wildfire. "Cashel is out again." Counting some escapades south of the border before coming to Canada, this was his third or fourth. The get-away became the chief topic of Calgary conversation. Home owners not only locked their doors when they retired at night, but moved organs and cupboards against them for added protection. A reward of a thousand dollars was posted for Cashel's capture. And in Ottawa, Paddy Nolan was in conversation with the Minister of Justice when the latter was handed a telegram. Breaking the conference to read the message, the Minister turned to announce: "Mr. Nolan, your man has escaped." The lawyer from the West grabbed his hat, saying: "Thank you sir, I'll be going."

Cashel stole another horse at the Andrew Smith ranch and was seen several times. The police were sure they had him surrounded and a special train stood ready to carry extra police officers out of Calgary. But the days passed and the clues evaporated. The police finally admitted they didn't know where Cashel was hiding.

For 45 days Ernest Cashel eluded the police. During that time he did not leave Calgary district, remaining around with the idea that he might help his brother John who was arrested and charged with aiding an escape. Ernest's final hiding place was seven miles east of the City where an abandoned shack with hay-stack close by offered the sort of protection he wanted. It was easy to excavate a den in the hay and he divided his time between shack and stack.

When the hiding place was finally discovered, Cashel was ready to shoot it out with the police and it was only when straw around the shack was set on fire that he threw down his guns and surrendered. This time the police made sure Ernest Cashel did not escape. The scaffold at the barracks was still standing. Just prior to going to his death on February 2, 1904, he confessed the shooting of Isaac Rufus Belt to Rev. George Kerby. A few minutes later, the story of Calgary's most noted criminal came to an end.

TROUBLE AT CITY HALL

Calgary's City Council was never noted for tranquility. Even in youthful years the waters of civic government were periodically rough. The first big scandal arose from the sale of city property. In bringing the citizens to anger it was a reminder, however, that elected representatives have a very real responsibility in guarding taxpayers' interests and should not under any cirmumstances be-come involved in personal transactions with the corporation or governing body of which they are a part. Through the years, the lessons were sometimes forgotten.

In March, 1904, the expanding City of Calgary had about 500 lots for sale and an urgent need for the money expected from them. Council, meeting on March 3, authorized, "That the finance committee be instructed to place a value on the lots of land held by the city ... and when the price is set they be put up for sale by the city treasurer."

That was the motion, but what, exactly, did it mean? Was the treasurer who was also the city clerk to proceed to sell the property without further reference to council, and was sale to be by auction or private treaty? The finance committee met very casually a couple of weeks later, took about 30 minutes to place valuations totalling $21,500 on the nearly 500 lots and, with no advertising whatever, most of the properties — certainly all the good ones — were sold before noon the next day. Purchasers were required to pay one-sixth of the total buying price in cash and had five years to pay the balance, with interest at six percent. They could buy one lot or as many as they wished. For a few hours the city hall was the scene of a genuine land-office business.

The first editorial reaction was that, "The speedy sale of these lots is a healthy sign." Almost at once, however, editors and citizens had second thoughts. Suspicion mounted. Why was the sale not advertised? How did it happen that friends of the aldermen got so many lots? And why were many lots sold at what seemed a fraction of their value? One citizen, who had a letter on file offering $100 a lot for certain properties, discovered the ones he wanted had sold for $35 each; and when he tried to buy them privately from the new owner, the price was $500.

Taxpayers were mad about what they called a "land-grab" and demanded an investigation. They weren't sure whether they had witnessed a display of incompetence or corruption, but they were determined to find out. Mayor Ramsay called a special meeting of city council and the chamber was jammed with irate citizens. The city solicitor, called upon for his opinion of the legality of sale, replied that, "If the resolution was legal and the city clerk acted within his powers, the sales were legal." That, however, satisfied nobody. One of the aldermen who had hoped to get some lots for himself made the loudest protest. He came down at 9 o'clock in the morning and the lots in which he was interested were sold. How was it, he asked, that prices were fixed at 6 o'clock at night and by 9 o'clock next morning, without public notice or advertising, the lots were practically all gone? Perhaps they were sold before the prices were set, he suggested. Anyway, as an alderman who wanted lots and didn't get any, he righteously proposed that Chief Justice Sifton be asked to conduct an enquiry.

The suggestion for an investigation wasn't accepted at the meeting. Some aldermen had good reason for hoping the public protest would subside without an exposure of all the circumstances. But the protest did not subside. Citizens sensing irregularities circulated a petition demanding a full investigation and the press gave it support. In the meantime, one real estate man, who had secured 75 of the lots, offered to give them up, but many other purchasers were reluctant to lose the benefit of good bargains, even when an independent law firm declared the entire sale to be illegal.

For days members of city council squirmed. The mayor announced that he favored sale by public auction, but Alderman Clarke insisted that nothing had been mentioned about auction selling when plans were being made. Alderman J. A. McKenzie, said to be a relative of one of the major purchasers, wrote a letter to the press, telling about seeing a light in the city hall the night the prices were set. Going in to find the reason, his gaze fell upon the list of lots and prices and he marked certain of the properties for Andrews and Devaney, who had given him a signed cheque with instructions to invest in Calgary land. None of the purchase money was his own, he insisted Alderman Macdonald, also, had some not-too-convincing explanations about how he happened to be involved.

Scandal at city hall was the talk of the town, and newspaper stories about the Russian-Japanese War in progress at the time were completely overshadowed. The demand for investigation became more ardent and the council, meeting on March 26, 1904, accepted the sale as being illegal, authorized the city clerk to refund all payments on lots and adopted a motion: "Moved by Alderman Macdonald, seconded by Alderman Clarke, that Chief Justice Sifton be authorized to hold an investigation of the sale of city lots."

By this time, all but one purchaser had surrendered claims to the lots they believed they had bought, and council instructed the mayor to appoint a special committee to revalue the controversial lots.

On March 28, Chief Justice Sifton opened the hearing and Calgarians crowded eagerly into the chamber. Nothing since the escape from local barracks of the convicted murderer, Ernest Cashel, had so exercised the city's people. One after another — land buyers, aldermen and city employees — were called to the stand. Some explained; some confessed; nobody could be very proud of what happened.

In due course the judge submitted his report and heads began to fall. In passing the resolution of March 3, authorizing the finance committee to establish prices and sell the lots, there was "gross carelessness" on the part of mayor and aldermen. Moreover, the committee itself was censured for taking its work so lightly — placing values on nearly 500 lots in half an hour.

Next, the judge concluded that Aldermen McKenzie and Macdonald had met on the evening prior to the sale with the clerk in the city hall office and prepared two lists. Next morning the city clerk had walked to his office with Alderman Irwin, arrived earlier than usual, and found a list of lots on his desk with a request from Alderman McKenzie to allot certain ones to T. H. Andrews and others to E. Devaney. Minutes later Mr. Blair had arrived with a list of lots he desired to buy. Alderman Irwin was then told that the lots were practically all sold, but after studying the list, he found two that he wanted.

The lists handed in by Alderman McKenzie and Mr. Blair, the judge noted, comprised about the same numbers of lots, over 270 in all, yet in no case were there duplicate applications. As for Mr. Blair's list, the judge could only conclude it was made up from information received from Alderman Macdonald. The report showed, also, that Aldermen Irwin and Hornby and City Solicitor Smith obtained lots, with only the solicitor paying the money for all and obtaining the receipt.

The first heads to fall were those of the two aldermen, McKenzie and Macdonald, who were found to have rendered themselves ineligible to sit as aldermen by having entered into contracts with the city. Aldermen Irwin and Hornby were considered to have escaped the effect of the ordinance by not actually paying any money or receiving any receipts.

The judge showed some sympathy for the city clerk, who believed he had the authority to sell the lots; but the particular blame attached to him was in allowing himself to be used by two aldermen for their own purposes in obtaining what promised to be a profitable bargain with the city.

Concluding his report, the Chief Justice believed the financial loss to the city would be small but reputations would suffer. Aldermen in the future would have to attend more assiduously to duties.

When the city council met on April 5, 1904, the chairs of the two disqualified aldermen were vacant. City Solicitor Smith and City Clerk McMillan resigned and their resignations were accepted. Next, the resignation of the city auditor was requested. Finally, Alderman Clark moved and Alderman Kerr seconded, that the entire council resign. If they were going to have a "house-cleaning," they might as well have a good one. On the streets and avenues there was support for the proposal that all the elected officials retire, and a petition was circulated. But in spite of petition and motion to hold a general civic election, the majority of council members were not in favour.

As it was, the casualties resulting from the blunders and indiscretions in the sale of lots stood at two aldermen, one clerk, one solicitor and one auditor. Another alderman submitted a resignation that wasn't accepted. A by-election to fill the two aldermanic vacancies was held on April 23, and in surprisingly short time public anger subsided. By the date of the next regular meeting of city council, things seemed to have returned to normal — instead of a chamber packed with agitated citizens, the city fathers had an audience comprising one lone and quiet spectator who was there because it was warmer than on the street.

That was the civic upheaval of 1904, when the men who sat on Calgary's city council learned the hard way that they should confine themselves to administration and leave civic business transactions intended for gain to others. It shouldn't be inferred, however, that a permanent peace descended upon city hall. As the record will show convincingly, the waters in Calgary's civic sea have never remained calm for long.

THE STRUGGLE FOR THE CAPITAL

Long before the Province of Alberta was created in 1905, Calgary people believed their city should be a capital; it had all the qualifying amenities. In the mid-'80's there was the report in a local paper that "the Dominion Government is seriously considering the abolition of Regina — that is to say the removal of the capital of the North West Territories, in which event there would be nothing left." Calgary promoters considered it a good idea and, quite openly, the Regina paper accused Calgary of trying to steal the capital, "injuring Regina in the eyes of the public and encouraging the idea that Calgary is the only place in the Territories fit to be a capital."

If the Territorial Capital were withdrawn from Regina, where would it be located? Calgary's Town Council could not decently ask aloud that the seat of government be snatched from Regina and placed beside the Bow River, but on January 18, 1888, a compromise proposal was approved for presentation to Ottawa, "to have the sittings of the North West Council alternate between Calgary and Regina."

"That's a smart idea," the foothills aldermen said to themselves, "and we'll let Regina keep a 50 percent interest in the capital." But the Dominion Government was not impressed and no change was made. Had the request been granted, Calgary might have established as good a claim to capital status in the new Province of Alberta as Regina did for itself in the new Province of Saskatchewan. As it was, the choice of capital site produced bitter inter-city rivalry with Edmonton, Calgary, Red Deer, Banff and Lacombe bidding for the honor in Alberta.

From the beginning of 1905, autonomy was the burning topic across the West. Under the leadership of Frederick Haultain, the prairie people obtained a federal promise of early action and they were impatient. The Calgary Board of Trade and Calgary newspapers became militant in their determination. Everybody in that city knew Calgary would be the best place for the capital of the new province to be carved from the westerly portion of the Territories. Nevertheless, local leaders were aware of the danger of overplaying their hands and decided to emphasize that they were not asking for "favors"; they wanted only impartial consideration — and if they got that, they'd get the capital. Edmonton's competition was what Calgary people feared most, but "What has Edmonton got to offer?" they kept asking; and besides, "Edmonton is too close to the North Pole."

As a matter of strategy, Calgary spokesmen were insisting that the provisional capital, likely to be named in the federal legislation, should go to some neutral point which would not be considered as a permanent location. It meant that neither Calgary nor Edmonton should be named as the temporary site. Calgary leaders proposed Banff for the temporary location — until Banff too began to show an interest in having permanent possession of the capital.

On February 2, a Calgary delegation headed by Mayor Emerson and including Major James Walker, W. H. Cushing and W. M. Davidson, left for Ottawa to wait upon the Cabinet and remain until the favorable assurances were gained. Unfortunately, an Edmonton delegation with exactly the same purpose went East about the same time. The northern delegates argued that Edmonton should be the provisional capital and also the permanent capital, and that no town like Banff or Fort Macleod within "the Calgary sphere of influence" should be considered.

Editorials from the two contending cities became steadily more bitter. One of the main arguments was about centre of population in the new province, and on this point the Daily Herald had something to say: "If the province were extended to the North Pole and every member of the remote Indian tribes was added to those of the white settlers, Edmonton would not yet be the centre of Alberta's population. Of course if it is the intention that Athabasca and the polar regions should be added to Alberta, the geographical centre would be nearer Edmonton than Calgary."

A week later, while bitter fighting in the Russo-Japanese war was international news and typhoid fever and political manoeuvring were important nearer home, the Calgary daily noted sarcastically: "Edmonton is a lively place, alright. To show the interest they do not take in the affairs of national importance, the leading editorial in one of the dailies last week was on the question of the dog catcher capturing a farmer's pups. That's the place to have a capital."

Meanwhile, Red Deer, Lacombe and Banff leaped or were pushed into the contest. Only Lethbridge displayed a superior and disdainful indifference. "Lethbridge is the only sane place in Alberta," wrote the editor of the Lethbridge Herald. "All the rest are capital crazy. Anybody knows that Lethbridge could be the capital by snapping its fingers, but we don't want it. We are going to be the commercial capital, not the political capital."

The Lethbridge editor then registered his choice in favor of Banff. If that place were selected, "No province could boast of a more picturesque seat of government." The attractiveness of Banff could not be questioned and C. W. Fisher, who sat in the Territorial Legislature, submitted a letter to Premier Haultain pointing out something even more unique about Banff's qualifications, that "although the times are peaceful and Canada desires peace, we ought to consider the possibility of war. If such an unhappy event should occur, what spot in the West could be so easily defended. A capital on the prairies would always be exposed to the danger of easy capture while Banff could in a few weeks be turned into an impregnable fortress." Fancy that as a 1906 argument in favor of Banff as the capital of Alberta.

Then there was Red Deer's bid accompanied by an offer of 50 acres of "choice land in the most commanding situation in the town." "We are in earnest about the capital," wrote the editor of the Alberta Advocate published in Red Deer. "We know that we have the strongest array of facts to present." After alluding to the purity of the water, the good drainage, excellence of climate and "noble river," the Red Deer spokesman reminded the legislators that with Calgary and Edmonton waging the most vigorous warfare for the capital, it would be only sensible to compromise and place the capital exactly midway between.

The so-called "capital fever" was highly contagious and still other centres contracted ambitious ideas — among them Blackfalds, whose spokesman offered a handy summary of the situation in these words: "Calgary is too far south . . Edmonton is too far north . . . Red Deer, a thriving and pretty little town, is situated too low in a valley, is muddy and has stuffy atmosphere. Lacombe is a smart, go-ahead prosperous town but there is positively no drainage." Finally, the crusader reached the real bleeding heart of his dissertation, that there is no town, "so suitable, so beautiful, so adaptable and so recommending," as Blackfalds.

All the while, the campaign to get the capital for Calgary was unrelenting. By way of good example, Calgary's Young Mens' Club held a Mock Parliament with the first measure being a government bill to name Calgary as the permanent capital of the new Province of Alberta. Opposition amendments were presented in favour of Edmonton, Red Deer and Hobbema but the make-believe bill passed in favor of Calgary.

On February 21, 1905, the real Autonomy Bill was introduced in the House of Commons by Sir Wilfred Laurier. It provided for two provinces to be named Saskatchewan and Alberta. Regina was to be the capital of the former and, to the supreme disappointment of the Calgary people, Edmonton was to be the provisional capital of Alberta. Each province was to have 10 representatives in the House of Commons and 25 members in its legislature. And as for the final decision about the site of Alberta's capital, that was to be left to the first legislature.

Edmonton, whose federal representative was Frank Oliver sitting on the government side, seemed to have triumphed over Calgary whose M. S. McCarthy was on the opposition side. But Calgary was not giving up; "the fight is just starting," said one of the local editors.

The new Act came into effect on September 1, 1905. Hon. G. H. V. Bulyea was appointed Lieutenant-Governor; and Hon. A. C. Rutherford, who represented Strathcona in the Territorial Legislature, was called to form a provincial government. The first general election was on November 9, 1905, and Rutherford's government was confirmed with a big majority.

The question of the permanent site for the legislative buildings was still unsettled when the first assembly was formally convened in Edmonton's Thistle Rink on March 15, 1906. Editorials were as pungent as ever, but Premier Rutherford admitted he favored Edmonton or Strathcona and the men of the South saw their case failing. In the final contest it was Calgary vs. Edmonton — North against the South — and the North won. In the legislature the vote was 16 to 8. For Calgary it was defeat with a painful sting but the fight was a good one. The capital decision practically coincided with the San Francisco earthquake — which meant that another city had been shaken much worse than Calgary.

AUTOMOBILES ON STEPHEN AVENUE

Some strange mechanical contrivances — self-propelled, of all things — appeared on streets and avenues soon after the beginning of the century.

The city which in recent years has boasted more motor vehicles per thousand of human population than any other city in Canada, received its first one, a steam-driven car, in 1903. Until that man-made wonder appeared, the most extravagant vehicle on Stephen Avenue was a London hansom — a low, two-wheel, two-passenger, horse drawn covered cab, with seat for the driver at the rear. It was brought to the town in 1895 and commanded a mixture of admiration and amusement as it rumbled over the rocks protruding from the frontier thoroughfares.

Rancher William F. Cochrane brought that Stanley steamer car known as a Locomobile to the district. The date of arrival has been disputed, but the Eye Opener of August 8, 1903, placed the event on record, referring to the machine as "the first automobile in Alberta."

As that sensation of its time came down Stephen Avenue, men stood to marvel at the sight. Road horses displayed less of tolerance and respect. Hackneys and Thoroughbreds considered well broken forgot their street manners, reared in panic, bolted and tried to kick their way out of the harness restraining escape. Nobody knew how many horses ran away but the accidents were numerous.

Away from the City the lack of roads or trails was no obstacle to Billy Cochrane, and he drove his famous car over ranch country, dodging badger holes and mud. On its first appearance on the Cochrane range, an uninformed cowboy, supposing the thing to be running out of control and taking the boss with it, dashed madly after the steamer and tried to capture it with his lariat. But Billy Cochrane liked his fun and the ultra-modern means of conveyance provided lots of it. Later the car was sold to Charles Jackson, who displayed it in Calgary street parades for many years; and finally, as a precious relic, it found its way to the Provincial Institute of Technology and Art where it was restored to working order by Stanley Green.

Calgary's next was a gasoline auto introduced to the City in the spring of 1904. This, a Rambler, was made in Wisconsin and brought to Calgary by John Prince, who made some local history by driving to Nanton in 5½ hours. Later in the same year J. J. Young, editor of the Calgary Herald and Member of the Territorial Legislature, bought a McLaughlin, and R. B. Bennett an Oldsmobile.

Bob Edwards of the Calgary Eye Opener observed that the "first thing a man with a new automobile runs into is debt," but it wasn't that way in Bennett's case. The first thing he ran into was a stone building, one in which Calgary citizens kept their savings.

His driving career was brief. Taking Mr. Edgar of the Hudson's Bay Company for a spin on an April evening in 1905, things of a mechanical nature went wrong. Derby hats were dashed to the ground and the dignity of Calgary's best groomed lawyer, at that time a Member of the Legislative Assembly of the North West Territories, was slightly injured. The one-cylinder car, after chugging its way along Stephen Avenue ,was turned with moderate skill at Centre Street but right ahead was a youth on a bicycle, taking traffic liberties such as young fellows on bicycles have never ceased to take. To avoid hitting the rider, Driver Bennett turned his car quickly, mounted the pavement and crashed violently into the wall of the Imperial Bank Building. Bicycle and building escaped injury but the car was damaged severely.

Cynics agreed that horsepower was much safer when the horses had it all to themselves and human life would never be free from danger in an automobile age.

Mr. Bennett rose in wealth and fame and became Prime Minister of Canada. Annually he travelled many thousands of miles but never again did he indulge in the uncertain pastime of driving himself.

By September of 1906 there were 10 cars in Calgary, and the owners were listed by City Clerk H. E. Gillies in response to a letter from the Deputy Provincial Treasurer: John Prince, J. J. Young, A. McKenzie, Fred Lowes, Healey Brothers, White and Grasswick, Fred Brown, Bert Stringer, Charles Jackson and Mr. Hillier. Mr. Bennett was no longer numbered among the car owners.

Ten primitive motor vehicles in 1906; and 75,000 offering comfort and more speed than anybody needed, 50 years later. That was the Calgary record which helped to explain why the city motorists were increasingly inclined to tear their hair while trying to locate parking places where they wanted and needed them.

But as the noisy early cars were becoming more numerous, the horsemen, fighting for their rights, became more hostile. Many and strange were the proposals made by horse drivers in whose eyes any car was a danger and a menace. Some rules the suffering horsemen about Calgary would have imposed upon car drivers in 1909 should be noted:

1. When an approaching team is observed the automobilist must stop offside and cover his machine with a tarpaulin painted to correspond with the scenery.

2. A driver approaching a corner where he cannot command a view of all incoming roads must stop not less than 100 yards from the turn and toot his horn before proceeding.

3. Penalty for speeding — a dollar for every mile per hour in excess of ten. Thus an estimated speed of 20 miles per hour would call for a fine of $10.

4. In case of autos making horses run away the compensation to the horseowner will be $50 for the first mile the horses run and $100 for the second mile, in addition to customary damages.

Not only did the horsemen become increasingly hostile, but car drivers became increasingly courageous in the trips they undertook. A few Calgary chauffeurs ventured as far as Red Deer and Banff in 1906. When the hidden hazards of strange trails were considered — country roads might be all right for horses but not for cars — plus the temperamental nature of 1906 motors, he was indeed a bold driver who would tackle a tour of more than a hundred miles.

Especially newsworthy was the account of an Edmonton man who made a journey to Calgary without mishap at that time. "From Edmonton to Calgary in a motor car, 200 miles in 11½ hours, was the record made by G. Corriveau of Edmonton the other day. Mr. Corriveau sold the machine, a 29 horse-power, four-seated affair, to W. H. White of Calgary and in company with his son, Mr. White and Mr. Lundy of Innisfail, made the trip to Calgary." Quite clearly the editor who recorded the expedition was properly impressed.

A few years later Calgarians read about a sensational driving record made by Fellow Citizen Ernie Hubbert, sales manager for

Canadian Natural Gas Company. Wearing goggles and a tight-fitting cap, Hubbert drove his Ford roadster from Cemetery Hill in Calgary to Okotoks in 46 minutes, "thus establishing a record for cars of its class." Officials who gave the starting signal and timed the mad drive took affidavits to support the accuracy of their figures. And word having been sent ahead about this race against time, scores of farming people and Okotoks residents were present to see the roadster complete its run with an average speed of 29 miles per hour. That was in April, 1913.

The Calgary speed limit at that time was 15 miles per hour, and on the day of the disastrous McCarty-Pelkey fight, about a month after the roadster made its record-breaking run to Okotoks, 50 Calgary motorists were charged with fast and dangerous driving. The number represented a big percentage of all the car owners and civic revenue was substantially raised.

The first closed car appeared on Calgary streets in 1911 and was greeted with laughter. "A greenhouse on wheels," it was called, though the correct name was sedan. Most observers agreed that it had no practical future, that the rattle of windows and the dangers of broken glass would be enough to condemn it. The touring type car was the thing, and if there was threat of rain a driver could take a few minutes to put up the top and button on the side curtains normally carried under the seat cushion.

One of the first closed cars seen in Calgary was conspicuous in other ways. It was one of the biggest and heaviest cars made and came to Calgary for Mrs. Lougheed, wife of Senator Lougheed. Seven thousand dollars would buy much of any commodity in 1911 and the huge, custom-made Peerless, with driver's seat securely partitioned off, bore the same relationship to cars of later models as the cumbersome steam engines of that period bore to handy farm tractors that followed.

Misunderstanding arose about the Peerless and delivery was never completed. The big car was unloaded, taken for a trial run over Calgary streets, and then placed in storage, the property of Cattleman Frank Collicutt. There, hidden and stationary, the leviathan of the automobile world remained for over 40 years, ultimately being rediscovered by one who recognized it as a rare relic. It was then bought for the Western Development Museum at Saskatoon where its working mechanism was revived. There, amid other mechanical curios of steam tractor years, the automobile wonder of 1910 found a permanent home.

But while gasoline power was becoming popular and promising to dominate on city streets and country roads, the position of horse stock was bound to change. Motor vehicles and horses seemed to be in direct conflict. They were in conflict and the position of the horses did change in a spectacular way. But nothing in the life of Calgary was more striking than the bonds of affection for and loyalty to horses, which remained unbroken.

HUNTERS, HACKS AND HALTERSHANKS

As the building of the Municipal Street Railway system in 1908 marked an acceptance of mechanization, Calgary was still a "City of Horsemen."

Horsehairs on one's coat were never considered a disgrace in and about Calgary. Nor was there ever a time when hacks, hunters and haltershanks were not acceptable topics for polite conversation. Horses had an essential place in the lives of ranchland citizens and readily became a part of local tradition. For at least half a century Calgary was acknowledged to be the "horsiest" city in the realm, with porches sheltering more saddles — stock saddles and flat saddles — per thousand of human population than in any other urban community.

Even on the Scottish Isle of Mull the Calgary name had an equine connotation. Many of the best ponies of the Highland breed were to be found there, and ponies bred by the Mackenzie of Calgarry House were considered to possess special excellence.

Though quick to adopt motive transportation, the Alberta City was the last to abandon hitching posts. Actually it never completely rejected those homely institutions, because every year at Stampede season a few are brought back as invitations to street-weary horsemen to stop and tie up.

Indeed, it is improbable that business streets and avenues anywhere witnessed more varied displays of good horsemanship and bad horse manners. The surrounding ranch country supported bronchos of all kinds, colors and degrees of meanness, and the men of the range weren't always particular which ones they rode or drove to town. For years run-aways on Stephen and Atlantic Avenues were so commonplace that local papers didn't report them unless a horse plunged through a plate glass window or somebody was carried away on a stretcher.

The main thoroughfares were the scenes of rather numerous harness races, but now and then one of the pleasure-bent horsemen came under the gaze of a policeman who neglected to turn his back upon the scene, and faced a charge of fast or reckless driving. Often enough to serve as a public reminder somebody appeared before the magistrate and paid a fine for "bronchobusting" on the main street, "to danger of pedestrians."

But the law officers had no thought of depriving the horsemen of all their fun, or spectators of the excitement; and a news item on September 27, 1901, noted: " a magnificent bit of rough riding on First Street West yesterday evening. Ed. Taylor of Macleod was riding a nasty, vicious broncho."

For many years the Corporation of the City of Calgary owned horses for street use, and purchase and sale were frequently on the agenda of city council. At least one candidate, in drawing public attention to his qualifications for the office of Mayor, noted "long and profitable experience with horses." What he implied was that nobody would sell the city a foundered or broken-winded horse while he sat in the Mayor's chair.

Local horses, however, provided problems in various forms for city fathers, as a perusal of minutes of council meetings will show. At the meeting on June 10, 1885, Councillor N. J. Lindsay, on behalf of his committee, reported the successful disposal of "the carcass of a dead horse which was rapidly decomposing" on one of the streets. On February 16, 1905, august aldermen proclaimed: "That on and after the 28th day of February, no more dead horses to be dumped on the exhibition grounds." And at the meeting of February 18, 1904, the Mayor and clerk were authorized "to issue a cheque in favor of Frank Hamilton for the sum of $40 in full of claim against the city for damages to horse, rig and harness caused by said horse falling into an open drain."

But there were more romantic sides to Calgary's horse history. A strikingly large number of local animals won international honors and admiration one way or another. A Hackney stallion

137

won the breed championship at Madison Square; a jumping horse made a world record; the Thoroughbred, Joey, distinguished himself in winning both races and human hearts; the unconquerable bucking horse, Midnight, bred by rancher Jim McNab of Fort Macleod, became a sensation of the rodeo world; the big black Percheron mare owned and exhibited by Hardy Salter had 45 grand championships to her credit. And so, the story of Calgary horses is one of achievement and color.

The Hackney stallion which won championship honors in New York in 1901 was Robin Adair, a stylish thing which had been in the ownership of Rawlinson Brothers of Calgary. But the most famous local horse at that period belonged to a draft breed; this, the "champion of champions" as he was hailed, was a Clydesdale stallion — Balgreggan Hero — owned by John Turner, who farmed on Calgary's South-West. For three consecutive years that horse was undefeated at the Winnipeg Exhibition, and he was selected to go with the Canadian exhibit to the World's Fair at Chicago. The Calgary pride in Balgreggan Hero resembled the kind inspired by winning hockey team in later years.

The first Territorial Stallion Show was held in Calgary in May, 1902, and provided classes for Clydesdales, Percherons, Shires, Suffolks, Hackneys, Standard Breds, Thoroughbreds and French Coach. It was something of an equine menagerie. The most coveted award was an inter-breed championship and it was won by a Clydesdale from John Turner's farm.

Calgary had a succession of outstanding jumping horses. Somebody recorded the view that it was due to the high altitude. Smokey, owned by P. D. McDonald, made a Canadian record in 1914 by clearing the bars at exactly seven feet. A Calgary-owned animal standing 13½ hands and performing at Brandon Winter Fair in 1922, made a six-foot jump, said to be a world record for pony jumpers.

But the jumper of them all was Calgary's Bara Lad, owned by Peter Welsh. On a local jumping course the temperamental gelding equalled Smokey's record, but his best marks were made away from home. At the opening night of Brandon Winter Fair in March, 1922, Bara Lad established a Manitoba record by jumping six feet, 10 inches; and next night he bettered his own mark by doing seven feet and one inch.

It was at New Westminster three years later that Bara Lad made a world record and ended his life. The bars were set at the forbidding height of eight feet and one and a half inches. Conversing spectators said it was impossible; and then they saw the amazing horse — ears back ,nostrils distended, and Louis Welsh in the saddle — spring almost tiger-fashion into the air and come down on the other side of the obstacle, a world champion. Six thousand horse-show patrons screamed their surprise and admiration. There was a sad epilogue, however; in making the winning effort the great and game horse injured himself internally, and five hours later he was dead.

Then there was Joey — the little Thoroughbred with the heart of a fighter and a personality that made Calgarians and others love him. For years he was the darling of the turf. In a sense he was an "ugly duckling." As a foal he commanded small attention, and he and his mother sold together for $185. But when he approached maturity, the indomitable racing spirit of the horse became apparent. Usually he was in front when the race ended, and his winnings totalled $37,000 to make him a leader among Canadian horses on Canadian tracks.

So well-known did Joey become, that when plans were being made for the Victory Loan Campaign in Winnipeg, it was decided that Joey should be brought from Calgary to officially start the program and subscribe some of his own earnings. Fact was that Joey was a recognized personality as well as a great runner. Even Winnipeg could become enthusiastic.

For long after his death the courageous little Thoroughbred was still a favorite; and as events showed, still in big money. On October 16, 1944, three years after the horse's death, Calgary was the scene of an auction sale at which the racing shoes of the famous American horses, Whirlaway and Seabiscuit, and the Calgary horse, Joey, were sold, with bids in terms of pledges to buy Victory Bonds. The shoes of the celebrated Seabiscuit, silver-plated and mounted on pieces of aeroplane propeller, brought pledges amounting to $10,000; Whirlaway's shoes went for $6,000 in pledges. But Joey had more friends than either Whirlaway or Seabiscuit and the bids for his last racing shoes went to a total of $40,000. It was Joey's last race and he was the winner. And, as fans were reminded repeatedly, Joey belonged to Calgary.

A lot of Canada's horse history was written or could have been written in the Calgary area. It should not have been forgotten that the first shipment of pure bred Percheron horses to go from this continent to the home of the breed in Europe went from Calgary; and that the most notable single shipment from France to Canada came to Calgary in 1909 — a band comprising 72 pure bred mares and three stallions bought by George Lane of the Bar U Ranch. They arrived just too late for the Dominion Fair.

Horse fortunes rose and fell, but the admirers of good hunters, hacks, drafters, ponies and other kinds remained loyal. The magnificent bronze statue in Central Park, erected in 1914 "In Memory Of The Brave Men Of The Province" who fell in the South African War, was seen by many who viewed it as a memorial to the soldier's horse as well as to the soldier.

And at a Rangeman's Banquet in Calgary many years after the streets ceased to be good places for displays of rough-riding, the toast of the evening was to the "cowboy's horse," and several hundred ranchers and pioneers stood to pay their respects. It was a solemn and lovely moment.

Clearly, no horsemen had more interesting memories than those at Calgary. They were such memories as an age of mechanization could not erase.

THE BLOODLESS BATTLE OF OLDS

The bloodless "Battle of Olds" took place well beyond the city limits, but Calgarians had a special interest in it and at least 60 citizens from the city witnessed the main events.

At 8.15 on the morning of Monday, June 3, 1907, a special C.P.R. train pulled out of Calgary carrying the invading force — 60 robust workmen described as "navvies," Inspector Duffus with eight officers from the North West Mounted Police barracks, and District Superintendent Niblock along with various other C.P.R. officials. Destination was the Village of Olds, 50 miles to the North.

Smouldering for more than a year was a dispute over a railroad crossing in the village. The people there made good use of the crossing at 3rd Street until, on May 3, 1906, railroad workers closed it, removed the plank sidewalk, and unceremoniously fenced off the road.

"Who do they think they are?" the villagers were asking contemptuously, at the same time goading their municipal council to demand re-opening of the thoroughfare. Acting upon citizen displeasure, the village fathers succeeded in obtaining an order from the Board of Railway Commissioners to have the disputed crossing opened. The railway authorities obeyed, but almost at once they closed a similar crossing at 2nd Street and local indignation turned to anger.

Was this a legal crossing? That was the question that had to be answered. People living in and about the village said it was, and therefore the municipality could insist upon the right-of-way. The Company maintained it was not a legal crossing, that the property belonged to the railway and could be closed at the Company's pleasure.

Assured by the village's solicitor that they were within their right in resisting street closure, citizens became bold and some belligerent. They'd fight it out if necessary. When railroad workmen removed the 2nd Street sidewalk and erected a fence to stop traffic, determined residents promptly relaid the walk and tore down the fence. The same thing was repeated, and then it was learned that a contingent of policemen and workers was on its way from Calgary to enforce the will of the railroad company.

Tempers flared and some hotheads favored arming homesteaders and other able-bodied men with clubs and pitch-forks. Better judgment prevailed, however, and there was no resort to weapons of violence. But when the special train from Calgary arrived at the hour of noon, more than 200 men and a few women from village and surrounding country were assembled at the crossing to furnish a welcome of sorts.

The train was stopped at the crossing, and after an uncoupling, half of the cars were placed on each side of the disputed roadway. Evidently it was part of the planned defensive strategy.

When 60 men and policemen emerged from the train, an Olds man was heard to shout defiantly: "Why didn't you bring the rest of Calgary? We'll take 'em on."

Superintendent Niblick, prior to departure from Calgary, had assured representatives of the press that he did not anticipate trouble, but the angry Olds crowd, headed by the village council and a battery of special constables, gave him reason to change his mind. Forthwith, Inspector Duffus read the Riot Act and the listeners, not quite sure what it was all about, were at least temporarily subdued.

With unwarranted complacency the Mounted Police went to dinner at a village restaurant. It was a mistake, but it wasn't the first time that hunger and the thought of fried pork chops had caused men to forget their purpose. Promptly at one o'clock, while the Mounties were still absent, Company Superintendent Niblock ordered his hired men to tear up the sidewalk and close the crossing by means of a fence. Just as promptly the village constables, with the Councillors and Justice of the Peace behind them, stepped forward and arrested Niblock. Simultaneously, citizens proceeded to demolish the road barricade as the workmen tried to put it up. And the seizure of Niblock was followed immediately by the arrest of his subordinates, Roadmaster George Bell and C.P.R. Constable Foy. According to newspaper reports, only Foy resisted — "drew his baton and stirred up considerable civic bile."

The Mounted Policemen, enjoying the good Olds food, were inconsiderately interrupted by a message to return quickly to the crossing. They responded at once, and sensing what had happened, Inspector Duffus ordered his uniformed men to release Superintendent Niblock and arrest the constables who had taken him into custody. "Use your guns if necessary," he was reported to have commanded.

The excitement was terrific, and as the Olds constables were seized and placed as prisoners in one of the railroad cars, it would have been easy to start a wicked riot.

"What's the matter with Olds?" a local man shouted. "Surely you're not going to be held up by a few Mounted Policemen."

Members of the village council stepped forward to urge the local mob to restraint. "We'll win this battle another day," one of them said. The wisdom of submission was recognized by most of the local people. And with the Mounted Police now pretty well in control, the work of closing the crossing went forward.

Charges and counter-charges followed. The C.P.R. men were charged with obstructing police officers. The Olds men were charged with unlawful assembly and assault. Inspector Duffus contended that Justice of the Peace Deane exceeded his authority in swearing in the special Olds constables. But the Justice of the Peace showed no inclination to retreat. He summoned the railway superintendent and the Mounted Police Inspector to appear before him at 2.30 o'clock that afternoon. The order was ignored and warrants for arrest were issued although, evidently, they were not formally served.

The legal confusion was entertaining if not embarrassing — two groups of police officers fighting for authority and trying to find reasons for and ways of arresting each other. But the Mounted Police had the advantage of greater numbers and the day ended with three Olds constables locked up, the C.P.R. encamped as victors on the field of battle, the Justice of the Peace still demanding arrest of the officer commanding the Mounties, and the village spokesmen appealing once again to the Board of Railway Commissioners to order an opening.

The special train returned to Calgary; Olds Constables Maybank, Harvey and Sinclair were released on bail of $1000 each; and C.P.R. officials Bell and Foy were released on $2000 each.

The Mounted Police came in for criticism on their performance during the day and seemed ready to drop charges, but the Olds Justice of the Peace entertained no such benevolent feelings. To make a long story no longer than necessary, the nearby village, which according to headlines was "Aflame With Excitement," settled down to quietude once again, notwithstanding the fact that the crossing remained closed for some time.

As the account of the day's events was reported across the country, it sounded like civil war. It wasn't that bad, but it was a day the Olds people and some Calgary people didn't forget.

A few days after the trouble at the crossing, revolution broke out in South America. A local paper suggested that following so closely upon the clash between Calgary and Olds personalities, the South American news was unlikely to command much of readers' interest.

BIGGER AND BETTER EXHIBITIONS

After knocking at the door of oblivion, the bankrupt Agricultural Society managed to pull itself together and the year 1907 saw the revitalized organization heading for bigger things. It was Ernie Richardson's first year with full responsibility of management and he had big ideas, among them a conviction that Calgary should accept the challenge of staging a Dominion Exhibition in the following summer.

Much had happened since that day, just ten years before, when the Agricultural Society, having lost its fair ground to creditors, was debating its next course of action — if any. Some people were saying that Calgary had seen its last fair or exhibition.

But interest wasn't dead, and after two silent years the minutes of a meeting held an May 19, 1899, show Mr. Van Wart moving and Mr. Johnston seconding "that the Exhibition be held on the old ground providing suitable arrangements can be made with Mr. Bennett."

Rental arrangements were made with R. B. Bennett, who held title to the property, and a fair was held in September. On the year's operations there was a surplus of $37.45 and the directors were encouraged.

At this point the reorganized Agricultural Society was known as Inter-Western Pacific Exposition Company, and directors became anxious to buy back the fair ground or acquire suitable land elsewhere. But with no money in the old treasury and only $37.45 in the new one, there was but small hope of purchasing property. Even the rent payable to Mr. Bennett for the use of the ground seemed formidable and went into arrears. Other locations were considered, including the biggest of the nearby islands in the Bow River, but the necessity of a $4000 bridge discouraged that idea.

Late in 1900 directors moved to ask the City Council to obtain a long-term lease on the old site and let the Company operate the plant. The mayor and aldermen, however, were not favorably disposed to leasing and suggested repurchase in the name of the City. Pursuing the idea, City Council meeting on February 8, 1901, was informed of "a communication from R. B. Bennett stating that the price of the Agricultural ground was now $7,000 plus $250 for back rental. On payment of the sum mentioned he was prepared to hand over the deeds to the City."

Members of the Council were divided in their views; Alderman Hatfield said derisively that he'd let Bennett keep the property but Alderman Young received support for his motion to offer "Mr. Bennett the sum of $6,500 with interest at seven percent from first of June." The offer went forward but Bennett refused to compromise, and when City Council met on February 14, 1901, purchase at $7,000 was approved. Thus the City of Calgary became the owner of the Exhibition Ground, and almost immediately an agreement to lease the property to the Company for a period of 20 years was presented and approved.

At the end of January, 1903, W. H. Cushing, president of the Board of Trade, announced that Charles W. Peterson, who had been Deputy Commissioner of Agriculture for the North West Territories, had accepted an offer to become the joint secretary of Board of Trade and Inter-Western Pacific Exposition. The salary was to be a handsome $2,000 a year. And later in the same year a young man with a Diploma in Agriculture from the Ontario Agricultural College came to be Peterson's assistant. He was E. L. Richardson, soon to be better known across the West as Ernie Richardson.

Four years after seeing Calgary for the first time Richardson assumed full management of the Exhibition and retained the responsibility for the next 33 years to witness the most spectacular changes. Though short in stature, he was long in imagination and showmanship and became the acknowledged "Dean of Exhibition Managers" across the West. When he retired in 1940 the Exhibition and Stampede attendance was nearly a quarter of a million — 500 times greater than it was at the first fair in Calgary — and still growing.

Ernie Richardson and fellow promoters of 1907 were pressing for three major concessions; they wanted the University of Alberta to be located beside the Bow River; they wanted the Federal Government to place the main body of its recently acquired herd of North American buffalo somewhere close to the City; and they wanted the Dominion Exhibition.

The idea of making Calgary the buffalo capital of the world originated with the "Hundred Thousand Club," Calgary's energetic "Booster Club" of that time. Major James Walker was named to convene a special committee, and with Ernie Richardson as strategist, a formal request went to Ottawa. With it went an application for a lease on half the Sarcee Indian Reserve for use as a buffalo range. The Indians liked the idea and all Calgary was enthused, but the Government was unimpressed and simply went ahead with the plan to place its recently acquired Pablo and Allard herd from Montana on the big prairie park at Wainwright.

Nor was the request for the Provincial University any more successful. Edmonton, which had gained the Provincial Capital in the face of strong Calgary claims, was now getting the University also. Calgarians were disappointed and bitter. Inter-city feeling produced unkind remarks and jealousy was no longer hidden. Edmonton, according to a local editor, wouldn't even let Calgary's claim to the biggest hail storm of the season go unchallenged. There was an urge to do something which would completely overshadow and even humiliate the Capital City — and Richardson knew it very well.

With a politician's paternal desire to ameliorate, Hon. Frank Oliver suggested that Calgary petition for the privilege of holding the coveted Dominion Exhibition in 1908, promising to personally support the request and see to it that the usual cash grants to help make the fair a success would be forthcoming.

Toronto held the first Dominion Exhibition in 1903 and Winnipeg held the second. Calgary was the sixth Canadian City to be accorded the distinction, and the dates for the ten-day event were fixed for June 29 to July 9, 1908. In accepting the task Calgary's

Richardson promised to make the show of that year the greatest event ever held in Western Canada.

The Federal Government promised a grant of $50,000, the Provincial Government $35,000 and the City of Calgary $25,000. Preparations began a full year in advance, and directors embarked upon a $60,000 building program to furnish new barns, exhibit buildings and an addition to the grandstand to accommodate a total of 5,500 people.

"If you want to have the time of your life," Ernie Richardson announced, "come early to the Dominion Exhibition and stay late."

The premium list showed an offer of $20,000 in regular prizes and $13,000 for horse races. And coupled with all the razzle-dazzle of the circus there was promise of street parades, Miller Brothers' Wild West Show from Oklahoma, roughriding contests, daily airship flights with Strobel's balloon-motor combination which in the previous year had won the airship race at St. Louis, Indian races, polo matches with Calgary, Millarville, Pekisko and Fish Creek competing, the Highlanders' Band from Hamilton, and the Iowa State Band for American Day on July 4.

Ten days before the opening Manager Ernie Richardson was stricken with appendicitis; but he refused to submit to an operation until the show was over, and the sick man carried on.

A mile-long parade in down-town Calgary marked the beginning of the Dominion Exhibition and also the birth of the now-famous Monday morning Stampede Parade. The Grand Marshal was the incomparable Cappy Smart of the Fire Department. No one else could have filled the role of Field Marshal as well as the Fire Chief. And the leading carriage, drawn by Calgary's proudest horses, carried Lieutenant-Governor Bulyea, Chief Justice Sifton, Senator James Lougheed and Exhibition President I. S. G. Van Wart.

The parade surpassed anything Calgary had seen. The biggest section told the history of the prairie country, with Indians followed in logical sequence by missionaries, traders, Mounted Policemen, railroad builders, cowboys and farmers. The Alberta Conference of the Methodist Church, meeting at Medicine Hat in a preceeding week, formally protested the proposal to include the Indians in the program, pointing out that the atmosphere of a city exhibition would corrupt the native people and revive "pagan customs" among them. But Rev. John McDougall, who knew In-

147

dians better than anybody else in the Methodist ranks, was in charge; and the only evidence of "pagan customs" came from members of the white race who discovered an exhibition booth at which it was possible to buy "strong cider" and something else with an alleged alcohol content of three percent.

Immediately after the parade the Lieutenant-Governor mounted the platform in front of the new grandstand, said all the right things about Calgary's wonderful climate, the prospects for a bumper crop, pigs and poultry as the salvation of agriculture, and officially opened the exhibition.

On that first day 25,000 people paid 25 cents each to enter the ground, and many contributed an additional 25 cents to sit on the grandstand to view the airship's ascent and other unbelievable things in entertainment. And nobody in that period went to a fair without visiting the barns. On this occasion the livestock entries made the greatest display Western Canada had experienced. Clydesdales, of course, predominated in the horse department, and Shorthorns in cattle. Hereford entries were light, consisting of a single herd owned by J. A. Chapman of Manitoba and a single bull from a British Columbia breeder.

There were a few tragedies — no exhibition escapes, it seems. A team of frantic run-away horses dashed down the midway and wrecked a few popcorn stands without killing any people. More serious was the accident during a high wind on the afternoon of American Day; a tent blown against the gas-filled balloon of Stobel's airship caused an explosion and the ship's destruction by fire. Jack Dallas, the usual operator, who admitted that air travel always made him sick, was burned rather severely and taken to hospital. But what cast the biggest shadow of gloom over the exhibition was the death of a pioneer, W. D. Kerfoot of Cochrane, the man who had brought the first big flock of sheep to the Calgary area 24 years before. Losing control of a frisky horse in front of the grandstand, he was thrown and killed.

What most people considered foremost in exhibition interest was the array of district displays — collective exhibits of district products as presented by Boards of Trade and Agricultural Societies in 37 different communities of the West. With good reason could Ernie Richardson say: "If you can't see all of the West, you can and should see the District Displays at the Dominion Exhibition."

Kelowna had a tempting arrangement of fruits; Prince Albert boastfully displayed lumber, furs, gold and wheat; Medicine Hat, describing itself as "the Town that was born lucky," featured the advantages of having natural gas; and Lethbridge presented reason to support its claim that "Lethbridge mines its own coal, makes its own flour, produces its own honey, grows its own fruit and vegetables, kills its own meat of all kinds, manufactures its own cloth and is more self-sustaining than any other district in the Province." But when the contest judges had finished their work, the first prize was won by Granum, second by Okotoks and third by Carstairs.

When the show ended after ten exciting days, the total paid gate attendance stood at 89,439 and the grandstand attendance at 52,635. On the entire undertaking the Exhibition Association lost some money; but Calgary people, temporarily forgetting the loss of a Provincial University, were satisfied and proud of the general performance. Even the neighbors in Edmonton were obliged to admit that it was a history-making achievement and had done much to win country-wide respect for both city and province.

Said Ernie Richardson: "We're only starting. Give us time and we'll show the world something in exhibitions."

A COLLEGE AND ITS FOUNDER

While denial of the Provincial University on a Calgary site still rankled, the community heard the voices of resolute men like Reverend George Kerby and Dr. Thomas Henry Blow. "If the Government refuses to provide for higher education in our City, we'll build our own colleges."

Not all the dreams came true, but at least George Kerby achieved his college dream — Mount Royal — the means of providing secondary education for some 10,000 students and giving them the added benefit of his fine and forceful influence. The College as Calgarians came to know it ultimately, serving 1500 or more pupils a year in its High School Department, University Department, Commercial Department and Conservatory of Music, might well have carried the name of "Kerby College."

A COLLEGE AND ITS FOUNDER

From the time of his arrival at Calgary George Kerby saw a need for more educational facilities. A secondary school with residence accommodation for the special benefit of young people from rural homes was an urgent necessity and he talked about it often. Realization began with the offer of land for a school and then the granting on December 16, 1910, of a provincial charter for a non-profit educational institution. The name was to be Calgary College but the Provincial Government saw objections. Premier Sifton phoned Kerby from Edmonton, telling that a new name was needed. Kerby paused momentarily and said: "Mount Royal." The Premier replied: "That will be satisfactory."

A Board of Governors was appointed and Kerby was searching about for someone whose name might be recommended for the important post of principal. It came as a complete surprise when the new Board requested formally that he become the principal. He needed a few weeks to consider, but his decision was to accept and devote himself completely to education.

In succeeding months George Kerby visited 65 colleges in the United States and Eastern Canada and returned to Calgary with lots of fresh ideas for the institution he hoped would become a full fledged University in time. Plans were drawn for a dormitory to accommodate 140 students. The College opened on September 8, 1911, and the enrollment in that first year was 189.

In the following year Victoria College honored the founder and principal with a Doctor of Divinity degree. The name of Kerby was becoming familiar in many parts of Canada. He was writing articles, books and poems; he was a popular Chautauqua lecturer; he became vice-president of the Canadian Authors' Society, first president of the Canadian Federation of Home and School Associations, and vice-president of the International Federation. Nearer home he was a Calgary School Trustee, member of Calgary Hospital Board, Chairman of the Board of Education and active in Canadian Club, Board of Trade, Rotary and so on.

They called him the "Calgary Dynamo," and for very good reason. At the time of his death on February 9, 1944, he was "Honorary Lieutenant-Colonel, Reverend George Kerby, D.D., LL.D., B.A., E.D., Principal Emeritus of Mount Royal College;" and titles indicated only a fraction of the activities of this churchman, educator, author, poet and lecturer.

When he accepted the call of the West in 1903, a Toronto man said with obvious disappointment: "Kerby's going to Godforsaken Calgary and he'll never be heard from again." But Calgary's Kerby was to become a national figure, and at the end of 41 years in his adopted community the press could state that: "Dr. Kerby did more than any other man to promote education and appreciation of spiritual values in this city."

George Kerby's birth was on a farm in Sombra Township, Lambton County, Ontario, and the date was July 18, 1860. Sometimes he dated his birth from that day on which he decided to extend his education beyond public school. Had he followed the example of most boys in the community, he would have put books away and given full time to farming. But on the evening of the day on which public school exams were concluded, the school inspector visited the Kerby farm, talked to the lad and repeated: "George, you can have an education — if you want it."

George Kerby decided he wanted it, went to high school and formed some ideas about going into the ministry. His parents were Anglican, but the only church in the home district was Methodist and in due course the young fellow attended Victoria College — edited the college paper, led the Glee Club, won awards in oratory, and graduated with first class honors in theology and arts. His first church charge was at Woodstock, then Hamilton, St. Catharines, Brantford and Montreal. He turned to evangelism and knew what it was like to face audiences of 10,000 people in California and Tennessee.

On January 2, 1903, the Calgary press reported a telegram from Rev. George Kerby of Toronto, accepting the call to Calgary's Methodist Church. "Mr. Kerby," the report indicated, "is about 40 years of age, an excellent speaker and a fine tenor singer."

He was slight and fragile in appearance; but in that summer of 1903, accompanied by an extremely capable wife, he struck Calgary like a July hurricane. After inspecting the church on the corner of 6th Avenue and 2nd Street West, he announced that it would be too small for the congregation he was determined to attract, and enquired if there was a bigger hall in town. Learning that Hull's Opera House was bigger, the minister replied: "Then we'll rent it until we can build a bigger church."

Before many weeks George Kerby was filling the Opera House at every Sunday service and making plans for a handsome new church at the corner of 7th Avenue and 1st Street West. Stone masons went to work and on February 5, 1905, Calgary's new Methodist

Church was opened with the Red Deer pioneer, Rev. Leo Gaetz, as guest preacher. Kerby's persuasive appeal on that dedication Sunday was for $10,000 and his enthusiastic congregation replied with $12,000.

The manner in which this preacher fellow broke with tradition worried or shocked a few people in the City and attracted others. Either way he was making church history. Just months after his arrival he was speaking boldly in favor of Church Union and making hazardous and unorthodox proposals about women's hats. Many people held to the belief that a woman's head should not under any circumstances be uncovered in a church; but when big hats and flourishing plumes obscured vision in the pews, George Kerby asked the ladies to take them off. According to the press account: "Quite a few acquiesced but a large number hadn't had sufficient notice to arrange their hair so left on their hats."

And, strange as it must seem, only three weeks after the new Methodist Church was opened, many Calgary people listened from positions in their own homes to the church service, very much as they were to do by means of radio in later years. The listeners in 1905, however, were receiving the sermon by telephone rather than radio. George Kerby, one might be sure, would be first in anything like that. "Nearly one hundred people availed themselves of the telephone connection with the Methodist Church yesterday and listened to the music and sermon," the newspaper related. "In the morning 23 people were all listening and at night nearly three times that number had connection with the pulpit. A Herald man was one of the listeners ... When Mr. Kerby announced the opening hymn, the sounds of the people turning pages could be heard. It seemed the minister's splendid tenor voice was singing a solo."

Ever anxious to bring young people into the Church, Kerby organized what may have been the most successful Young Men's Club in all Canada. Meetings were held at mid-afternoon every Sunday and average attendance in 1907 was close to 500. The church basement was enlarged and renovated to provide club rooms and gymnasium, open daily between 10 o'clock in the morning and 10 o'clock at night. Even a New York newspaper was sufficiently interested to direct one of its writers to get the complete story for publication.

And let there be no mistake about it, Calgarians were hearing dynamic preaching. They heard fearless sermons about "Calgary's

Moral Mudholes," and straightforward messages about the need for better welfare programs. "The deadest man in God's world is the one who shuts his eyes so that he cannot see the tattered garments of the poor; who stops his ears so that he cannot hear the cry of the hungry; and who shuts his hand so that he cannot help a deserving fellow. God save you and me from being mean and small in our charities."

He departed boldly from religious sectarianism. "Denominationalism has had its day," he believed. He fought for the principles of brotherhood; and immigrants from many lands found him understanding, though on occasions they may have misunderstood him, as on that Sunday when he extended his friendly hand to a New Canadian girl leaving his church and said: "Can I come and visit you sometime?"

"I think not," she replied, blushingly. "I got one feller now an' one's 'nough.

In June, 1942, the striking little man with white hair, sharp features and well trimmed chin whisker, officiated at his 31st and last Mount Royal convocation — his last because at the age of 82 he was retiring. Following him in office would be Aberdeenshire-born Rev. John Garden with the distinction of having been the first pupil to enroll at Mount Royal.

Speaking at his last convocation the little principal and philosopher noted that he had made mistakes but hoped some profit had come from them. "The person who does not know how to profit by his mistakes drives the best schoolmaster out of his life," he said.

"Perhaps he made some mistakes," a listener whispered, "but it was a lucky day for Alberta when he accepted the counsel of a friend, Timothy Eaton, to whom he went when deliberating about accepting the call to Calgary, back in 1902."

Less than two years after retiring, the founder passed on, leaving living monuments like Central United Church with one of the biggest congregations in Canada, and Mount Royal College, extending the horizons of education. Calgarians mourned the passing of a great citizen and read again his book, Broken Trail, and some of his poems like "A Thought":

A COLLEGE AND ITS FOUNDER

"You ask me for a thought,
A thought to find a place
Upon the painted canvas of your Art,
Where stand the hills of God
Amid the glory of the dawn.
One thought alone is worthy such a place —
A thought unstained by selfish plaint,
A thought of beauty and of truth,
A thought of honor and of right,
A thought of power —
The power to hold and keep
When all else fails.
A thought of man, of God, of Him
Who bore upon the cross
The load of human guilt,
The weight of human wrong.
A thought that speaks
In every tint and hue and color-tone
Your brush has made.
These thoughts of God, and man and human need,
The sum of each and all
Can only be —
The thought of love."

Mount Royal College fulfilled the hope of its founder, but the same could not be said of Dr. T. H. Blow's Calgary University.

"Give me land and I'll build a University," this man with admirable zeal was saying in 1909. Thanks to W. J. Tregillus, a good site was obtained west of the City on the Bow River side of the old Banff Coach Road, and considerable money was subscribed. Calgary University was described as something of which citizens would be proud.

On November 29, 1910, R. B. Bennett presented a bill in the Alberta Legislature to incorporate the Calgary University. There was opposition on the ground that one University was enough in a young province; nevertheless, the bill passed.

Calgary people were jubilant. The City was entering its notable real estate boom and more donations of cash and property came to the Board of Governors, on which sat Dr. Blow, R. B. Bennett, W. J. Tregillus, James Short, J. S. Dennis, William Georgeson and Harold W. Riley.

Not waiting for buildings, the Board authorized that lectures be given at the Public Library, starting in October, 1912. The courses in English, history, classics and mathematics had four full-time professors; and various other classes had part-time instructors. Calgary's scholarly Kent Power was Dean of the Faculty of Law and some celebrated lawyers of later years received their basic instruction under him.

But Alberta had one Provincial University, and degree-granting privileges were not to be given to another. It was a burning issue and once again it appeared as a contest between the Cities of Calgary and Edmonton. A commission was appointed to help resolve the difficulty — three University presidents, Walter Murray of Saskatchewan, Robert Falconer of Toronto and Stanley Mackenzie of Dalhousie — and in 1915 the group declared against degree-granting powers for more than one Alberta institution.

For Calgary people the only comfort in the Commission's report was a recommendation for the establishment of a Provincial Institute of Technology and Art — at Calgary.

The "Tech" was built and it flourished. But in view of failure to obtain degree-granting status and the grim distractions of World War I, the plan for Calgary University was abandoned. Calgarians with dreams of a local University campus were obliged to wait until the University of Alberta accepted a policy of decentralization — which it did ultimately.

THE STAMPEDE OF 1912

Calgary's stampede history began in the spring of 1912 when a long-geared itinerant cowboy — more talkative than most — blew into the City. The name was Guy Weadick, already well-known in the rodeo world. Born in New York State, he ran away from home and learned to ride, rope and talk the cowpuncher's lingo in Montana. Moreover, he was a showman as well as cowboy and had some big notions about staging a rodeo of international championship calibre — also a conviction that Calgary at the heart of the Canadian range would be a good place for it.

THE STAMPEDE OF 1912

The city Weadick encountered was approaching a feverish peak in its real estate boom and the man on the street was finding it difficult to give reasoned thought to other things. There was a new City Hall and the Public Library was under construction. Immigrant newcomers were conspicuous. The most fashionable of women's hats were as big as barrel-heads and the smart males wore patent leather button boots. And for $1000 a person could buy a 25 horse power Overland car complete with five lamps but without top or windshield.

Weadick wasn't a total stranger, having been in Calgary on two previous occasions — once when he and Negro Will Pickett were touring the country as vaudeville cowboys and later while riding with Miller Brothers' Wild West Show at the Dominion Exhibition in 1908.

In the course of the second visit, Weadick became friendly with H. C. McMullen, who was Livestock Agent for the Canadian Pacific Railway. They talked about Calgary as an ideal place for a big rodeo — one with historical as well as entertainment value — and they agreed that Weadick should return at some time to promote the idea.

As a Wild West Show performer, the young cowboy travelled to many part of North America and Europe. Sometimes he was in trouble with the Old World society which could scarcely be expected to understand a brash young cowboy from the West. A Parisian barber who thought he recognized an insult challenged the reckless Guy to a pistol duel, and it wasn't a simple matter to persuade the touchy fellow to compromise by resort to fists. The cowboy had more experience with fists than with pistols.

But Weadick didn't forget Calgary and his friend McMullen. In March, 1912, he returned, this time with a travelling companion, Tom Mix. As Calgarians saw Weadick at that time he was altogether magnetic, looking and walking like a Roman soldier. Business men with whom he talked on the subject of a rodeo for Calgary were impressed; but most of them concluded that his scheme was too big for a city of 60,000 people.

"Why don't you try El Paso or Cheyenne or Pendleton where they've had rodeos before?" many people asked. "We did all right with the Dominion Exhibition four years ago but a show such as you're talking about might ruin us."

The best encouragement continued to come from McMullen, who repeated that if the problem of financing could be solved, Weadick's show would succeed. Together they went to see George Lane, who ruled the Bar U Ranch but was frequently in residence at the Alberta Hotel. The cattleman, sitting in the rotunda, listened patiently. Silence indicated interest and the interview was concluded when Lane said: "I want to talk to some friends about this; I'll see you in a day or two."

The friends with whom Lane talked were Pat Burns and A. E. Cross, and the very next day a request was made for the use of the Exhibition Park. A. J. McLean came in with the other three cattlemen and together the "Big Four" agreed to back Weadick's plan to the extent of $100,000, the only condition being an insistence that contestants and patrons get a "square deal." It was settled in short order; the dates would be September 2 to 5; George Lane would be chairman and Guy Weadick, manager.

Planning was on a gigantic scale — $20,000 for rodeo prizes; 200 Mexican longhorn cattle imported by Gordon, Ironside and Fares for the contests; 300 of the meanest horses obtainable to come from A. P. Day of Medicine Hat; and invitations to be circulated to reach cowboys in all parts of the continent. Even a replica of notorious Fort Whoop-Up which had flourished before the coming of range cattle and broncho horses was included in the plans. It was Weadick's idea to bring the old trader, Fred Kanouse, to run the "Fort."

As usual, the Indians were the first to arrive. Some 5,000 of them pitched tepees on the ground, so many that the Inspector of Indian Agencies for Canada thought he should be present.

The big show started with a street parade and an estimated 80,000 people saw it. Leading the parade was the famous cowboy band, mounted, from Pendleton, Oregon.

On opening day 25,000 people watched the Stampede contests. Among them were the Duke and Duchess of Connaught and daughter, Princess Patricia, who came to spend a day and remained for three days in spite of unfavorable weather. On the second day it rained in torrents, but 13,000 spectators accepted wet clothes and remained to the end of the program.

Sure enough, the top North American cowboy and cowgirl performers were present to compete. Even Mexican Bandit Pancho Villa sent his best rider. Such a show was bound to produce thrills

— lots of them; but for Canadian spectators the highlight of the week was the performance of Tom Three Persons from the Blood Indian Reserve near Cardston. At that he very nearly missed the contests completely. Paying for some misbehaviour, he was spending time in the Mounted Police cells at Fort Macleod until the day of the events, and it was on a plea from the Inspector of Indian Agencies that he was released in time to ride.

One word on everybody's tongue was "Cyclone," name of the wicked bucking horse imported from the United States. Rarely had the big black been mastered and he was known to possess qualities of a man-killer. When it was learned that Tom Three Persons had drawn this horse for the finals in the broncho riding event, the common conclusion was, "Well, that'll be the end of the show for Three Persons."

As on other occasions the powerful horse leaped explosively from the chute, pitched, jack-knifed, did everything except somersault. It was Cyclone at his wickedest, but this time the famous horse could not unseat its rider. Finally, the exhausted horse gave up and Three Persons got out of the saddle, a champion.

That most of the high honors would go to the more experienced rodeo performers from the United States was expected, and when the big Alberta Indian was declared the winner the crowd went nearly wild in exultation. The two heroes of the week were Tom Three Persons as broncho riding champion, and Calgary's Clem Gardner as champion all-around Canadian cowboy.

"Do you think the Stampede would make a good annual event?" Guy Weadick asked through the medium of the prize list. "If so advise us. This is some country."

About the success of the event there was small reason for doubt. In spite of wet weather it more than paid its way, and the $100,000 guaranteed by the "Big Four" backers was not needed. But the Stampede did not become an annual event — not at that stage anyway. Weadick resumed his world travels, staged cowboy vaudeville in London and introduced rodeo to New York. In August, 1919, he was back in Calgary, briefly, to direct a Victory Stampede; but it wasn't until 1923 that he returned to stay because only then did the Calgary Exhibition adopt the Stampede as a permanent feature of the summer show with Weadick as its manager. Thereafter, Calgary's midsummer classic was conducted as a combined event — Exhibition and Stampede.

In 1952 Calgary celebrated the 40th anniversary of the first Stampede, with Guy Weadick as the special guest of honor. A few months later that Prince of Western Showmen who stamped his personality on the Calgary Stampede died in Los Angeles. The body was brought back for burial at High River, downstream from his Stampede Ranch. The funeral service was conducted exactly as Guy would have ordered, his saddle horse following to the graveside. Somebody standing nearby said: "The Calgary Stampede will be Guy's best monument."

And as for the Stampede of 1912, Weadick's first great Canadian triumph, those people who had cautiously considered it to be a huge gamble were right. It was. But when it succeeded in commanding the attention of the ranching world, Calgary's citizens were proud, and agreed that as a city achievement it outranked the Dominion Exhibition of four years before.

Then, with the Stampede over, Calgary interest returned to real estate and the easy profits to be made in rapid-fire turn-over of Elbow Park lots.

THE MAD YEARS IN REAL ESTATE

"Make a million dollars? Easiest thing in the world," said an old timer, "if a man just knew enough to buy Calgary real estate at the right time — and get rid of it at the right time."

But how was one to know that a corner lot at 7th Avenue and 2nd Street West, priced at $150 in 1895, would sell for $2,000 in 1905 and $300,000 in 1912? Andrew Carney, who sold the Town of Calgary "a hill for a cemetery" at $70 an acre, recalled offering Jack Lineham a half interest in five acres of what became Mewata Park for $300. Said Lineham: "Here's the $300 if you want it, but I don't want no half interest in that property. I wouldn't give you $300 for the whole outfit."

For some years the increase in property values was slow and unimpressive. By 1910, however, the pace was quickening and the incidence of boastfulness mounting. "For its size," wrote one of the editors, "Calgary has most cities faded to a whisper even now and it will have them all lashed to the mast when the warm weather comes." The editor was right, and by 1911 the city was feeling the grip of one of the mad real estate booms in Canadian history. A few people made huge fortunes and almost as many lost fortunes of similar magnitude.

"Everybody has a lot in mind," said Bob Edwards. "Either he wants to buy it or he wants to sell it." The 8th Avenue optimism was infectious and fabulous, and by the end of 1911 any thought that the boom would ultimately end and prices collapse seemed to disappear. If anybody harbored fears, he didn't have the courage to admit them. The aim of the city's "100,000 Club" was to realize a population corresponding to that figure by 1915; but in 1912, while Calgarians were being carried away by their own enthusiasm, the name was revised — it became the "Quarter Million Club."

"Nothing but a catastrophe can even temporarily impede progress," an editor wrote. "The cow town of yesterday, the city of 55,000 today, will be the metropolis of tomorrow." The thing to do was to "put your money in real estate instead of the bank."

Even the person with modest means could speculate and did. Lots were sold with initial payments as low as a dollar. At one stage, lots in Belfast and Fairview districts were being offered at $250 each, payable at a dollar a week for five years. According to the announcements, at the end of a purchaser's five year's of payments, when the last dollar would be paid, the lots would be at the heart of the city and "big skyscrapers will be going up all around." A lot could mean a fortune.

Every few days lots were being offered in new subdivisions with names no longer familiar to Calgary people — Hiawatha, Sarcee Garden, Northalta, Pullman, Haysdale, Marlborough Place, Majestic, Strathdude, Manitou Park, Balaclava, Pasadena, Columbia Gardens, Sarceedale and so on. They were nice names, but most of them belonged far from the centre of the city and the majority of the subdivisions were difficult to find.

Lots sold in Eastern Canada and in England were in many instances far beyond the city limits. But that didn't seem to matter much; in most cases the property was bought without inspection and purely for purpose of resale. It didn't matter, therefore, if it was somewhere below the high-water mark in the Bow River. In early 1912 certain lots were reported to have changed hands three times in three hours with sellers averaging profits of $1,000.

The spirit of the boom was everywhere and citizens accepted it as their duty to notify friends living elsewhere about the opportunities awaiting them in the foothills metropolis. In March, 1912, the Board of Trade proposed an Advertise Calgary Day on which every Calgarian — man, woman and child — would be expected to write at least one letter to an acquaintance in another part of the world, pointing out the benefits of Calgary as a place to live and own property.

If the boom had a peak, it came in October when F. C. Lowe and Company was offerings lots in Roxboro district. Here was something new — something with a fresh attraction — home sites with graded streets, sidewalks, curbs and electric light poles already provided and trees planted. Each lot carried a $3500 building restriction and during the day on which the property was offered, October 21, over $100,000 worth of lots were sold. Even an American vaudeville actor seeing Calgary for the first time that day became a victim of the enthusiasm and bought a Roxboro lot.

Fred Charles Lowe, said to be Calgary's first millionaire, will be remembered as one of the dashing personalities during the gay years. Born at Brampton, Ontario, he came to Calgary in 1902 and worked for a life insurance company until the attractions of real estate induced him to start in business for himself in 1906. His main office at the south-west corner of 8th Avenue and 1st Street West became one of the busiest in the city. With two brothers joining the firm, the business turnover mounted and branch offices were opened at Lethbridge, Edmonton and New York.

Lowe drove the biggest land deals and the biggest cars. His firm opened much of the south part of the city, Elbow Park, Elboya and Windsor Park. In that pre-bulldozer period, the ingenious Lowe resorted to well-directed streams of water as a means of cutting away part of the Elbow River bank and improving the topography for building purposes. And as for cars, he had four at one time — two of them being Pierce Arrows costing around $5,000 each. When in California in the winter of 1912-13, he took a fancy to a racing car winning on a Santa Monica track, bought it and brought it to Calgary to add to the wonder of his performance. They might have called him "Mr. Boom," but when the boom faded, so did Fred Charles Lowe.

Naturally, the Calgary business climate at that time attracted real estate agents — hundreds of them. Real estate offices outnumbered grocery stores by two to one. For the year 1911 City License Inspector Manarey could report 443 real estate licenses. "This means," he said, "that there are that many offices located in Calgary. Figuring five men to the office, which is considered a conservative estimate, there are 2,000 men in the city selling or connected with real estate." Such a total of real estate salesmen would represent more than 10 per cent of the adult males in the city — and the number was considerably higher in 1912. In the new Maclean Block opened in that year, three-quarters of the offices were occupied by men offering houses and lots.

Pointing a warning finger at 8th Avenue, an itinerant evangelist had something to say: "Woe unto you, real estate men; your folly is like that of Sodom. Repent before you reap destruction." But there was no evidence that the warning changed anything, and the boom went its merry course.

Then to add to the mad excitement, there was a gold rush to the Ghost River near Morley — more or less in Calgary's "back yard." It started in February, 1912, when 62-year-old Terence Brady reported his discovery of a bonanza on the river. Briefly it made competition for the real estate trade; but when Calgarians heard that tests showed the "gold" to be iron pyrites they returned to speculation in lots with renewed vigor.

Nor was the rapid-fire turnover in lots without backing in building. Building permits jumped from five and one-half million dollars in 1910 to over 20 millions in 1912. It was the biggest increase reported by any Canadian city; but building operations, like the boom itself, dropped abruptly and not until 1949 was the 1912 volume equalled again.

The year 1913 had a sobering effect and some of those who had been driving automobiles went back to horses and buggies. There followed years of dormancy and years of moderate growth; but ultimately the city's growth pace quickened again, this time with the sounder and better impetus furnished by a new-found oil industry.

Forty-six years after the boom of 1912, the City of Calgary embraced 75 square miles of surface, had a population of one-fifth of a million, ranked tenth among the cities of Canada in point of size, and fifth in volume of bank transactions. It took longer than once anticipated, but the dream of 1912 was being fulfilled.

THE MAWSON MASTERPIECE

Replying to a question about the city's population at a certain time in 1911, one of Calgary's tobacco-chewing, sidewalk philosophers replied, "Stranger, I wouldn't venture a guess; it was 55,000 last week but Heaven only knows how much more it is today."

In the preceding six years the Calgary population more than quadrupled, and at last the City Fathers, under Mayor Mitchell, were becoming conscious of the need for guidance to a boom-time development which was spreading aimlessly like fire in stubble. River banks were being invaded by builders; main streets were increasingly congested with buggies and wagons; and real estate promoters were selling lots in areas which could never be serviced with sewers and water mains.

At a meeting of City Council on November 13, 1911, the necessity was acknowledged and the mayor authorized to appoint a committee to prepare a "comprehensive and extensive scheme of City Planning which will meet the requirements of this city for its future development."

A Planning Commission was appointed and it concerned itself with many things — street lights, tree planting, cleaning up vacant lots and improving the standard of Calgary garbage cans — but seemed unwilling or unable to tackle the major planning problems.

So it was until October 4, 1912, when Thomas Mawson was in Calgary to deliver a public lecture under the joint sponsorship of the Women's Canadian Club, the I.O.D.E., and the Planning Commission. The speaker, a middle-aged Englishman with an infectious sort of enthusiasm, had a reputation as a planner. He was from Liverpool University and had carried out planning assignments for big European cities. He spoke with an Englishman's authority and his skill in salesmanship far exceeded that of most academic people. Here, it seemed, was the Moses for whom Calgary had been waiting.

The public meeting in the High School was a big one and dignified by R. B. Bennett's consent to be chairman. Mawson related the costly mistakes made by certain other cities. There was London, for example. "We allowed the short-sighted greed of a few individuals to baulk Sir Christopher Wren's plan for rebuilding after the great fire of 1666 ... and now, 250 years afterwards, we find that we have spent 20 times the cost of his scheme in more or less futile attempts at patching up old mistakes."

Convincingly, Mawson urged immediate planning to ensure that Calgary be "the point from which will radiate an incentive in commerce and industry and some day in arts, letters, music and science." How could any good citizen be indifferent?

Editorial writers added their support and enthusiasm swept the city. Said one real estate man: "We'll build a New Jerusalem right here on the banks of the Bow." Exactly ten days after Mawson's lecture, the Planning Commission submitted a report to the City Council, recommending "the engaging of Thomas Mawson of Liverpool, England, or some other expert regarded as possessing equal qualifications, to investigate conditions in Calgary and make report covering the traffic and housing problems, and a comprehensive scheme of parks, playgrounds, boulevard drives, a proposed civic centre and such other matters as generally come under the head of 'City Planning.'"

The Council adopted the report, approved a grant to the Planning Commission and, forthwith, invited applications for the task of re-designing the city. And none but planners of world renown need apply.

Mawson, in submitting application, explained what he proposed to do: "My preliminary plans for Calgary would include a street and boulevard plan showing ... improvements to existing streets ... new streets for the relief of traffic; and boulevard drives for the beautification of your city. I would suggest, within the limits you think possible, the plan on which the city should develop, with the main arterial roads clearly indicated ... position of bridges, playgrounds, riverside walks. I would also give a plan for a civic centre ..."

On January 20, 1913, the City Commissioners reported: "We now recommend that Mr. Thomas Mawson be appointed to this position at a salary of $6,000 for complete preliminary plans." A few days later the Council authorized Mawson "to begin work at once."

By the time the great planner faced up to his task the real estate boom was subsiding, but Mawson was in no way discouraged as he began sketching a course for a city of half a million people and "three million persons engaged in farming close to Calgary." Clearly he was unfamiliar with Western Canadian conditions, but for a brief spell he was a Calgary hero. Even after many real estate firms were failing, Mawson continued to sketch sky-scrapers for his dream city.

Many of his ideas were sound — others costly and impractical. He recognized the need for street widening in certain districts, also for more bridges and subways; but so did many other people before and after him. In relieving down-town traffic, he pointed out, bridges would be needed at Centre Street, 4th Street and 14th Street West. As for the Centre Street bridge, he debated between a high-cost high-level structure, and a more economical low-level bridge fitted with an elevator service at the north end to raise and lower street cars and other vehicles between the bridge and street level. The inevitable delays to be created by traffic elevators to raise and lower street cars and other things caused no evident concern, and with the optimism of a cigar-smoking stock broker, Mawson obtained firm bids from manufacturers who could furnish the hoisting machinery. Had his idea for a low-level bridge been carried out, riders on the Thorncliffe and Mount Pleasant bus lines might still be making part of their regular trips in a vertical direction.

Mawson wanted to completely reconstruct the business section — lay it out like a wagon wheel with spoke-like streets radiating in all directions from the hub. With so much of down-town Calgary already fixed by construction, however, it was impossible to carry out that part of his dream and his only hope was to get a few radial routes leading from the centre of things.

In neither the business nor the residential sections could Mawson see reason for the grid or checkerboard system of laying out streets and avenues; "monotonous regularity," he said. Mount Royal district with its curves and confusion of streets won his admiration and he favored duplicating the plan. He'd have the fewest possible square corners — hateful things at any time. "Your grid-iron system of planning," he said in his report, "leads to great loss of momentum owing to all fast wheeled traffic having to pull up every time it approaches the end of a block."

Although it was a horse-and-buggy period, Mawson didn't overlook the possible impact of motors. Calgary should seek to attract "the increasing number of persons who visit places of

165

interest by automobile." The way to do it — have "automobile trails where high speeds could be obtained." Few people talked about tourists, but of them Mawson said, "No more desirable class to attract to your city."

To his eternal credit he advocated more parks, natural park reservations, extensive tree-plantings, and preservation of the river-banks for public enjoyment.

But Mawson liked nothing better than to sketch new and massive buildings. With the imagination of a true artist, he completely re-designed the Calgary Exhibition Ground, adorning it with palace-like structures. The C.P.R. depot of his imagination would have made an ornate headquarters for a World's Fair. And straddling Centre Street would be the Market Place covering several blocks, and, in Mawson's view, the most important institution in down-town Calgary.

But nothing in the notable report entitled "Calgary, Past, Present and Future," dated April, 1914, was as overwhelming as the conception of a Civic Centre. Even by costs of that time, it would have been a multi-million dollar undertaking, resembling the dream of an Oriental potentate more than the administrative workshop of a frontier city.

The Centre was laid out on both sides of 4th Street West and extended to the river and across to Prince's Island. The natural course of the river would have to be changed but that was a small matter. On the Island there would be a Museum, and on the south side, close to the river, City Hall, Post Office, Auditorium, University, Library, Art Gallery and numerous other public institutions. It was a fabulous design, and had it been carried out the cost would have been crippling. "But," said Mawson cheerfully, "this is how Paris has been made so beautiful and there is no doubt that Calgary can do it too."

THE McCARTY-PELKEY MATCH

Calgary's most notable boxing event in all its years was the McCarty-Pelkey fight which ended disastrously and plunged gay holiday crowds into mourning.

Boxing commanded local interest and men meeting at the Alberta Hotel or Chan's Pool Room discussed their favorite heavyweights just as those of a later date talked quarterbacks. For its local popularity the sport owed much to ex-champion heavyweight of the world, Tommy Burns, who came to Calgary in 1909 to share a retail clothing business with his friend Jim Sewell. After losing the heavyweight crown to Negro Jack Johnson in a wicked grudge match in Australia — stopped by the police in the 14th round — Burns was retiring and Calgary was to be his home. The short and stocky ex-champion became a local idol and interest in his sport began to soar.

Occasionally Burns yielded to community pressures and boxed an exhibition match at the Sherman Rink or Manchester Arena, and was assured of a big and admiring audience. One of those no-decision six-round matches was in early 1913 with a young fellow, Arthur Pelkey from Chatham — around Calgary long enough to be regarded as a local boy. Though short on experience, his performance against the ex-champion of the world impressed everybody, especially Tommy Burns, who offered immediately to train him for some big matches. At the same time, Burns was promoting local matches and capitalizing on Calgary's spurt of enthusiasm.

After giving Pelkey a terrific build-up, Burns billed the famous McCarty-Pelkey bout as a 24th of May attraction in 1913, and boxing fans the world over wondered how the Alberta city qualified for such a match, because Luther McCarty of Chicago was regarded as the strongest contender anywhere for the world championship crown still held by Jack Johnson. A San Francisco writer, noting the program Burns was embarking upon, said, "Calgary will become the hub of the boxing universe."

Title-holder Jack Johnson wanted a match with McCarty and his manager wired Tommy Burns suggesting the contest be in Calgary. But Burns was bitter at Johnson because of ring conduct and chose to let him wait. Burns' reply made his feeling clear: "Would be impossible to match Johnson here," he said; "I would not have him at any price. He will have to look elsewhere for a match as I am keeping the game clean in Calgary. Regards. Tommy Burns."

Anyway, the dominant topic on 8th Avenue was "boxing," just as it had been four years earlier when John L. Sullivan, who believed boxing should be taught in public schools along with geography and arithmetic, had spent a week in the city.

Pelkey was regarded as Calgary's boy and McCarty was no stranger. A former Oklahoma cowboy, McCarty had worked in Calgary and did some of his first boxing there a couple of years earlier. Many local people remembered the big fellow well. In the meantime he boxed his way up the ladder, and when he arrived back in Calgary for training in early May, 1913, his was a famous name in boxing circles.

Advertising for Tommy Burns' 24th of May program at the Manchester Arena told about two preliminary bouts beginning at 11.30 a.m. The feature, of course, was the 10-rounds McCarty-Pelkey event with Ed. Smith of Chicago as referee. Tickets went on sale at Tommy Burns' new store, 213 8th Avenue West, ten days before the holiday — $2.00 for general admission, $5.00 for ringside seats and $6.00 for box seats. The advance sale was brisk and sports writers from as far as Chicago made reservations at Calgary hotels. It was the sporting event of the year.

Weeks before the match, McCarty, with the added experience and the title of "White Heavyweight Champion of the World," was a 5 to 1 favorite to win; but as the day approached the betting became just about even, largely because of Tommy Burns' faith in Pelkey.

By 10 o'clock on the morning of the big test, holders of rush seat tickets were lined up for half a block at Manchester Arena, and at 12.30 the preliminaries concluded, the two heavyweights entered the ring. Both were fine physical specimens, tall and handsome. The applause was deafening. The boxers shook hands and retired to their corners to receive their gloves. At that moment, a person, Reverend William Walker of St. Augustine Anglican Church, climbed into the ring, uninvited. He tried to say a word to the crowd and then reminded the boxers that the "Great Referee" stood over them in this bout, all powerful above the one selected by the sponsor to see fair play.

The clergyman stepped down and the bell sounded to start the match. The two giants smiled boyishly, circled, exchanged a few light blows, a heavy blow or two, and then — after only one minute and 40 seconds of the first round — McCarty reeled and went down — never to get up again.

As 7,000 fans roared with excitement, the referee counted to ten. McCarty's body was motionless and doctors were called. The noise subsided. The shouting turned to whispers. Doctors lost no time in resorting to artificial respiration, to morphine and brandy — but there was no response. The great McCarty was dead.

The referee was shocked. Pelkey looked dazed, and as soon as death was confirmed he was taken to police headquarters as a material witness and released on $10,000 bail. Shadows fell across the City of Calgary. And on Sunday night, 36 hours later, Tommy Burns' Manchester Arena where the match was held burned to the ground; cause of fire, unknown.

There was an immediate demand to put a stop to boxing and even the City Fathers discussed a prohibiting bylaw. Editorializing, however, the Calgary Herald said: "There will be, arising out of Saturday's tragedy, an inevitable inclination on the part of many people to condemn boxing as a sport. That would be wrong. Boxing is just as manly and fair a sport as it ever was."

McCarty's death was almost instantaneous, doctors agreed. There had been a hemorrhage caused by a dislocated neck, presumably from a blow to the chin. The boxer's body was sent to Ohio for burial.

Then there was the Coroner's Jury; it found Luther McCarty to have come to his death "accidentally." But even in the face of that verdict, a charge of manslaughter was laid against Pelkey. The legal firm of Clarke, McCarthy, Carson and McLeod was retained to represent Pelkey; and A. L. Smith, a junior member of that firm and one whose name became well known to Calgarians, handled the case.

The Crown pointed to a legal difference between a prize fight and a boxing match, trying to establish that the 24th of May event fell into an illegal category. But finally, Pelkey was acquitted, as most people believed he deserved to be. He had lots of admirers and they cheered when he was cleared of anything that might have been construed as irregular. As expressed by the Calgary Herald: "No person ever contended that Pelkey harbored the most remote intention of injuring or killing the unfortunate McCarty ... Pelkey has conducted himself in Calgary in a manner that is in keeping with his reputation as a thorough gentleman."

But the fact remained that Calgary lost its enthusiasm for boxing, temporarily at least. Most people were not ready to accept the judgment of the great John L. Sullivan, when he appeared at the Empire Theatre in Calgary a short time before that: "Compared with football, boxing is a pink tea." Moreover, the prophecy that Calgary would become the "hub of the boxing universe" was blighted.

Tommy Burns was through with promoting but not with boxing. After several years he left Calgary and accepted important matches on the Pacific coast and elsewhere, demonstrating all over again that a man of five feet, seven inches, provided he had a long reach and extraordinary footwork, could be a great boxer.

Bob Edwards of the Calgary Eye Opener was on the friendliest terms with Burns and prophesied that sooner or later, he'd become a preacher, adding that, "If he does he should find it as easy to put his men to sleep as in the days gone by." Bob was right, but the great fighter did various things before the prophecy was fulfilled. He operated a pub in London and a speakeasy in New York. And in 1935 he "got religion" and became an evangelist. Thereafter he had nothing good to say about boxing. There was too much hatred about it, he said.

In 1955 the only Canadian to wear the world's heavyweight boxing crown died at Vancouver. His age was 74 years and his life, from the time of leaving Hanover, Ontario, where he was born, was one of unusual activity and color. Many Calgarians retained vivid recollections of his residence among them. Said one: "He had a grip like a steel vice; I couldn't use my right hand all one summer after a handshake with Tommy Burns."

As for the McCarty-Pelkey match, Tommy Burns didn't want to talk about it — didn't want to think about it. It was the saddest day in his ring career, he admitted.

OIL AND WAR

Calgary's first claim to the title, Oil Capital Of Canada, came in 1914, just a couple of months before World War I was casting its ugly shadow across the country. The real estate madness had run its course and 8th Avenue business was dull — until that day when discovery well blew in at Turner Valley. Over night the excitement typical of a real estate boom or gold rush was revived. Oil became the city-wide topic of conversation and even weather was neglected.

Until 1947 most of Alberta's oil history was written in the South of the Province; and Turner Valley, considered to be a Calgary suburb, was Canada's major producing field. The search for oil began with a crusty frontiersman distinguished by long grey hair and an Oxford accent — Kootenai Brown — who squatted beside the Waterton Lakes in 1868. Brown told of preparing a mixture of kerosene and molasses and giving it to his Stoney Indian friends, saying: "If you find something which tastes and smells like that and oozing from the ground, let me know about it." Evidently he was directed to a scum of oil on inter-mountain water but did nothing more than gather enough of it to lubricate the axles of his wagon.

At some time in the '80's Lafayette French, another foothills worthy — trader, rancher and prospector — suffered a gunshot wound in a leg and a squaw dressed the injury with something French identified as oil. At the time he thought little about it, but later he told Government Surveyor A. P. Patrick and together they set out to find the source of that oil or find the squaw who could direct them to it. After long searching they located the squaw, and by bribes of the magnitude of a pony and gun she was induced to lead the men to the place on Cameron Brook where oil seeped from the ground.

Reports about oil seepages on Cameron Brook reached Ottawa and Dr. Alfred Selwyn, director of Canada's Geological Survey, made a journey to the remote area in 1891. According to his report he found a gang of men erecting a derrick beside a tributary of Waterton River, preparing to probe for oil. Evidently the drillers struck a good supply of water.

But Patrick didn't lose interest in what the squaw pointed out on Cameron Brook and after a few years he succeeded in winning the support of John Lineham and John Leeson, familiar names in Calgary. The Rocky Mountain Development Company resulted and drilling started in 1901. A year later there was an oil strike at 1020 feet and the flow was reported to be 300 barrels a day. Immediately there was a stakers' stampede. Businessmen in nearby Pincher Creek organized the Pincher Creek Oil and Development Company to drill on an adjacent site and the Lineham company prepared for expansion.

Oil was being produced, sure enough, and early in 1903 the Calgary Herald reported that, "John Lineham came in yesterday from the Rocky Mountain Development Company's oil property west of the Blood Reserve. Mr. Lineham brought back with him a barrel of the oil which has been tapped at 1020 feet. An analysis shows the oil is 15 percent stronger than the best oil in Petrolia, Ont."

The optimism was typical but the boom faded quickly. There was no refinery in the country; transportation presented problems, and if the well ever yielded as much as 300 barrels in a day, it wasn't for long. The more accessible Turner Valley was beginning to arouse curiosity. Ranchers told about gas seepages along Sheep Creek and oil slicks on the water.

"Gas has been discovered in considerable quantities on Sheep Creek, 21 miles from Calgary," the Herald reported in 1904. "This information was brought to the City yesterday. Prospectors uncovered a vein of coal there and while the workman was lighting his pipe there was an explosion and the shanty caught fire. Much difficulty was experienced in extinguishing the blaze."

Natural gas strikes were made at Alderson and Medicine Hat, and now there was the prospect that Calgary residents would have the convenience of gas in their homes. It was a prospect realized in 1912 when gas was piped from Bow Island.

Meanwhile, Turner Valley had a resident who pioneered in developing the silver mines at Cobalt, Ontario, and retained the inquisitiveness and hope becoming to a prospector. He was William Stewart Herron, who bought a farm east of Okotoks in 1901. When hauling coal from Black Diamond, Herron noticed oil seepages as he crossed Sheep Creek. The showing so fascinated him that he bought the land on which he had made the observation, obtained the mineral rights at the same time, and moved there. That was in 1911.

There was oil under his feet, Bill Herron was convinced; and in his determination to interest others, he invited William Elder and A. W. Dingman to drive from Calgary for a visit at the ranch. Story has it that with the business men as spectators, Herron produced a frying pan and a couple of eggs, lit a trickle of gas issuing from a point near the creek and nonchalantly proceeded to fry the eggs.

The demonstration was convincing and what followed was the formation of the Calgary Petroleum Products Company — ultimately taken over by Royalite Oil — with Dingman, who had gained some knowledge of oil in Pennsylvania, as managing director. Drilling on Herron's property commenced on January 25, 1914. Methods were still terribly primitive and progress was slow. But on May 14 the pioneers made their historic strike at a depth of 2718 feet. "Dingman Number One," they called it; and in blowing in, the well was signalling the first major oil field in the British Empire.

Word reached Calgary in the evening, and within hours the new enthusiasm threatened to surpass anything experienced during the memorable real estate boom. Every automobile in the city was requisitioned to take directors, spectators and would-be millionaires over the bad roads to the field next day. Those who couldn't get places in cars hired buggies. Hardly a business man remained on 8th Avenue.

At the well-site visitors sniffed the liquid, tasted it, rubbed it between their fingers and were convinced. The flow was said to be some four million cubic feet of wet gas per day and some light oil. The latter was so good that car drivers pumped it into their tanks in unrefined state and drove away.

During the following days scores of new oil companies were organized to sell gushers. Some of the companies had acreage, some didn't. Only a few ever drilled wells and still fewer found oil. The cost of drilling was an obstacle and the lack of experienced drillers was another. But while the excitement lingered, it didn't seem to matter about a company's prospects — everybody wanted to buy shares, especially if they were engraved impressively and carried a gold seal. Calgary brokers were so busy that some abandoned the use of cash-boxes for incoming money and used their waste paper baskets. Customers standing in line were as impatient as crowds of a later date buying tickets for a Stampeder football game. An estimated 500 oil companies sprang into existence in the space of three weeks, and Calgary saw itself becoming the Oil Capital of Canada — perhaps the industrial capital of the world.

The opening of the Palliser Hotel at the beginning of June coincided with the peak of the oil frenzy, and for the benefit of people who monopolized the new lobby chairs, plotting their Turner Valley fortunes, the Calgary Herald offered a set of rules, the salient points being as follows:

"No well shall be drilled before 6 a.m. or after 3 p.m. Operations at that time are liable to disturb paying guests while in the midst of beautiful dreams of vast wealth and permanent gushers.

"No more than one well shall be drilled in each leather chair or sofa during one time interval. It is exhausting to the furniture.

"No dry holes will be tolerated in the lobby. All wells brought in must be in the thousand barrel class or better.

"No well drilled in the lobby shall stop at shallow sand. Every well must run down to deep pay and represent an outlay of not less than $100,000."

It was the spirit of the time. And "Dingman Number One" was living up to advance notices. Oil was hauled by six-horse team to Okotoks; and as a means of convincing Eastern Canada that the Turner Valley oil was real, a barrel of it was taken to Toronto a couple of weeks after discovery. The man who accompanied it was Calgary Alderman T. A. P. "Tappy" Frost, a former Baptist minister. In Toronto, where many people clung to the idea that no good thing could come out of the far West, "Tappy" Frost placed the barrel of oil on display in a big store and stood by it ladling out samples in tiny vials until the supply was exhausted.

But with investments being made recklessly, disappointments were sure to follow. Enthusiasm was already waning when, on August 4, exactly 82 days after discovery, newspapers screamed the startling news: "Great Britain Declares War Against Germany."

The Turner Valley boom collapsed and did not return until 1924 when Royalite Number Four came in from a deeper zone to establish a new Valley landmark. Unfortunately the well caught fire and burned for weeks. But when the blaze was extinguished the well's great resources were evident. Production close to a million barrels in the next seven years removed any possibility of doubt.

War was to change many things. The spasmodically booming City of Calgary had sent its sons to battle before and was just attending to the unveiling of a splendid monument to the South African War veterans when the call for volunteers came again.

A political convention was in session at Calgary when war was declared and at once Dr. Michael Clark, Member of Parliament and orator extraordinary, proposed a resolution to end all political manoeuvring while the international struggle continued. At the same time all Commanding Officers in Alberta were offering themselves and their units.

As the war effort progressed Calgary played its noble part, furnishing men, women and materials. City people had reasons for special interest in certain units but loyal pride in all. Men in uniform became increasingly conspicuous on streets; railroad depots were the touching scenes of departures; heart aches sprang from growing casuality lists; and pride mingled with sadness as people studied the reports of combat at Ancre, Vimy Ridge, Hill 70, Amiens, Passchendaele, and so on. They were names meaning sacrifice, bravery and honor.

The price of wheat and cattle increased and business was brisk, but while war continued there was no enthusiasm for promotional drives in the field of oil.

"ALMOST TOGETHER"

Lists of war casualties were pathetically long, and midwinter of 1916-17 gripped the foothills country when the West's most dinstinguished frontier missionaries — Roman Catholic Father Lacombe and Protestant Reverend John McDougall — passed on, almost together. It was like the end of a church era.

Though their devotions differed in form their work among Indians and early residents of the country about Calgary was almost exactly parallel. And their respect for each other was admirable.

Equally colorful were their lives. It was in Calgary that Father Albert Lacombe was named to be president of the Canadian Pacific

Railway — for one hour. It was at the Mounted Police Barracks late in 1875 that Reverend John McDougall delivered a Sunday sermon which was the first in the district.

Coming to Fort Edmonton in 1852, Father Lacombe was the first of the pair to reside in what is now Alberta. The incident involving his elevation to the presidency of the C.P.R. occurred soon after the railroad was built to Calgary. Company officials inspecting the new line knew all about Father Lacombe's help in keeping the Blackfoot Indians from mischief when their natural inclinations were to tear up the rails as the road-builders laid them down, or better still, to go on the war-path and annihilate all workers who were defiling Indian country with iron tracks and smoke-puffing monsters.

Knowing that he and his party would be in Calgary, C.P.R. President Sir George Stephen wired to invite Father Lacombe to lunch with the directors in their private car. The priest, then in charge of the local Parish of St. Mary, accepted; and when all were assembled, Director R. B. Angus moved that Sir George step down from office and Father Lacombe be elected president for an hour. The motion was approved, Sir George vacated the chair and the priest accepted office, at the same time nominating Sir George Stephen for a one-hour term as Rector of the Parish. The temporarily retired president smiled to show his pleasure and said: "Poor souls of Calgary; I pity you."

Next day Father Lacombe accompanied the C.P.R. party eastward as far as Gleichen, where he had a date to keep with friends on the Blackfoot reservation.

Perhaps one facet of his ancestry sharpened his devotion to the native people. In 1695 Indians stole a French girl from her home beside the St. Lawrence River and carried her to Sault Ste. Marie where one of them claimed her for his wife. Five years later she was recovered along with her two babies. To one of those children Albert Lacombe could trace ancestry, and it was on the St. Suplice farm from which the girl was kidnapped that Lacombe was born in 1827.

He studied to be a missionary and as a young priest worked at Pembina, south of Fort Garry, for a couple of years. Then, having obtained permission to go farther west, the year 1852 found him at Fort Edmonton, a thousand miles beyond Fort Garry. Bishop Tache came that way and together they chose a site for a church at St. Albert. Thereafter, Father Lacombe was found building a church, building a historic bridge across the Sturgeon River, trying to maintain peace between the tribes, working to cure victims of small pox, enduring all the frontier vicissitudes, and even on occasion boiling his moccasins for food when everything else failed.

He was called back to Winnipeg for a few years, but in 1882 he came to take charge at Calgary where Fathers Doucet and Scollan had erected a church in the autumn of 1875, the first church at the new settlement.

Upon his arrival at Calgary, Father Lacombe and Father Doucet filed on homesteads on section 10-24-1-West of 5, land now at the heart of the City and still known as Mission District. A legal matter concerning transfer of his homestead land to the church took Father Lacombe to Ottawa a few years later. When he failed to get an immediate answer from the Honorable Minister to whom he presented his problem, he announced with good humor and firmness that he would "camp" right there in the government office for a few days — or weeks if necessary. He had slept in worse places and his determination was convincing enough that the government decision came quickly and the little Father was on his way with the answer he sought.

In his last sermon, at St. Mary's Church in 1913, he said: "Many years ago I stood on this ground and pictured to myself the time when a great Cathedral would stand here. At that time there was no church at all. There is now this beautiful church. In time there will be a Cathedral and a Bishop here, and I hope that time will not be far away. God bless you, people of Calgary, God bless you."

He died at the Lacombe Home on December 12, 1916, age 89. A special train carried his body from Calgary to the North for burial at St. Albert, but his heroic heart remained at the Lacombe Home built on land given him for the purpose by Pat Burns.

The McDougalls? Calgary was not the only place in Alberta with a claim upon them. Reverend George McDougall was a missionary at Norway House and sons John and David grew up to understand Indians and Indian ways. In 1862, when John was 20 and dedicated to the Church, he and his father travelled to Fort Edmonton and the younger man decided to stay. Next year the entire family followed, locating at Victoria, 90 miles north east of Edmonton.

Reverend John became an expert horseman and hunter. Living off the land and being prepared to resist hostility were necessities, and when need arose he'd have to make a thousand-mile trip to Fort Garry or the 600-mile trail journey to Fort Benton.

In coming to Morley beside the Bow River in 1873, John McDougall's purpose was to bring the Church to the Stoney Indians. His wife, who accompanied him, was the first white woman in the South. They were joined by David and his wife, David coming to trade with the Indians. At the end of 1873 the McDougalls were driving cattle — 11 cows and a bull — from Fort Edmonton to Morley. These would be the first breeding cattle to graze in the Valley of the Bow River.

Prior to the coming of the Mounted Police, Reverend John McDougall was commissioned by the federal government to go among the Indians to inform them and explain what the new force would mean. It wasn't an easy assignment but John McDougall was the man who could do it most effectively. And while carrying out that mission, he encountered the unexpected request to conduct a Christian marriage in wild and Godless Fort Whoop-Up. Amid a crowd of strange characters the ceremony was performed while the father of the bride shouted out now and then, "Marry 'em strong, John; marry 'em strong so's no man can part 'em."

The police post was completed on the Calgary site in 1875, and John McDougall was granted permission to conduct a church service in the barracks. With a few policemen and I. G. Baker Company men sitting on benches, the Methodist missionary preached Calgary's first church sermon.

Shortly after that there was tragedy in the McDougall family. It was winter time and they needed meat. Reverend George went along with his missionary son and they shot six buffalo. While the young man quartered the carcasses, the elder was riding back to their tent to prepare supper. But George McDougall lost his way on the snow-covered prairie about ten miles north of Fort Calgary, and days later his frozen body was found where he perished.

After conducting services at the police barracks, John McDougall held Sunday church meetings at the I. G. Baker store at

Calgary for some time, and in 1877 directed the building of Calgary's first Methodist church. He never ceased to be active, and when the Riel troubles gripped the West and Father Lacombe was working to prevent the Blackfeet from going on a bloody warpath, McDougall was going to the Crees. He attached himself to the Frenchman's Butte column and tramped, ate and slept with the soldiers. Worried settlers who knew the weakness of their defences could never forget their debt to those two missionaries working for peace.

"Preacher John" and "Man of Good Heart," as the Indians called them, died within five weeks of each other. It was the City of Wetaskiwin rather than the City of Calgary that obtained a unique monument to them — a single monument honoring a Catholic priest and Protestant minister — honoring them together.

CALGARY CLAIMED A PRINCE

According to Mayor R. C. Marshall, who welcomed His Royal Highness, Edward, Prince of Wales, in September, 1919, it was Calgary's "proudest moment."

Somebody wrote that the Calgary enthusiasm fell short of expectations, but when the Prince appeared on the platform in front of the grandstand at Victoria Park, an estimated 40,000 people roared their pleasure, and when the day ended the royal wrist was blue and swollen from shaking eager Calgary hands. There was nothing wrong with the western brand of fervour that greeted the heir to the throne.

It was less than a year after the end of World War I, and soldier re-establishment was uppermost among the country's problems. Calgary, having granted tax-exemption for soldiers' homes in 1918, was making a serious effort to meet its obligations. To those who turned out to cheer, the Prince was seen as a war hero who shared in the dirty work of trench warfare, as much as a member of the Royal Family.

It may have been Prime Minister David Lloyd George's idea that the Prince should visit Canada for the purpose of reinforcing bonds of loyality which might have been strained by four years of war. Prince Edward, a handsome 25-year-old with youthful color in his cheeks, was the person to perform the service most effectively.

Calgary was wearing its best face for the occasion. Some of the stores remained closed from Saturday night until Wednesday morning. The special functions were the public reception at the Exhibition Grounds, a civic luncheon at the Palliser Hotel, a garden party at the home of Sir James Lougheed, and a military ball for which 8th Avenue stores brought in appropriate shipments of fine dresses. At all of these appearances the Prince was magnetic and feminine hearts fluttered. At the ball where plans had been made to have him dance with the "right people," he made it quite clear that he could choose his partners without advice. Before leaving the Calgary district the Prince removed any doubt about his ability to identify a good horse or a pretty girl half a mile away.

It was planned that the Prince's third day in the district would be spent quietly and restfully with Rancher George Lane at the big Bar U spread. There the visitor saw an autumn round-up of 3500 cattle and insisted upon getting into a stock saddle and helping the cowboys. Rain fell but the Prince refused to seek cover until the regular ranch hands quit. The result was a thorough wetting but there were no ill effects. The royal guest had tried his hand at everything except the use of the branding iron, refusing because "I might inflict some unnecessary suffering on the calf."

There was an inspection of a band of Bar U Percherons going to England, and there was to have been a morning expedition across the range to shoot sharp-tail grouse or ducks. To pursue the hunt the Prince was called at 7 a.m., and George Lane was getting a horse-drawn cart ready for the trip. The visitor said he'd prefer to walk and George Lane, unspoiled by convention, replied, "All right, Prince, but you'll walk alone."

The Prince did walk alone, walked seven miles and liked every bit of it. He didn't get a lot of shooting but he saw foothills and mountain scenery which he couldn't forget. That night, in the quiet of the ranch house, Britain's Prince of Wales admitted a love for the district and George Lane replied, "Say Prince; why don't you buy a ranch here, buy the one you walked over today. It's the Beddingfield place and I can get it for you."

The Prince continued on his tour, but exactly four weeks after his departure, Calgary people read with special glee: "Prince of Wales Buys Beddingfield Ranch." "The Western spirit," said the Prince in commenting about it while making his way back eastward, "is a very catching one. I want to feel I have a home in the West."

The choice of ranch location was good, as everybody admitted. The 1600-acre spread adjoining the Bar U on the west was about 60 miles from Calgary and afforded excellent grass, water, game and scenery. Part of it had come into the Beddingfield family as early as 1883.

At the time of purchase there were 150 cattle and 400 horses on the place, but on George Lane's advice the Prince's plan was to stock it with pure bred cattle, sheep and horses from British herds and flocks. Professor W. L. Carlyle was already on his way to England with the shipment of Bar U Percheron mares, and he would help select breeding stock for the new ranch program — Shorthorns, Shropshires and Thoroughbreds.

Pioneer Rancher George Lane, who was as much at home on 8th Avenue as he was on the hills beside Pekisko Creek, was the author of it all and was being congratulated. Britain's future king would now have business interests in the Calgary district.

Nobody could foresee the surprises and changes time would unfold; but for weeks following announcement about the ranch deal, Calgary asserted a special claim to the Prince. More than to most cities, he belonged to Calgary. Emmeline Pankhurst, the world famous suffragette who rocked a nation, came to Calgary some days after the ranch purchase was announced, but not even the story of her triumph in winning the franchise for British women in the previous year was enough to attract more than slight interest after the exciting royal fare to which Calgarians had been treated. The Prince of Wales belonged to them.

THEY BURIED BOB

It was a day Calgary people wouldn't forget; it was November 17, 1922. Trees were bare of leaves and falling snow signalled oncoming winter. It was the day they buried Bob Edwards and Calgary saw the biggest funeral in its history. It seemed to mark the end of a "free-wheeling" era in the life of the City, when restraints were minimum and men had no fear of individuality.

"Old Bob is gone," sorrowing citizens told each other and proceeded at once to recall some incidents of charity or mischief in which the editor of the West's most astonishing paper had played dramatic parts.

For almost 20 years the Calgary Eye Opener had the unchallenged distinction of being Canada's prime journalistic controversy, and Bob Edwards the most misunderstood editor. Shocking a few readers, offending some, and entertaining many, the paper seemed to defy all the accepted rules of business administration. Here was the spectacle of a newspaper carrying but little news, going to press with an irregularity that would normally bring a publisher to ruin, sometimes banned from the mails, and all the while, if popularity were the measure, a flourishing success. Notwithstanding unorthodox behaviours, the influence of its pages and a circulation going to 33,000 — highest of any paper published west of Winnipeg — were enough to bring most editors to envy.

"The subscription to this paper," wrote the editor, "should be $10 per annum but owing to slight irregularities and an occasional punk issue, we knock off nine."

But in journalistic character this product of a one-man newspaper staff was no more extraordinary than the chunky, unconventional, sometimes inebriated creator, Bob Edwards. Fearless in writing and warlike toward insincerity when he sensed it in public figures, he managed to mix his unequalled humor with serious subjects. Quite a few of society's straight-laced and self-righteous individuals feeling his jocular barbs pronounced him objectionable and sinful. Some, indeed, hoped for the day when he would be run out of the City. At the same time, those who sought to know and understand this man, whose name became almost synonymous with that of his adopted city, discovered sterling qualities of generosity, honesty and loyalty behind a facade that sometimes appeared terrifying and usually frivolous.

As a humorist this strange fellow possessed gifts like those which projected Mark Twain to fame. Without evident effort he furnished no end of entertainment for the people across the homestead country, thereby rendering a service.

Nothing about the Eye Opener was commonplace. It treated serious subjects with humor and it ridiculed dull customs robbing men of their individuality. There was its sparkling Society Column, basically a rebuke to the sham and snobbery the editor sensed on the fashionable society pages. "This is no country for society magazines," he wrote, and then proceeded to record the most widely read society notes of those years.

Some of the names were invented, while others, like those of Mrs. Fulham, who kept pigs and periodically disturbed the peace, and "Hippo" Johnson, who escaped from the Mounted Police while awaiting trial for cattle stealing, were real enough. And so, "Mrs. Fulham gave one of her delightful musicales," now and then; and "Hippo Johnson, the charming beef assimilator, has been the guest at North West Mounted Police Barracks in Macleod for several weeks. The other day he reviewed the Guards and mentally expressed great satisfaction with their inefficiency. Shortly after, he took leave of his entertainers ... and is now chasing scenery over the mountain tops."

In many instances where fictitious names were used, Calgary people were able to identify the individuals inspiring the satires. No doubt the neighbors recognized "Mrs. Alex. F. Muggsy," and "John Moran" and "John Swalligan":

"Mrs. Alex. F. Muggsy, one of our most delightful West End chatelaines, has notified her friends that her usual Friday Musicale is called off for this week. Her husband, old man Muggsy, has been entertaining his own friends with a boozicale for a change and is in an ugly mood."

"John Moran of Sunnyside who was killed last week by being run over by a Ford car was good fellow and deserving of a more dignified death. There will be a sale of empty bottles at the Moran residence Saturday to defray funeral expenses."

"We take pleasure this week in publishing the picture of Mr. J. B. Swalligan, one of Calgary's most prominent and esteemed citizens. It is not at all unlikely that Mr. Swalligan may run for the Council this fall, in which case he will be elected by a sweeping majority. He is one of the most hospitable men and justly popular. With commendable forethought Mr. Swalligan stocked his spacious cellars with hundreds of cases of Scotch before the dry blow fell and it is the delight of his life to assemble around him a bunch of choice spirits and celebrate passing events, preferably birthdays. Generous to a fault with his whiskey, he is the idol of the city. (Stop press: Just before going to press we learn that the provincial police have raided Swalligan's place and seized all his booze. No more parties at Swalligan's. This removes all further interest in Swalligan and he will retire to the obscurity where he belongs. He is a poor fish and never was any good. Our jails and lunatic asylums are filled with Swalligans.)"

The Eye Opener's editor was born in Edinburgh, Scotland, in 1864. Left an orphan at an early age, he was taken by an aunt and given an opportunity for the best in Scottish education. After graduation from Glasgow University he travelled in Europe, dabbled in journalism and resolved to try cowboying in the United States. But life in a Wyoming stock saddle did not satisfy him; and in 1894 the plump young Scot with classical education, a billycock hat and no remaining money arrived at Wetaskiwin, North West Territories. After working at various jobs about the town he decided to start a paper. Accordingly, after arranging with an Edmonton firm to do the printing, Bob Edwards launched the first newspaper between Calgary and Edmonton. It was to be the "Wetaskiwin Bottling Works" because it was sure to be a "corker," but friends advised otherwise and the paper appeared as the Wetaskiwin Free Lance.

At first the paper was received with cordiality but plain and unvarnished reporting produced opposition and the editor moved to Leduc and then to Strathcona. At the latter point his paper was scheduled to be the "Strathcona Strathcolic" but it ended up as the Alberta Sun. Still the way of a small-time editor was hard and before long Edwards was moving again, this time to work for a daily in Winnipeg.

Anyone knowing him would understand that he couldn't successfully work for wages. He couldn't adapt himself to regular hours and conventional methods, and before long he was making his way back West — this time to High River where his friend Jerry Boyce had the Astoria Hotel. There on March 4, 1902, the

Eye Opener was born. Again, a town's reception to its first paper was good and Bob hoped that High River with its carefree spirit of the range would be forbearing.

At first the place filled all expectations. "High River," he wrote, "is the greatest place on the line. Any town that pays the preacher and supports the editor is so close to Heaven that a man can hardly sleep for the singing of angels."

But High River, too, proved fickle and trying. When Bob was drinking he was drinking too much; and when he swore off, life was dull. "If anyone desires to know exactly what it feels like to be utterly lonesome, marooned on a rock in the Pacific, as it were, let him become a teetotaller in High River."

Then there was trouble between the Eye Opener and the Methodist Church and Bob was moving again. Discouraged, he came to Calgary and early in 1904 his paper appeared as the Calgary Eye Opener. As time proved, it was the right move. Community and editor sort of adopted each other.

Even though punctuated with difficulties, the Calgary years were Bob Edwards' best. His humor, his criticism and the quality of his writing were indicative. City fathers discovered that they had a new critic. "Instead of another license inspector," they read, "the council should appoint a civic laundryman to handle the dirty linen." And digging and obstruction on the main avenues inspired dialogue that citizens of a later period would appreciate:

" 'I'm glad I am a child,' remarked the infant protege as it poked its head out of the baby carriage and cast a critical glance up 8th Avenue.

" 'Why, my darling Skookum-wookum?' asked the fond mother.

" 'Because I stand a show of living for 75 years and perchance seeing the day when 8th Avenue will be free from incumbrances in the shape of excavations, gravel heaps, sand mounds, mortar beds, pipes, barricades and street corner loafers.' "

Periodically, the Eye Opener seemed to shake more than the community. So it was in 1906, when the paper reported a banquet tendered by the Calgary Board of Trade in honor of Peter McGonigle's release from penitentiary where he had served time for horse stealing. That McGonigle was nothing more than an Eye Opener brain child was not enough to pacify Lord Strathcona, who read in his English paper of his alleged message of congratulations and good wishes for further successes to the horse thief,

McGonigle. Reluctantly, the noble Lord decided against suit.

There was one major libel suite and, strangely enough, the Eye Opener's editor was the plaintiff rather than defendant. But it was upsetting and caused him to leave Calgary for a couple of years. He bounced back, however, and Calgary had a welcome for him as he resumed his usual unsteady way, publishing the Eye Opener "Semi-occasionally," roasting the hypocrites in public life and society, getting drunk too often, and fighting for social reforms — municipal hospitals, votes for women and mothers' allowances.

He might call himself a Conservative but he was really a fighting reformer, as his stands on provincial autonomy, transfer of natural resources, conservation, and Senate reform would make clear. He was even advocating a natural gas pipeline from Alberta to Winnipeg as early as 1912. And when the provincial plebiscite came in 1915 the drinking man Edwards was unmistakably on the side of prohibition.

Finally, the editor who had pestered the politicians accepted a nomination in the provincial election of 1921, made one speech of 60 seconds duration, refused to use his own paper to further his political cause, and was elected with a very large vote.

"Politics," he said, "is a good game but a damn poor business." He sat through one session of the Alberta Legislature and died before the next. Now the friends were burying, but not forgetting, Bob Edwards — the man who, more than any other, contributed to Calgary's refreshing distinctiveness. It required two cars to carry the flowers; and people from all walks of life — from Lieutenant-Governor of the Province to men whose clothes revealed their poverty — were present to pay their tributes to the strange editor they had grown to love.

Unfortunately, not many copies of the fabulous Eye Opener survived. The few to be saved became treasured relics. One copy went to share company with a flask of well-seasoned whiskey in a sealed cavity in the stone marking the Bob Edwards grave at Union Cemetery beside the Macleod Trail. Even at the end of life's trail there was nothing usual about either the Eye Opener or its editor. Both were part of an uninhibited city rich in personalities and rich in the charm of being natural.

THE "BOMBING" OF CITY HALL

Tax-ridden citizens may have considered it on other occasions, but only once did a plot to "bomb" Calgary's sandstone city hall come to light. Silently the door of the mayor's office opened; a masked man shoved a black bag along the floor; a fuse sputtered for a moment; but the result was nothing more serious than two broken windows and some shattered civic nerves. Jack Miller, Calgary's city clerk from 1911 to 1955, was an eyewitness and many of the details are as he recalled them.

It was late in March, 1922. Weather was still crisp enough to call for winter underwear and storm windows, and there was snow on the ground. Calgary was having unemployment troubles and city commissioners were doing their popularity no good by proposing to cut civic wages. The mayor was the target for criticism. A brick had been tossed through a city hall window, and the mayor was the recipient of at least one threatening letter that said something about the use of dynamite.

Among those who heard about a threat to blast the city hall and kill the mayor was an affable and able young Oklahoma Indian employed as a reporter by the Calgary Herald, Buffalo Child Long Lance. In his late 20's, the ramrod-straight Long Lance came from south of the border in 1916, enlisted with the Canadian army, served with distinction in France, was wounded in action, and on discharge with rank of captain, accepted a position with the Calgary newspaper. He proved an able writer. Canadian and United States magazines wanted his stories about Indians, and journalism brought him closely into touch with the Blackfoot Tribe on which he became an acknowledged authority. As an athlete, Long Lance was one of the best in the country. Among his special skills were boxing and wrestling; and when Jack Dempsey went through Calgary, the young Indian was matched with him in two exhibition bouts — one in wrestling and the other boxing.

On hearing of the threat to blast city hall, Long Lance looked appropriately serious. It would indeed be a tragedy for Calgary to lose its city hall, built at a cost of $300,000 and opened only eleven years before. And it would be more serious to lose a good mayor and his team of top-ranking officials — all in one explosion. But neither the reporter nor the city clerk with whom he conferred believed the danger to be real.

For weeks there had been a dearth of city hall news, a state of affairs no self-respecting reporter could long endure. Eager to get a story — create one if there was no better way — Long Lance bounded up the steps at city hall just as the mayor, commissioners, city treasurer and solicitor were going into a committee meeting in the mayor's office to consider the latest threat.

The city officials wore solemn expressions. A heartless maniac might at that very second be lurking in a shadowy corner — waiting his chance to touch off a bomb that would blow city hall and everybody in it to smithereens. Naturally the civic faces were grave.

Halting briefly to assess the tense situation, the reporter entered the city clerk's office and engaged Jack Miller in a moment of conversation. Instantly an idea was born. Reporter and clerk made their way to the second floor of the building where E. H. Fletcher, city plumbing inspector, kept some equipment. Without disclosing the purpose in mind, some pieces were borrowed — a black leather tool bag heavy with a pipe-fitter's wrenches, and a pressure gauge of a kind inspectors use in their work.

With quickened step the Indian strode away to visit an 8th Avenue store. Minutes later he was back with a red bandana handkerchief and a length of fuse such as men use in blasting rock. Behind the closed doors in Jack Miller's office the two men made some pseudo-technical adjustments. All was ready — the pressure gauge tied with its imposing face protruding ominously from the opening of the leather bag, fuse in place with one end in plain view and the other buried in the bag, and red handkerchief tied about the reporter's face, leaving only eyes uncovered.

By this time the commissioners and their associates were sitting with His Worship the Mayor as chairman. Nobody sat comfortably. Threat of violence had made officials about that circle more restless than usual. A snap from somebody's fingers or the slamming of a door could have triggered the committeemen into a frenzy.

While the mayor was speaking, hinges on his office door squeaked just a little — then a little more. All eyes turned to the opening to behold a masked man, stealthily easing a suspicious appearing black bag along the office floor.

For a brief moment the city officers stared at the black eyes showing above the mask. It was easy to see them as those of a criminal — some cruel sadist with regard for neither human lives nor civic property.

Package delivered, the door closed; and civic officials realized they were sharing the office with what had the appearance of a bag of dynamite. There was the horrible spectacle — black bag, an intricate mechanism with graduated dial protruding, and a burning fuse becoming shorter every second.

The thought of impending disaster gripped everybody in the office, as the Indian plotter and the city clerk observed through a slight opening in the doorway. In panic one member of the committee dashed for safety, and others who could, followed. A newspaper man attending the meeting — although unaware of the plot — plunged under the mayor's desk; Commissioner A. J. Samis escaped by the rear door, left the building through the north exit, and didn't look back until he was on the opposite side of 7th Avenue. The other commissioner, Angus Smith, chose a more direct way of quitting the danger zone and plunged straight through the nearest window, double-paned as it was at that season. Only when he struck the ground, some ten feet below, did he venture to glance back, expecting to see the city hall being blown apart like a firecracker. And while some members of the committee found it easy to run, mayor, solicitor and treasurer appeared "frozen" to their chairs and waited in terror for the explosion, and the end.

But the blast didn't come, and after a period of waiting some courageous soul ventured back to peer into the black bag and found it to contain nothing more deadly than a plumber's pipe-wrench.

Buffalo Child Long Lance had his story and wrote it for the paper, but when the circumstances became known the editor fired him promptly. The city solicitor, according to Jack Miller, interceded on the reporter's behalf and tried to win forgiveness, but it was all in vain. The editor was anxious to obtain news for his pages but not by such rough and unethical methods.

The evening newspaper of March 29, 1922, carried "An Apology: Wednesday morning, B. C. Long Lance, a reporter on the staff of the Herald, opened the door of Mayor Adams' office at the City Hall and placed inside a bag which had the appearance of an infernal machine, with fuse attached and burning."

THE "BOMBING" OF CITY HALL

"All present thought that some person with a grievance planned to blow up the City Hall, and there was an immediate rush to escape from the room. The thought was natural in view of the fact that threats against city officials have lately been heard and considering that a rock was hurled through Mayor Adams' window Tuesday."

"Commissioner Smith, in attempting to open a window to escape from the room, was badly cut about the hands and face."

"The Herald deeply regrets this occurrence and that this indignity to His Worship Mayor Adams and the commissioners and other officers of the city was suffered by them through the act of a member of its staff, and tenders its sincere apologies . . ."

The powerful and handsome young Indian left Calgary and did newspaper work in Winnipeg and public relations for the Canadian Pacific Railway. Banff saw quite a bit of him and Calgary saw him again now and then. At the onset of the Stampede in 1923, a band of Blackfoot, Sarcee and Stoney Indians raided the city hall and kidnapped the mayor, George Webster, taking him to a downtown street where he was obliged to pay for his release by frying flapjacks for pedestrians and singing cowboy songs. Who was the Indian who conceived the idea and led the braves? Buffalo Child Long Lance, of course.

Wherever he was, the magnetic fellow was as conspicuous as a plug hat at a Calgary Stampede. He seemed to hold a special attraction for wealthy widows and sometimes he was in trouble. Always, however, he was refreshing. He was on friendly terms with Irving Cobb and Bob Fitzsimmons and Will Rogers. He played movie parts in Hollywood, was acclaimed a great success, and his name might have become famous had it not been for tragedy.

A few years after leaving Calgary he wrote an alleged autobiography giving a vivid description of Blackfoot Indian life. Actually, Long Lance was part Cherokee and his experience with the Blackfoot was limited, but the book was good reading nevertheless. And then one day in March, 1931, Calgarians read where "The Chief" was found dead in a palatial American home at which he was a guest — bullet in his head. The circumstances were not very clear. The verdict was given as suicide but his friends had doubts.

Said Jack Miller: "He was an unforgettable character — should have remained in Calgary."

THE BISHOP'S RECORD

When he came from England to Red River in 1868, Reverend William Cyprian Pinkham was the youngest clergyman west of the Great Lakes; and at the time of his retirement at Calgary on August 7, 1926, he was the oldest consecrated bishop in years of service in the Anglican world. Nor was he quitting then; at age 81; he was saying, "I want to be useful as long as I live."

The city in which he was retiring was a strangely different community from the one he had adopted about 40 years before. The trees he had planted as seedlings were now full blown and mature; fine and lasting churches had taken the place of temporary structures; stone-strewn streets were overlaid with pavement, and population had increased exactly 100 times.

When he came to make his home in Calgary in 1887 his Diocese of Saskatchewan extended from Manitoba to the Rockies and northward to the Arctic Circle — roughly 300,000 square miles, they said. For that far-flung mission field the Church needed men and money and the Bishop set out to get both.

"I've been a beggar all my life," he said, and others could have added that as such he was a great success. When he travelled to England he returned with funds for church building in Calgary and elsewhere, and even when he visited his charges in the North he inspired generous donations for the work. At Onion Lake, where he confirmed 48 Indians on one trip, the collection plates came forward to the altar loaded with offerings which included seven bars of soap, five skins of mink, one towel, two mugs, a leather jacket and a stone pipe.

The Bishop was a Newfoundlander by birth — born November 11, 1844 — but the family went to England and lived in Devon. Graduating from Augustine's College, Canterbury, William Cyprian went the same year as missionary to Red River in what was still called Rupert's Land. There he met the attractive Jean Drever, a native daughter from Scottish parents, and recognized a prize. The third time they saw each other the clergyman proposed, and in two months they were married. There being no jewelry store nearby, the Red River blacksmith was commissioned to hammer out a wedding ring. That he did, making the very acceptable ring from a gold coin.

Other Drever girls married Colonel J. F. Macleod of Mounted Police fame, J. A. Mackay who became Archdeacon Mackay, and J. P. J. Jephson who practiced law in Calgary.

Pinkham in 1881 was appointed Archdeacon of St. John's Cathedral in Winnipeg, and in 1887 Bishop of Saskatchewan with headquarters at Calgary. Until he moved to "Sunny Alberta," he said, he had never been frostbitten, but one of his earliest adventures in the far West proved both chilly and dangerous. It might have cost him his life. He was making a winter trip to Fort Macleod, by stage coach, of course, and a storm came out of the north west. Wind blew with hurricane force and the air was full of snow. All landmarks were blotted out and the driver was practically helpless. The stage horses, losing the trail, began to wander aimlessly.

With no shelter, travellers and horses were out all that night. The danger of freezing to death couldn't be overlooked but there was no despair. With the Bishop leading, half perished passengers joined in singing hymns and psalms and so the night passed. In the morning there were frozen cheeks, noses, ears and fingers, but the driver took his bearings from the sun and drove southward across trackless prairie, coming in time to the Oldman River — 18 miles east of Fort Macleod, 18 miles off the trail.

On another trip by stage, when the driver was found to be incapacitated by drink, the Bishop of Calgary mounted to the top of the coach and took charge, driving the four-horse team with skill that marked him a good horseman.

The Bishop's contribution to education should not go unnoticed. When Manitoba's first School Act was passed, Pinkham was appointed to the Provisional Board of Education; and in coming to Calgary he was appointed, almost at once, to the Territorial Board of Education and became the board chairman.

And while he was working for church and education, Mrs. Pinkham was struggling to get a general hospital in Calgary. Some of the first funds came unexpectedly. A Chinese dying in a Calgary hotel willed his trousers and the money in the pockets to the clergyman who had befriended him. The pockets were found to contain about $100 and this money was put aside to start a hospital fund.

Mrs. Pinkham organized a Women's Hospital Aid Society the year after her arrival and was its president for a long period. "Our principal way of raising money," she said, "was by dances and suppers at the old Hull Opera House. I once carved 12 turkeys for one of those meals."

Soon after the Bishop came to Calgary, his Diocese of Saskatchewan was divided and he became the Bishop of Calgary, the office he held until retirement. It was a singular tour of service. In his long association with the West in general and Calgary in particular, Anglican Bishop Pinkham's record resembled that of Roman Catholic Father Lacombe and Methodist Reverend John McDougall.

On July 17, 1928, the tall, dignified man with luxuriant white beard and broad face which might have fitted the Apostle Paul — that Anglican member of early Alberta's ecclesiastical "Big Three" — went to his rest. Few men had lived so unselfishly; few men had so endeared themselves to their fellows.

THE MEMORABLE BIRTHDAY PARTY

The huge birthday party at the Palliser Hotel on July 6, 1931, was Calgary's tribute to a distinguished pioneer, and there was nothing quite like it before or after. The guest of honor was round-faced and affable Patrick Burns, better known as Pat or "P.B.", of whom Mayor Andrew Davison read from the official address: "The City of Calgary is today celebrating with enthusiasm the seventy-fifth birthday of its best-loved citizen . . ."

In the initial plans, the party, coinciding appropriately with the first day of the Calgary Exhibition, was to be a local affair. Gradually, however, the guest list became national in scope and then international. Among the 700 people who sat down to the birthday dinner, nearly every province and many parts of the United States were represented and special guests included two provincial premiers and three lieutenant-governors. People from every walk of life were there to pay eager respect to the man Alberta's Premier Brownlee described as "a grand pioneer, a true Canadian gentleman, a philanthropist and prince of good fellows."

Of course there was a birthday cake — and what a cake! It was a gift from the Exhibition Company, but there was one difficulty — it was too big to be taken into the Palliser Hotel so it was placed on the platform in front of the grandstand at the conclusion of the evening performance, where it was cut into 15,000 pieces and passed to the patrons.

That rich fruit cake with 75 candles measured eight feet square at its base, had three layers, and was seven and one-half feet high. Its weight exceeded 3,000 pounds, and those who wanted the recipe could have it: 380 dozen eggs, 285 pounds of sugar, 304 pounds of butter, 380 pounds of flour, 12 pounds of spices, 115 pounds of raisins, 290 pounds of currants, 190 pounds of mixed peel, 190 pounds of cherries, 160 pounds of nuts, 160 pounds of dates, 60 pounds of candied pineapple and 2½ pounds of salt. Nor was that all; there was still the icing, taking an additional 160 pounds of sugar, the whites of 340 eggs, and so on. It was a culinary masterpiece, even in its artistic appearance, and when the last patron left the grandstand on that birthday night, the great cake had disappeared.

At the birthday dinner, Lieutenant-Colonel J. H. Woods, as chairman, recounted Pat Burns' contributions to the life of Calgary and, indeed, that of Canada. The guest of honor was the poor boy, handicapped by limitations in education, who became a leader in Canadian industry. It was the sort of success story people have always loved.

The compliments came thick and fast and the modest Burns was embarrassed. He was presented with an oil painting of himself, the work of Kenneth K. Forbes of Toronto. The incoming telegrams of congratulations were so numerous that the chairman said he could not consider reading them all at the time. One, however, was from the Prince of Wales, one from Prime Minister R. B. Bennett; and one from the Clerk of the Privy Council, which stated: "His Excellency, the Governor-General of Canada, on the recommendation of the Prime Minister, has been pleased this day to summon to the Senate of Canada, Patrick Burns, Esquire, of the City of Calgary, in the Province of Alberta."

Guests whispered to each other, "He's now a Senator," and then, spontaneously, there were three rousing cheers for "Senator Burns," the man who 41 years earlier had come into Calgary with neither capital nor fanfare — the man who could become a millionaire without losing a friend.

During that "Burns Week," as it was designated by the Calgary Industrial Exhibition Company, local people heard a good deal about the young Irish-Canadian who came to Western Canada in 1878. He was born at Oshawa, Ontario, and while he was still an infant, parents Michael and Bridget Burns took their family to Kirkfield. There Pat obtained an unfortunately small amount of schooling; and there he made the acquaintance of neighbor-boy Willie Mackenzie, who was to become a member of the noted firm of railroad builders. Mackenzie and Mann, and through whom Pat Burns began his climb to success in the meat business.

Pat was 22 years of age when he and brother John travelled to far-away Manitoba. At Winnipeg they learned about good homestead land at Tanner's Crossing, 160 miles west and north. To that place, later called Minnedosa, the two young fellows walked in five days. And after selecting homesteads, they walked back to Winnipeg to get work on the new C.P.R. grade east of the city.

After saving enough money from his wage of $25 a month, Pat invested in a team of oxen and wagon and rode to the homestead, intending to make it his home. Neighbors came together to help build a cabin and then, with walking plow, the ambitious young fellow broke some land for crop. But from the beginning Pat Burns was recognizing business opportunities beyond the boundaries of his quarter-section farm. He undertook to do freighting between Minnedosa and Winnipeg; and he hauled hay to Brandon.

One of his Clan William neighbors recalled Burns buying thin oxen in the autumn, fattening them until near spring when he would build pole racks on sleighs, load up with hay, hitch a team of fattened oxen to each sleigh, and start over the snow trail to Brandon. At his destination he would sell the hay, dismantle the hay racks, and sell the poles for fire-wood, sell all the fat oxen except one team, load all the spare sleighs and harness on one sleigh, and drive back to the homestead.

Having kept in touch with his boyhood friend, William Mackenzie, Burns received the offer of a job supplying beef for the workers where contractors Mackenzie and Mann were building a railroad in the State of Maine. Taking it, he found such enterprise profitable and one meat contract led to another. In 1889 he was supplying beef for a thousand hungry men building the Qu'Appelle, Long Lake and Saskatchewan Railroad north from Regina, and in 1890 he arrived at Calgary to render the same service along the new grade being built toward Edmonton.

At Calgary he was a total stranger when he hired a horse and buggy and drove into the country to buy cattle for delivery at his slaughter camp beside the grade. He worked night and day. Expanding operations made financing difficult, but as settlers discovered, Burns was honest; if he couldn't pay all cash for steers and cows, he went back and made settlement as soon as he collected for his meat.

He wasn't seeking publicity, and not until late in the season when 28 head of his cattle went astray did he rate newspaper recognition. To a young business man with limited resources such a loss could be ruinous, and people about him wondered if he could overcome it. But 15 years later they had their answer when a Southern Alberta newspaper reported: "One of the best known ranching men of the West is Patrick C. Burns of Calgary. He is the Armour of this part of the world and is sometimes called the Cattle King of the British Northwest. He shipped 3500 carloads of beeves last year and he has now about 20,000 head in his yards. He has a big trade with Manitoba, British Columbia and Alaska. At the beginning of the Klondyke gold discovery, he got $1000 a piece for steers at Dawson."

That Klondyke venture was typical of the man. Late in 1897 and throughout 1898, thousands of fortune-seekers were flocking over the forbidding routes leading to Dawson City, deep in the hinterland of the North. Great volumes of food, especially meats, were needed, and Burns was one of the first to ship cattle to Skagway on the coast, drive them over the dangerous passes and trails and, finally, slaughter them beside the Lewes River and raft the carcasses down to Dawson City. It was a four or five-months task to deliver beef from Calgary steers at Dawson City, but it was Burns beef more than any other that fed the miners in the far North.

His small slaughter house built in East Calgary in 1890 led to massive plants in various cities and to business connections extending around the world. The original slaughter house burned down in 1892 and was promptly rebuilt. Fire struck again in 1913, taking his large new abattoir in Calgary. It was the city's biggest fire up to that time; but before the firemen left the scene of the disaster, Pat Burns was making plans for a still bigger plant.

In addition to having large and modern abattoirs in various parts of Canada, Pat Burns acquired a hundred or more retail meat stores in Alberta and British Columbia, 65 creameries and cheese factories, about 30 wholesale provision and fruit houses, extensive ranchers at scattered Alberta points, interests in oil wells, coal mines and real estate. He was the busiest man in Calgary but never too busy to help people in need or support some worthy cause.

In 1912 when plans were being made for the first big Calgary Stampede, the men who backed the project and carried the financial risk, with no possibility of personal gain, were Ranchers George Lane, A. E. Cross, Archie McLean and Pat Burns; the "Big Four" people called them. When Burns workmen went to the Village of Midnapore to paint the little Roman Catholic church, the operation made the Anglican church on adjacent property look shabby by contrast and the broad-minded Burns gave instructions: "Boys, you better paint their church too." And while Calgary was honoring Pat Burns on his seventy-fifth birthday, he was quietly giving instructions for the distribution of 2000 birthday roasts of beef to needy families in the city and 4000 meal tickets to single unemployed people. It was little wonder that by 1931 there was no name better known across the West than that of Pat Burns.

It wasn't easy for those round about to get used to calling him Senator Burns; but he didn't care. At first he didn't even like the Senate Chamber — apart from the joy of sitting with his old friend and fellow-rancher, Senator Dan Riley. But he found increasing satisfaction in it and served faithfully though not noisily.

Early in 1937, six years after the big birthday party, death claimed Senator Pat Burns, took the pioneer of whom Mayor Andy Davison said: "Calgary's best-loved citizen" — the one who was Calgary's first industrial tycoon and who demonstrated that a man can become a millionaire and win a million admirers at the same time.

THE PRIME MINISTER

Nothing for some years after the Prince of Wales chose to buy a ranch close to Calgary gave local people such prideful satisfaction as sending fellow-citizen R. B. Bennett to Ottawa to be Prime Minister of Canada. The year 1930 belonged to the Conservative Party, R. B. Bennett and Calgary. Bennett was the only Calgarian, and indeed the only Albertan, to achieve the high office.

Following the financial crash of one year before, depression was tightening its hold upon the country. More and more men were out of work; wheat was netting Alberta farmers about 50 cents a bushel; choice steers were down to 5½ cents a pound and retailers were selling pickled beef at six pounds for 49 cents.

Voters were asking themselves if a change of government and Bennett's leadership would bring improvement. His policies seemed attractive: protection for industry, improved transportation, outlet to the sea for Peace River, development of the St. Lawrence Waterway, the Trans-Canada Highway, and other necessary steps to end unemployment.

The formal and dignified Bennett was not one to command public affection, but his oratory and his convictions were impressive and the people, especially in Calgary, had faith in him. In the federal election on July 28, 1930, Dr. G. D. Stanley won in Calgary East and R. B. Bennett in Calgary West, both Conservatives and both elected with big majorities. Across the country the Conservatives had 137 seats, the Liberals 85 and the United Farmers of Alberta 10. The King Liberal Government had been overthrown and the people of Canada were calling upon the leader of the Conservatives, Calgary's Bennett, to form a government.

For 33 years the citizens of Calgary had watched this lawyer and politician whose eyes were fixed upon the uppermost rungs of life's ladder. He stood out like a plug hat such as he sometimes wore. "On the platform he is without a peer in all the western country," wrote an observer as early as 1901. "In appearance he strikingly resembles the portraits of Robespierre. Tall and slight, clean shaven, with a forehead not very broad but singularly high from which his hair, somewhat long and straight, is brushed carefully

back, he has an appearance that would command attention anywhere."

It may be too soon for the historian's assessment of his states-
manship, but not too soon to study and enjoy Bennett's amazing
career embracing service at no fewer than five levels of government — town council in his native province, Legislative Assembly
in the North West Territories, Legislature of the Province of
Alberta, Canadian House of Commons and, finally, the British
House of Lords. It stands as a half-century record unlikely to be
equalled.

Richard Bedford Bennett, ultimately Viscount Bennett, had
many loyalties; but, in the main, he belonged in the western
community where he was known as "R.B."

But wherever he chose to live Bennett must be seen as one
of Canada's best manifestations of vibrant ambition realized by
dint of determination and hard work. His mother believed her
boy was born to be great and he never took his eyes off the goals
she helped him set. Moreover, it was his belief that every person
should strive to achieve nothing less than the maximum for which
he has capacity.

He was very much a part of his background. The parents were
of United Empire Loyalist stock, the father a shipbuilder of modest
means at Hopewell, New Brunswick. There Richard Bedford was
born in 1870. For his native province there was lifelong affection.
According to a Calgary reporter: "R. B. Bennett delivered an
eloquent address on Tennyson last night and proved conclusively
that the poet was of the best New Brunswick lineage."

As a boy he acquired a fine respect for honest work, education,
temperance and the "Grand Old Party." When school mates were
playing and fishing, young Bennett was engrossed in books. At
no period in his life was there much time for non-productive
amusements.

For a while he taught school, and at the age of 19 entered
the Dalhousie Law School. At once his actions identified him as
academic rather than athletic.

Graduating in 1893, he was called to the Bar of New Brunswick, became a junior law partner with L. J. Tweedie, who was
destined to become Premier, and then Lieutenant-Governor of his
province. And it was there in Tweedie's Town of Chatham that

young Bennett made his political debut when elected to the local Council.

Senator James Lougheed of Calgary wanted a junior law partner and was difficult to satisfy. Acting upon advice from Dean Weldon of Dalhousie, however, Lougheed went to Chatham and persuaded Bennett to come to the West.

Calgary, with frontier recklessness, was a shocking change for the refined young Maritimer. He didn't smoke, didn't drink, didn't care about boxing and horse racing. In a sense he seemed a misfit. Mixing with the masses never came easy and had it not been for political ambition and a fondness for making speeches, his name might have been unknown outside of legal circles.

As it was, when church or club wanted a polished speaker, thoughts turned to Bennett and he never disappointed. With special pride the temperance forces placed him on their platform at every opportunity. The old pages tell that, "An interesting address was given in the opera house last night by R. B. Bennett, M.L.A., on temperance. It has been his proud claim that never has a drop of liquor passed his lips. The opera house was crowded."

Quickly Bennett realized that Calgary offered more than a place for legal practise. It was an area of opportunity — a good place for one with the Bennett brand of ambition. Now and then he revealed those deep convictions of purpose, strengthened by thought of his mother's hopes. The press told about a largely attended meeting of the Young Men's Club, the special attraction being an address by R. B. Bennett, with the title: "Aims and Ambitions Which Should Animate a Young Man's Life":

"Many concrete examples of well known men of ancient and modern history were cited as illustrating the benefits from having a definite aim and of adhering to it, no matter what forces opposed. Cicero, Demosthenes, Disraeli, Stevenson, Gladstone, Carnegie were mentioned as men who, whether their aims had been praiseworthy or not, had accomplished much in life by keeping steadily in view one clear purpose." But as those who knew him would appreciate, no name would illustrate the moral more fittingly than that of the speaker.

And in 1898, just over a year after his arrival in the West, the young orator was elected to represent Calgary in the Legislative Assembly of the North West Territories. When he repeated that political victory in 1901, he "had a band out in the street," according to the press, "and delivered an address, pledging himself to live and die in Calgary." His legislative record was good and the best debates in the Assembly were those between Bennett and Premier Haultain, both Conservatives but not always in agreement.

In his profession he was proving to be an able counsel, with the thoroughness and decision to make a great judge. In court he found himself most frequently on the opposite side to another famous lawyer, Paddy Nolan. Probably the old sandstone Court House heard no more brilliant debate than when Bennett appeared for the plaintiff and Nolan for the defence. The latter's arguments had more spontaneity and warmth, Bennett's more preparation and finish.

Bennett remained in the Territorial Legislature until 1905 when, owing to defeat at the polls, he was out of politics for four years. In 1909 he was returned to the Provincial Legislature, and in 1911 resigned to enter the federal election, winning in Calgary East with a big majority. Thereafter, the name was known across Canada. For a short period in 1921 he was Minister of Justice in the Meighen Government, and for another short time in 1926, Minister of Finance.

Calgary's Bennett was now a man of wealth, partly due to friendship in New Brunswick years with Harry and Jennie Sherreff. The latter became Mrs. E. B. Eddy and much of the Eddy Company stock came ultimately to Bennett. But wealth made no difference to his way of life. He contributed generously and quietly to charities, but he continued to save odd bits of paper for scratch-pad purposes and indulged in few luxuries more extravagant than eating chocolates.

More dreams were being realized when, at the Winnipeg Convention in 1927, Bennett, with protectionist and imperialistic leanings, was chosen to be national leader of the Conservative Party. Energetically he threw himself into the federal election contest of 1930, convinced he could end unemployment and "blast" his way into bigger export markets.

He and his party were swept into power but it was an unfortunate time to be in power. Canada was in grievous trouble and the Prime Minister was certain to be held responsible for the state of the nation. Canada, like much of the world, was feeling the cold clutch of economic depression and there was the added problem of severe drought across the Mid-West. Unemployment and unrest mounted and Bennett came in for more and more criticism. Even personal faults which might have been overlooked in more normal times were recited to his political detriment. He resented criticism and interference; he was not careful enough to be on good terms with the press; he dominated his cabinet more than a wise Prime minister should; and in the cold light of depression his failings were magnified. Politically, it was a bad time to be in power, as it was a good time for Bennett's opponents to be in opposition.

The depressed state of the nation's economy did not respond to Bennett's remedies. He was coming to recognize the need for sweeping changes in social legislation, but in this he failed to convince the voters and in the general election of 1935 he was re-elected in his Calgary seat but his party was defeated.

Bennett, the hard-working, serious man who resented criticism, was unhappy in being demoted to Leader of the Opposition, and in 1938, he resigned from the House of Commons and left Canada to live in England. Juniper Hill in Surrey became his home. Some people said he had deserted the land in which he had achieved wealth and fame. But England had long held attraction for him. As early as 1912 there was a rumor of his going there and entering politics. In 1941 he was raised to the Peerage. He became Viscount Bennett of Mickleham, Calgary and Hopewell, and sat in the House of Lords. Presumably he wanted the title, however little a man of his stature and record needed it. Perhaps it was a figment of the Bennett ambition, another goal set for himself.

In England he continued to be active, largely in Red Cross and war service. And there, on June 26, 1947, death took the wealthy and famous bachelor, probably a lonely man. But he had won the reward he sought — success — something achieved every day. Even in gaining the Prime Ministership he was fulfilling a youthful declaration of intention.

One may speculate about how his life would have been changed if he had married. He confessed to similar speculation.

And in Calgary, where he could be re-elected to the House of Commons even in a year like 1935, a person could hear long after his departure: "He should have stayed here."

But striking as Bennett's political part in the '30's will appear, he was obliged to share the Calgary stage with some other skillful actors — including one by the name of Aberhart.

MORE OF POVERTY AND POLITICS

Instead of reacting favorably to change of government, the depression became worse, especially for farmers and working people. Wheat which netted farmers 50 cents a bushel when Bennett was elected brought 25 cents three years later, and the price of steers declined to a ruinous three cents a pound. Men out of work collected in hostile knots on Calgary streets or "rode the rods" in moving aimlessly from place to place.

The public patience was running out. All established institutions like railroad companies, chartered banks, manufacturers and the capitalistic system itself were favorite targets for criticism. Nor did the two old political parties — Conservative and Liberal which had served Canada since Confederation — escape denunciation. "It's time for a change — perhaps a radical change." many who set themselves up as students of political affairs were saying. And when such statements were made, more and more people were ready to listen. The harsh economic climate of the time was inviting unorthodox remedies.

Two new political parties were born at that period and, strangely enough, both had their birth in the City of Calgary. One was the Co-operative Commonwealth Federation, better known as the C.C.F. In a manifesto of 1931 the United Farmers of Alberta sounded the call for co-operation between farmer, labor and other groups in bringing about a better social order. The political pot bubbled and boiled; and while Prime Minister Bennett was hopefully acting as host at the Imperial Economic Conference at Ottawa, an important mass meeting of farm and labor groups was held in Calgary's Legion Hall — held on the evening of July 31, 1932.

Thirteen hundred people crowding inside fanned sweating faces with their hats, and many more tried to attend but were turned away. E. J. Garland, M.P. for Bow River was chairman, and the speakers were former Methodist minister J. S. Woodsworth, M.P., Alderman M. J. Coldwell of Regina, who appeared as leader of the recently-formed Farmer-Labor Party in Saskatchewan, and Robert Gardiner, M.P., president of the United Farmers of Alberta.

Speakers said that new economic principles were needed and everybody present seemed to agree, with cheers. There was a clear call for action and Mr. Woodsworth, sensing the feeling of the meeting, declared: "I would rather be a member of this conference in Calgary which has for its aim the co-operation of farm and labor groups than of the Imperial Conference at Ottawa. It is of greater importance to the future of Canada."

The name, Co-operative Commonwealth Federation was agreed upon; and next day Mr. Woodsworth, the man who would "rather be the leader of a crusade than the Prime Minister of Canada," was chosen to be the first president of the first National Council of the new party; and Norman Priestly, well known to Calgarians, was elected secretary. The new farmer-labor-socialist movement would be "A federation of organizations whose purpose is the establishment in Canada of a co-operative commonwealth in which the basic principle regulating production, distribution and exchange will be the supplying of human needs instead of the making of profits."

Calgary people watched the launching of the new party but were not carried away by it. For them there was no overwhelming appeal in socialism, not even at a time of depression. But the period immediately ahead held political excitement centred in their city which they found more difficult to resist. At first it was at the provincial level, but with Calgary Teacher and Preacher William Aberhart as the driving personality, the movement became something to attract the eyes of the world.

From the beginning of the Province of Alberta there had been only one change of government — one change in nearly 30 years. A Liberal Government remained in power for the first 16 years and was then overthrown by the United Farmers of Alberta. Well over half of the provincial population was living on farms in 1921, and the so-called "class government" elected that year was still in power when the adversity of depression and drought was making life miserable for any group holding public office.

As the C.C.F. Party was being created, Calgary people were finding reason for new interest in fellow-citizen William Aberhart, principal at Crescent Heights High School. When he wasn't teaching or preaching his fundamentalist religion, he was studying the economic theories of Scottish Major C. H. Douglas and growing in conviction that therein lay the cure for the curse of depression. When currency is scarce, governments should create it by writing cheques.

Aberhart, from an Ontario farm and a Presbyterian home, came to Calgary in 1910. He was 31 years of age, hard working and ambitious. His own formal education was completed by means of night classes and correspondence, but he was a student in a broad sense all his life. As a teacher he quickly distinguished himself; and as an administrator he was so orderly and exacting that he wasn't popular with teaching colleagues, who found it difficult to meet his standards of efficiency.

Lifelong religious zeal and a leaning toward the ministry led him to teaching Sunday School and Bible Classes in Calgary churches. And then, with the support of a growing number of followers, he started the Prophetic Bible Institute.

Being a man of unusual vigor and working capacity, it was quite possible for him to combine education, religion and politics and be a leader in all. As his program developed he made his economic theory a bedfellow with his religious teachings, and by 1934 his radio and platform messages were polished blends of religion, politics and economics. The response was something to warm a crusader's heart; interest was spreading like fluff from a withered dandelion.

Aberhart loved the public platform, and in captivating an audience neither R. B. Bennett nor Michael Clark could rival him. He was a six-footer, heavily jowled, almost completely bald and 250 pounds in weight. In speeches he was voluble, caustic and witty, and listeners loved it all. In everything he did he was a dominant personality.

Fervently he believed he held the solution to the problem of depression and unemployment — just as he had long held the answer to the salvation of souls. And even though very few people understood his explanations in the field of economics, they were impressed by his enthusiasm and railings against the moneylenders and the financial "bigshots" who were contributing to human misery.

At first, as Aberhart and his young secretary, Ernest Manning from a Saskatchewan farm, expressed their confidence in the Douglas proposal of Social Credit, it was not held out as a political issue. The principle was one to be adopted by any political party, they pointed out. And various groups, including the U.F.A. Government, were sufficiently impressed to authorize studies of Social Credit and determine how it might help the sick economy. Aberhart appeared before the U.F.A. convention early in 1935 and talked for hours. People were feeling desperate. Even Prime Minister Bennett at that time was saying, "The economic system must be reformed. What we call the crash of 1929 was simply the crash of the system."

But as months passed it became clear that no existing political party was ready to adopt Aberhart's suggestions, and his actions and speeches became more and more like those of a man who would do it himself. He was working hard and working long hours. Ever a man who hated wasting time, he was teaching throughout school days, preaching at weekends, and addressing gatherings having the character of revival meetings at nights. If a student needed extra tutoring, the only time available was at 7 a.m.

A provincial election was called for August 22, 1935. The U.F.A. Government was in ill repute and it was an excellent time, amid frustration and discouragement, for anyone with a fresh message. Business on 8th Avenue was distressingly dormant, markets were paralyzed, Calgary's population at 83,000 was lower than it had been a few years earlier, and Mae West was about the only name that would bring a smile to men's faces.

And as Aberhart grew in fame he didn't escape criticism. Rapidly he was becoming the most controversial person since Bob Edwards. Was he the Moses to lead the people of Alberta out of financial bondage or was he a political phoney? Most people had extreme views one way or another. One editor described him as the "Pied piper who is to drive the rats away from the capital city." "Social Credit," proclaimed another, "is public enemy number one." At the same time a correspondent writing to the press described Mr. Aberhart as God's chosen leader: "Jesus walks every moment by his side. I often think that God will not let him suffer much longer with the jeers and cruel things folk are saying about him and He may taken him away from us, to live with Him in Glory." And from still another pen came the call, "Arise, oh ye people of Alberta and worship Aberhart who will lead us to the Promised Land and the Kingdom of God."

The crowning pre-election selling point was the promise of the Social Credit basic dividend — a $25 a month gift to every adult in the province. And at a time when the City of Regina was witnessing a three-hour street fight between police and unemployed with heavy property damage and 100 people reported injured, $25 a month sounded like manna dropping down from above.

Election plans began to crystallize at a two-day convention of Aberhart followers in the Prophetic Bible Institute, April 4 and 5. It was the first Social Credit convention and all the provincial constituencies south of Red Deer were enthusiastically represented. While a local editor was accusing Aberhart of "using a tabernacle built in the name of religion to promote what is rapidly becoming a political party," some firm decisions were being made in it, among them that Social Credit candidates would be nominated in all constituencies and that Mr. Aberhart working with a small advisory committee would have power to select all candidates.

Climaxing the convention with evangelical zeal, the leader, on the concluding evening, blasted his critics, left no doubt about being ready to fight it out, and followed a few days later with advice to his followers to boycott a certain Calgary newspaper because it had been unfair to him.

The campaign became hectic and rough. Critics called Aberhart a "lead pencil man." He described the U.F.W.A. as the "Undernourished Fool Women of Alberta," and so the campaign went.

The election day result, however, was a landslide victory for William Aberhart and his Social Credit Party, more decisive even than the election of 1921 when the Liberals were swept out and the United Farmers of Alberta were swept in. Every candidate representing the former government was defeated. Social Credit candidates were elected in 56 of the 63 Alberta seats. The City of Calgary, on a heavy vote, elected E. C. Manning, Fred Anderson, Mrs. E. H. Gostick and John W. Hugill, all from Social Credit; J. J. Bowlen from the Liberals, and John Irwin from the Conservatives.

The Province was assured of having the first Social Credit Government in the world and Alberta bonds dropped in price immediately by one to two dollars. Citizens in conversation expressed some surprise at the general result, but agreed they didn't have much to lose and it would be all right to give this thing a trial — even if its intricacies were quite beyond their comprehension.

Mr. Aberhart had directed campaign policy with skill, but had done so without being an active candidate in the election. Now, with victory, a caucus was called and it was agreed that one of the elected members would resign and the leader would contest a by election to gain a seat in the Legislature. The member for Okotoks-High River resigned, Aberhart ran there, was elected, and took office as the seventh Premier of Alberta. Two other Calgarians entered the cabinet, Mr. Manning as Provincial Secretary, and Mr. Hugill as Attorney General.

Now, what would the new government do about the $25 dividends? It began boldly. Eighteen days after the election there came an announcement from Edmonton that, "Preliminary steps in preparation for province-wide registration of Alberta citizens for the Social Credit basic dividends of $25 monthly will be started immediately."

However workable Mr. Aberhart may have considered his famous plan for dividends, the practical obstacles became painfully clear and the responsibility of office proved a harsh teacher. It wasn't easy to withdraw promises, and supporters who failed to understand the difficulties wanted their dividend payments — and quickly. Others heaped ridicule upon the false hopes and naive promises. The fact was that the Province was desperately short of money and lacked the sovereign power to make basic monetary changes.

Actually, the Premier proved more conservative than many of the economic reformers who had climbed on his political wagon. He did set up a Social Credit Board and bring Douglas experts to the Province. Advice from the latter led to a special session of the Legislature in 1937 and some radical bills which were ultimately disallowed. Little in the way of Social Credit was ever realized; but the government was returned in 1940, even in the face of an attempt to combine the opposition groups.

Calgary's William Aberhart died in 1943 and was succeeded in the office of Premier by Honorable E. C. Manning, with whom the founder had been closely associated in both church and party. The passing removed a skillful and distinguished leader, and even those who opposed him would concede readily that he contributed much to Alberta story.

But any way one looked at it, Calgary seemed to be the storm centre in that period of political turbulence.

THE MEMORABLE PRAYER MEETING

From the 10th day of September, 1939, Canada was at war with the German Reich, the decision having been made deliberately to stand side by side with the Mother Country. It was the onset of World War II, and although Canada was hopelessly unprepared, the nation's resources were mobilized quickly to furnish men, women, equipment and food to meet needs nearer the battlefields.

Calgary, with Currie Barracks and Lord Strathcona Horse, was already a garrison city. But to the call for volunteers there was a ready response and men in uniform were at once conspicuous on Calgary streets.

Business became brisk; unemployment practically ended, and farmers heard a clear call to produce more of bacon, beef, butter, cheese and eggs — more of almost everything except wheat.

For a while there were military reverses to try the staunchest hearts, the fall of France in June, 1940, followed by the evacuation of troops from the Hell-like beaches at Dunkirk. But everybody believed the main test was still somewhere in the future. More and more Calgarians and other Canadians were over there, taking part in the Battle of Britain, the costly attack at Dieppe, the campaigns around the Mediterranean, and preparing for the major invasion.

After being forced out of France the Western Allies were building strength for the return — the grand assault upon Hitler's continental stronghold. When the forces poised in the United Kingdom would invade Europe was the subject of everyday speculation. Certainly, when it came, it would mark the most crucial day of the war. It happened on June 6, 1944; the mightiest invasion force in history landed from more than 4000 ships and established a thin bridgehead along 100 miles of the Normandy coast, in North Western France.

On that D-Day, while a warm noon-day sun beat down upon Calgary, 15,000 citizens, more than one-sixth of the total population of the city, tried to crowd onto 1st Street West, between 7th and 8th Avenues. They were there to pray. Arranged long before by the Calgary Ministerial Association, the service was to be held on Invasion Day, whenever that might be. The miraculous escape of Allied troops from the German trap at Dunkirk was still fresh in memory and many people were convinced that prayer alone explained it. On this day there was the added urging from the King: "At this historic moment, surely not one of us is too busy, too young or too old, to play a part in the nationwide, perchance worldwide vigil of prayer as the great crusade sets forth."

Calgary boys were at that solemn moment among those fighting for survival on the French coast, just as Calgary boys were among those who were advancing triumphantly upon the City of Rome.

As if by magic the word went around down-town Calgary. Stores closed at 11.20 a.m., and at 11.35 a military band led the huge host of earnest people in the singing of O Canada. Usual street noises having ceased, the singing could be heard at Mount Royal College, almost a mile away. Reverend Edward Lawlor, representing the Calgary Ministerial Association, was chairman and Reverend C. E. Reeve led the gathering in the prayer for victory and a peace free from fear and aggression.

While 15,000 heads were still reverently bowed there was a minute of silence; and then two hymns: O God Our Help in Ages Past and Abide With Me. The service ended and Calgarians returned to their duties. In the words of a Calgary editor: "It was an occasion and a demonstration of community unity that will long live in memory." It was one of Calgary's finest moments.

Eleven months later Germany capitulated, and 14 months later atomic bombs fell on the Japanese Cities of Hiroshima and Nagasaki to bring World War II to an end.

August 15, 1945, was declared V-J Day, and Calgary along with other communities celebrated with thanksgiving and revelry. In the evening, with Calgary City Council as sponsor, a gala outdoor frolic was held at the Exhibition Grounds and 20,000 people attended. The program began with a service of thanksgiving and concluded with singing and entertainment, while flames from a huge bonfire on Scotsman's Hill seemed to symbolize the warmth of human joy. In the down-town section, where the celebrations assumed more reckless forms, there were some broken windows, and an exasperated Fire Department answered no fewer than 41 false alarms.

Said Andy Davison, in his 15th year as Mayor of the City "This is the day we have long been waiting for, marking as it does the most terrible war the world has known. Citizens of Calgary have every reason to feel proud of the magnificent contribution which has been made by their sons and daughters on many far flung battle fronts. Calgary men served with distinction, Calgary airmen fought magnificently, Calgary sailors surprised the world with their gallantry, and Calgary girls played their part in Canada's war effort and gave full support to the fighting men."

End of the War! It was hard to believe. After nearly six years it was reality. It would mean many things: relaxation of gasoline and food rationing, promise of less water in the whiskey, more nylons for the girls and, best of all, the return of the boys and girls from overseas.

After a couple of months the first units were returning and Calgary had a warm welcome for them. And as time passed, quite a few ex-service men who saw Calgary for the first time as trainees during the war years came back — to make homes in the city of their choice.

Back in 1928 citizens of Calgary and district made Central Park the site of an imposing cenotaph, dedicated to the memory of "Those Who Died, 1913-18." Now, at the end of World War II, there was added to the inscription: "And 1939-45."

THE '48 INVASION OF TORONTO

Nineteen hundred and forty-eight was "Grey Cup year." It was the year a Calgary contingent invaded Toronto, paralyzed the city, turned the Royal York Hotel into a mad-house, shocked eastern people into friendly submission, and returned with the Canadian football championship. The experience was good for both Calgary and Toronto.

Calgarians might know more about baseball, hockey and curling; even lacrosse was popular long before the first rugby game was played in 1901 with "English, Welsh and Scotch against Irish and Canadians." The first Calgary Rugby Football Club was organized on May 22, 1901, and 16 interested players turned out for the initial practice a few evenings later.

For many years thereafter, the supremacy of baseball and hockey was unchallenged but rugby football was winning friends. In 1907 Earl Grey, who had been Governor-General of Canada, donated the Grey Cup to the Canadian Rugby Union, and the first cup winner was declared in the following year. In 1921 Calgary Tigers, captained by W. L. "Squib" Ross, won the western championship, playing on the Hillhurst field and defeating Winnipeg Rowing Club 13 to 6. The winners then challenged for the Grey Cup, but the challenge was ignored and there was no East-West final.

Not until 1921 did a Western team go east to compete for the Grey Cup, and on that occasion the original Edmonton Eskimo team was beaten by Toronto Argonauts 23-0. But time changed many things. The Winnipeg Blue Bombers of 1935 were the first Westerners to win the handsome trophy. And when Calgary did it in 1948, it was the fourth time for the West and first time for Alberta.

Tom Brook was the president of that famous Stampeder team and Les Lear was the coach. In the line-up were great football names like Strode, Aguirre, Rowe, Spaith, Hanson, Kwong, Thodos, Pantages and so on. The team had power and precision and went through the Western Conference series without losing a game. In the Western final played at Mewata Stadium that fall, it was Calgary Stampeders vs. Regina Roughriders and the score was 17 to 6 in favor of the "Stamps."

Ottawa Rough Riders were the Eastern champions and from the moment it was known that the Stampeders would meet them at Varsity Stadium for the one-game Canadian final, preparations went forward for a pre-game, Calgary-style show such as the East had not seen before.

That game in Toronto on November 27 was a thriller from start to finish. Governor-General Viscount Alexander kicked to open the game. Twenty thousand spectators were in their seats. Coach Les Lear was dressed for play and went into the Calgary line in the second half of the game. For the last nine minutes there was unbroken suspense. The Keith Spaith to Norm. Hill sleeper play for a touchdown, and Woody Strode's part in setting things up for a second touchdown by Pete Thodos, were feats from which heroes emerge.

As for the people in the East, the game was only part of the entertainment, and long after they had forgotten the score or the name of the vanquished football squad, they talked about the street parade, the bright clothes, the prancing horses and the general pandemonium produced by a trainload of Calgarians.

Nobody can say exactly whose idea it was; but on short notice Harry McConachie accepted the chairmanship of a committee to arrange for a special train to carry fans, horses, chuckwagons and anything else needed to blazon the name of Calgary across the East — Toronto in particular. It seemed that nearly everybody wanted to go. Rugby might lack the traditions of hockey — the Stampeder hockey team won the Allan Cup just two years before — but nothing could dampen the local enthusiasm for the power-laden Stampeders of 1948.

The Stampeder Special was a 13-car train. A baggage car carried piano, musical instruments for a cowboy band, and miscellaneous equipment; another car was for the Buckhorn Ranch chuckwagon and a dozen Palomino and pinto horses. And the passenger list represented a cross-section of Calgary — children who couldn't be left behind, three patients from Belcher Hospital, an Indian chief or two and an 86-year-old woman. A thousand Calgary fans who couldn't go, and some who were following in a special Trans-Canada Airlines plane, were on the platform to shout farewell.

The train arrived at Toronto on Friday morning, and 250 Calgarians wearing 250 ten-gallon hats and Western clothes to match seemed to take over the Union Station and then the street in front of the Royal York for reels, square dances and song. Traffic was blocked and ordinary business was rudely suspended. Three Calgary ladies in bright Western clothes stopped the Toronto Stock Exchange when they arrived on the trading floor. From a chuckwagon parked in front of the Royal York hotel, rangeland pancakes were fried and passed out to business men and office girls who couldn't quite understand it. The Eastern city hadn't seen anything like it, and at first its people didn't know whether to be alarmed or amused.

Was this a preliminary to a football game or was it a full scale invasion by a horde out of the Old West? Toronto citizens weren't entirely sure, but after thinking it over they found themselves becoming part of the fun. By parade time next day — certainly by game time — most of the local people were Stampeder fans.

The Ottawa Rough Riders arrived at Toronto's Union Station about the same time as the Calgary train drew in, but somehow went almost unnoticed.

THE '48 INVASION OF TORONTO

The Saturday morning parade from the Royal York to Varsity Stadium was essentially a Calgary show, with leading personalities in Western dress and riding the colorful horses brought two thousand miles for the purpose. Toronto's Mayor Walker, who said he hadn't been in a saddle for 25 years, found himself on a Calgary favorite, Archie Currie's stylish parade horse, Stonewall Rex, one with a story book career embracing everything from the experience of being stolen by horse thieves to that of winning show-ring honors. Toronto's traffic police were obviously puzzled but decided to close their eyes; and only when the driver wanted to take his Buckhorn chuckwagon around the playing field, race-fashion, was there any real restraint.

Betting on the game favored the Ottawa team, but by starting time the cheering confirmed the new-found popularity of the Stampeders. There were 500 Calgarians in the stands, but the spectators catching the Calgary enthusiasm and roaring in support of the Western team outnumbered all others. One Toronto man occupying a good seat admitted he was so fascinated by the antics of the people in big hats and colored shirts that he completely missed the first touchdown of the game.

When the gun sounded to end the gridiron battle — Stampeders victorious with a score of 12 to 7 — the crowd broke in roaring disorder. The goal-posts were ripped from their places and the winning players were almost mobbed by their affectionate admirers.

That evening the Royal York hotel took on the appearance and sound of a New Year's eve celebration with music and square dancing. One enterprising fellow at the end of the lobby was sawing a goal-post into small pieces and selling them as souvenirs at one dollar each. The hotel management wondered how many of the fixtures would survive. Of course, the Calgary players were mobbed for signatures; and the Grey Cup, in the keeping of Stampeder President Tom Brook, was filled and refilled with champagne. The East had seen nothing like it. Said one editorial writer: "The old western spirit isn't dead. Not by a jugful."

And while Toronto was the scene of a victory celebration, back in Calgary plans were being made for a home-coming befitting conquerors. The coincide with the return of the Stampeder Special, a civic half-holiday was declared. By a pre-arranged delaying action to ensure a favorable time for arrival, the train was

214

five hours late in pulling into Calgary. A thousand people were at the station to see the Stampeder Special depart; ten thousand were there to see it return, and the street parade that followed was a mile long.

Beyond a doubt, Calgary belonged to Les Lear and his players. Woody Strode said he wore out two fountain pens furnishing autographs. And those who made the speeches and congratulated the players said Calgary had derived a million dollars worth of publicity and good will — to say nothing of a Grey Cup.

A ZOO ON THE ISLAND

At the mid-point in the 20th century as Calgary, with population of 120,000 and confidence in its new might, celebrated the seventy-fifth anniversary of its founding, it had many "showpieces," like the new million-dollar Stampede Corral at the Exhibition Ground, the Provincial Institute of Technology and Art, the Reader Rock Garden, fine homes and so on. Nothing, however, brought more pride than St. George's Island in the Bow River and its collection of birds and animals sharing the lovely setting with life-size models of pre-historic monsters. Proof of popularity was abundant. An estimated half million people a year were visiting and enjoying "The Island."

But the Calgary Zoo, rated biggest in Canada and one of the best anywhere, didn't achieve its eminence without patient struggles on the part of devoted and public-spirited citizens.

For years there was controversy about a suitable use for the 42-acre St. George's Island and some weird proposals were offered — a prisoner of war camp, a dog pound, an isolation hospital, an exhibition ground and a beer garden. The ultimate decision to make it a zoological park was a good one, and Calgarians have seen their zoo — at small cost to taxpayers — become one of the best educational and amusement investments in the City. They have seen it expand to display nearly a thousand bird and animal specimens as steady boarders demanding their respective and special kinds of feed and care. Meeting the nutritional needs of animals as different as African lions, polar bears, Rocky Mountain sheep, anteaters and ring-tail monkeys could be no small task in itself, and meant the provision annually of tons of porridge, bread, grain, fruit, hay, vegetables, nuts, fish and horsemeat.

Back of it all was a man with a dream; the man was Dr. O. H. Patrick, first president of the Calgary Zoological Society and founder of Dinosaur Park. It was he who called a meeting at the Board of Trade office on October 28, 1928, to consider the formation of a Zoological Society. The decision was to organize and Dr. Patrick emerged as first president; William B. Reader, Superintendent of Calgary Parks Department, as vice-president; and Hon. R. B. Bennett, Pat Burns and A. E. Cross as patrons. The new society had no assets but lots of ideas.

A few birds and animals were quartered at St. George's Island at that time but nobody flattered the unorganized collection by calling it a zoo. Back in 1922 a black-tail deer from the Johnny J. Jones travelling midway was presented to the Calgary Street Railway system. That was the starting point. But with no suitable place to keep it, the fawn was looked upon as a liability and finally given a paddock at Bowness Park. There it remained for two years and then was transferred to St. George's Island. The deer's presence there seemed to invite other wild life gifts — mostly pigeons, hawks and owls, for which cages were provided. A citizen with a bear cub was ordered to get rid of the thing and turned it over to the park. Next came a goat which had outlived its popularity in a Calgary back yard, and City Clerk Jack Miller added a swan he captured. To this small and polyglot collection somebody contributed a kangaroo, but its demands for the costly comfort of electric heating shortened its period of residence on the Island. For the feeding of the few animals in misfit cages, the park caretaker was responsible.

In 1929, while the newly formed Zoological Society was proposing to take over the task of building a real zoo, a Bow River flood just about washed away the goat and bear and what enthusiasm there existed for a big zoo at that location. But Society directors concluded they could prevent a repetition of flood and before the end of the year an arrangement was made whereby the City of Calgary would be responsible for park maintenance and the Society for providing pens and paddocks and animals to occupy them.

At this point in the summer of 1929, Thomas Baines, who had been employed on the wild animal park of the Duke of Bedford in England, was hired as curator. As those who watched the Calgary Zoo in after years recognized clearly, it was a fortunate appointment, the Baines skill and devotion being largely responsible for success. During the next quarter of a century Tom Baines, who was one of the first people in Canada to be made a Fellow of the Royal Zoological Society of England, was absent only for six years of service during World War II.

Tom Baines' first zoo inventory, on December 14, 1929, showed 34 birds and 20 other animals, more than a third of the latter being porcupines; and an initial undertaking was to load everything in the zoo, except the two bears and three deer, on one truck and set up a display at the Calgary Poultry Show.

Before the end of that year, however, a four-section pen was constructed for coyotes and wolves, and in the next year several deer paddocks were built. Each season saw building additions; in 1932 the first heated building for monkeys was erected; and, incidently, one of the baboons acquired at that time was still enjoying zoo life in 1958, at age 29 — the "grand old man" of the Monkey House. And to further increase interest in the Island, one of Calgary's first log houses, bearing date of 1883, and a Vancouver totem pole were brought there about the same time.

But the infant Zoological Society was not escaping reverses and troubles — not by any means. In the first year of operations Curator Tom Baines was severely injured by a fallow deer; moreover, the list of animal losses was alarmingly high. Some of the losses were due to natural causes but what disturbed society officers most was the extent of thefts. Boys seemed to have the impression the zoo was keeping animals for their convenience, and during 1930 the animals stolen from pens included numerous pigeons, five rabbits and 59 guinea-pigs. And on one occasion four silver foxes were taken. Until 1937 the lack of a good fence made theft prevention difficult.

As one might expect at a zoo, troubles came in varied forms. Now and then animals escaped. Buster, a California seal, had several weeks of freedom in the Bow River and neighboring irrigation ditches. No real harm came from that, but on another occasion vandals released two coyotes and before morning there was a sickening trail of dead guinea pigs and birds. Until a proper fence was constructed stray logs created destruction now and then, but the most trying experience faced by the young Zoological Society was the flood of 1932.

A ZOO ON THE ISLAND

An ice jam caused the flood waters to rise rapidly and menace the lives of 500 birds and animals then in the Park. By the time Society officers reached the Island in response to a call for help, flood water was two feet deep in most pens. Foxes, coyotes, skunks and the like were removed promptly. Fortunately, many of the cages and shelters were built on stilts or with upper stories and their occupants were able to remain above water. Animals in outside yards sought high ground or climbed on top of shelters.

Losses seemed inevitable. Logs in the swirling flood broke fences, including those enclosing the water fowl. Ducks and geese swam all over the Island and half a mile down river. Workers didn't expect to see them again. A baby big-horn sheep was born at the peak of the flood and transferred to the manager's residence; and all the while there was fear that the bridge above the Island would be taken out and carried onto the area of the zoo to do crushing destruction. All night Tom Baines, Dr. Patrick and Lars Willumsen worked and watched; and then the water dropped as rapidly as it had come up.

Zoo officers prepared to count their losses, but to their surprise the water birds were seen making their way back to their enclosures where the fences were being repaired. When a count was made, every bird except one was back. Nine days later, the lost duck returned and was seen trying to find an opening to the enclosure. The gate was opened and the homesick duck entered, glad to be back. The flood was a bad experience but it passed without loss of life.

Very shortly, however, steps were taken to build dikes to prevent recurrence of floods. And general improvement continued. In 1936 a thousand trees and shrubs were planted on the Island. Animal population grew steadily. When the Banff Zoo was disbanded in 1937 quite a few of the specimens came to Calgary. Animal inventories were becoming international in character. A zoological "Who's Who" by this time would show distinguished animal personalities from every continent and numerous countries.

At the depth of depression in the '30's the Dinosaur Park project to complement the zoo was started, and Finnish-born John Kanerva, with artistic touch and lots of patience, went to work creating dinosaur replicas from steel and mortar. Dr. Patrick's objective when he spoke at the annual meeting in January, 1936, was 40 models. Eighteen months later he reported that 20 models including two big ones were finished. When Dr. Patrick resigned in 1944, after 16 years as president of the Calgary Zoological Society, the collection of synthetic dinosaurs was acknowledged to be the most notable in the world.

In various ways St. George's Island has attracted international attention. In a recent single year the Calgary Zoo made no fewer than 50 exchanges of animal specimens with zoos in many parts of Canada, the United States, England, Ireland, Denmark and elsewhere. Near home the co-operative arrangement which gave both the city administration and the Zoological Society a working interest proved a good one.

St. George's Island seems to have been created for park and zoo. Young folks who flock to the Children's Zoo, an innovation of 1957, and older people who attend with enthusiasm, agree. Eighty-four thousand youngsters went through the Children's Zoo in the first 66 days after it was opened.

There is good reason for proclaiming the Calgary Zoo as one of the best educational and entertainment features in the Province of Alberta.

But for students of nature, those life-size models of terrifying reptiles which slithered across the swamps of Alberta a hundred million years ago may hold about as much of interest as the modern things like grizzlies and pronghorns. Moreover, they're cheaper to feed.

DINOSAURS IN THE PARK

Ugly and terrifying reptilian forms, constructed lifesize in iron and concrete, began taking their places as sentinels at St. George's Island in the mid-'30's, reminders of animal life on this continent 60 or 100 million years before Carmichael the polar bear was born. As though resurrected from the primitive past, they proved well able to fire human imagination, making small boys ask, "What if they all came to life?" and sending shivers up the spines of adults not completely sober.

Visitors entering the Island at a morning hour some years ago saw a dishevelled man dashing madly toward the river. The runner was a transient who had arrived in the city on the previous day, and after celebrating unwisely with a riverbank party, had wandered aimlessly in the darkness of midnight and finally lay down on the park grass to sleep.

Awakening in broad light of day, the stranger was understandably horified to find himself surrounded by dinosaurs with gaping mouths and hideous faces. To one with a heavy hangover those monsters were infinitely more real than the snakes and pink elephants he had seen before. It was easy to imagine them closing in to devour him and the natural impulse was to escape. Story has it that he missed the bridge but waded and swam his way to safety beyond the Bow River.

Biggest of the Island dinosaurs is the swamp-dwelling vegetarian, Brontosaurus — better known as "Dinny," 90 feet long, 34 feet high and 65 tons in weight as it made its awkward way through tropical everglades. Most ferocious in appearance is Gorgosaurus, the wicked carnivore called the "Tyrant" of its time. And weird to the point of being nigh unbelievable is the big-bodied, small-brained Stegosaurus and that horny-headed creature, Styracosaurus, looking as though it belonged in an extremely bad dream.

Not all the reptiles of that period were big. Some were as small as present-day lizards. Some fancied the water as the place to spend their lives; some favored the high ground and some flew about like clumsy birds. In a multitude of shapes and sizes they flourished amid the magnolia and cinnamon trees and other tropical vegetation in these parts, many million years ago.

Calgary's special interest in dinosaurs lies in the fact that fossilized remains of most of the reconstructed specimens on display were discovered nearby. From the eroded badlands along the Red Deer River, a paleontologist's paradise, have come all sorts of fossil treasures. The area with its fantastic landscape, its earthy formations like cones, pyramids and giant mushrooms, has been especially fruitful in the bones of dinosaurs which sank in the mud when the Drumheller wheat county was a marshy delta beside a great inland sea extending from the Gulf of Mexico to the Arctic.

Climate and topography in that ancient period were strangely different. The Rocky Mountains did not exist and both animal and vegetable life were primitive. Nevertheless, marine life in a thousand forms bred in that shallow inland sea and finally deposited itself as sediment on the sea floor to give rise to the oil and gas we now find thousands of feet underground. At the same time, rank-growing tropical plants flourished in the sour swamps and the residue from them accumulated to be transformed into coal.

It was the Mesozoic Era — Age of Reptiles — but that strange animal society disappeared. Why the disappearance? Why did the pre-historic horse become extinct on the American continents? And why the ultimate failure of the elephant and camel which lived here at one time? Biologists would like to know. Certainly the climatic changes between tropical and glacial times were extreme and other environmental changes would be correspondingly great.

Perhaps it was shock of changing temperatures that "tipped the balance" against the big reptiles; perhaps it was feed failure; perhaps disease. Anyway, those "living tanks" with armour-plated hides and pitifully small brains, quit completely. Only because mud-trapped skeletons fossilized and remained securely hidden until exposed in recent times by forces of erosion, do we have any record of them.

With the passing of time, pressure from deep in the earth produced the Rocky Mountains and caused the low country formerly marked out by inland sea and delta land to become high country. Then as the Red Deer River cut a torturous route through the floor of the ancient delta and river-side erosion advanced, dinosaur and other secrets from a period when the earth was comparatively young have been uncovered.

The first discovery of dinosaur remains in Canada was in the area now marked by South-Western Saskatchewan in 1874, G. M. Dawson of the Geological Survey being the discoverer. Ten years later, J. B. Tyrrell, Dominion Government Geologist, found dinosaur bones in the Red Deer valley while inspecting seams of coal. The real significance of the area was not appreciated for some time thereafter, but in 1909 Dr. Barnum Brown of the American Museum of Natural History visited the valley and took bones from it.

The most extensive work of discovery and recovery, however, was conducted by the Sternbergs. Charles M. Sternberg, who became a paleontologist of world renown, discovered a complete dinosaur skeleton in 1912 — a "duckbill" to be seen today in the National Museum at Ottawa. Another "duckbill" skeleton unearthed north of Jenner by Charles Sternberg in 1915 is laid out for all to see in the Fossil House at St. George's Island. Since 1912 scientists from many parts of the world have beaten paths to that fossil wonderland in Central Alberta; and bones from Red Deer Valley have gone to scores of museums.

Digging dinosaur skeletons is not a job for the tourist or casual curio hunter, and fortunately the highly technical work of recovery has been left to men of science. Consequently, the story about those primitive animal forms has been systematically pieced together. The shapes and sizes of bones have given reliable descriptive information about sizes and shapes of the living animals, and with guidance from paleontologists of international standing many of those giant dinosaur creatures have been re-created in cement.

Construction was started and carried forward by the Calgary Zoological Society while Dr. O. H. Patrick was president and driving force. Nowhere did dinosaur reconstruction advance farther than at Calgary, where the actual work of shaping and building life-size models was carried out mainly by Calgary citizen John Kanerva. Today, some 30 specimens occupy positions of prominence to bring exclamations of wonder from visitors.

What is the technique? How are the St. George's Island specimens made? After excavated bones have been measured and assembled, a scale model is constructed, usually a small one. Its shape and general characteristics must be exactly in keeping with body shape indicated by skeleton, otherwise the scientific critics would have good reason for protest.

Having fixed upon a suitable location, the next step in dinosaur construction consists of providing a proper base or foundation of concrete, with steel reinforcing rods protruding where the feet and legs of the monster will rest. On the base so provided, a metal framework approximately the body shape considered to be correct for the finished model is constructed and iron lath and mesh are attached. The metal skeleton is then ready for application of cement — both inside and outside the form.

Next there is the matter of modelling the head, tail and toes to properly fit the characteristics indicated by the 60-million-year-old skull and other bones. It is not a small job, either in time or materials required. Into reconstruction of the mighty Brontosaurus beside the Bow River at Calgary went 125 tons of inert material, to say nothing of study and patient work.

Finally, the park models are painted; and herein the scientists can offer the sculptors little or no guidance. Instructions can be given about the exact length for a leg-bone or the width between the eyes, but nothing from the fossil beds furnishes indication of color.

It is the student's right to speculate. Was the giant Bronto-saurus, largest land animal the earth has known, a brightly colored thing blending with swamp foliage, or did it possess dull color like that of the elephant? One guess is as good as another and no confidence can be placed in the artist's choice of colors. But shape and size in the St. George's Island dinosaurs are not guess-work; they are according to the fossilized "blueprints" embedded in mud ages ago when Central Alberta was a land of tropical wonder; "blueprints" of some of the weirdest animal forms that ever walked the face of the earth, things that would seem to belong to night-mares and fairy tales instead of land that is now Alberta.

THE BIG "WORK HORSE"

As Calgary moved into the second half of the 20th Century, Calgary Power Company was like a mighty and modern "work horse," having matured from a diminutive and wobbly baby "foaled" beside the Bow River. Behind it were imaginative pioneers offering electricity to light homes when bull-teams were still bringing the freight from Fort Macleod and Stephen Avenue had witnessed nothing more mechanically complex than a democrat with springs.

Founders of the parent company, having installed a water wheel to utilize the Bow River flow over the Eau Claire Lumber Company's mill dam west of the present Centre Street, sought approval from the Town Council to erect poles and string wire. The water wheel generated 280 horse power and the wires were connected to serve five Calgary customers.

He was a bold householder, however, who would exchange his time-tested kerosene lamp for electric lights — "hot hairpins in bottles," as somebody described them in 1889. Electric power was mysterious, almost alarming, and most citizens chose to let reckless neighbors experiment. But 65 years later, Calgary Power Company was generating 300,000 horse power, serving directly and indirectly

223

THE BIG "WORK HORSE"

150,000 customers, and furnishing much of the drive for the wheels of Alberta industry.

For the beginning of the Calgary Power story, however, one must search still farther back in the misty records. Kutusoff Mac-Fee, with a name for a fictional hero and a nose for business opportunity, was an Ottawa lawyer. He saw big trees — spruce, jackpine and fir — in the country west of Calgary, and in his enthusiasm went to the acknowledged woodsmen's capital, Eau Claire, Wisconsin, seeking advice.

Three authorities on the subject of lumber responded; I. K. Kerr, William Cameron and Dan Donnellan lost no time in journeying to Calgary, then at the end of the railroad, proceeding from there to Morley by team and wagon and then along the Kananaskis River by saddle horse. On the return journey the adventuresome prospectors took to canoe and travelled from Morley to Medicine Hat that way.

The report about timber resources in the country over which they conducted reconnaissance was favorable, and Lawyer MacFee secured a lease comprising a hundred square miles bounded by the Kananaskis, Bow and Spray Rivers. A new company, the Eau Claire and Bow River Lumber Company, contracted to work and develop the valuable timber limits, and in 1886 logging camps emerged — one at Silver City on the Bow and one on the Kananaskis. Machinery for a mill was shipped to Calgary.

Each winter thereafter, several million feet of timber were cut and made ready for the spring break-up when logs would be floated down to Calgary. Until 1944 log drives were annual events with all the danger and excitement associated with the better-publicized drives in Eastern Canada. In the spring of 1887, six of the log drivers were drowned on the Kananaskis.

Kerr became president of the lumber company; and another Eau Claire man, Peter Prince, for whom Prince's Island in the Bow is named, became general manager. Together they promoted numerous Calgary business enterprises — a flour mill, an iron works, a ranch, a grocery firm and the Calgary Water Power Company, which was ultimately taken over by Calgary Power Company.

By means of the dam built in 1886, water was raised and channelled along the south bank of the Bow to drive the wheel and saw mill located close to the foot of the present 3rd Street West.

And in 1893 the Dominion Government granted Water Power License Number 6 to permit use of a 12-foot head of water for power purposes.

But Prince was offering to sell electricity well in advance of the license. His water-driven A.C. generator was installed in 1889 and the minutes of the Town Council show that on June 27 of that year, "A communication was read from P. A. Prince offering to supply the Town with Electric Light at certain rates if allowed the privilege of putting up poles, etc., for a period of ten years."

The communication was referred to a committee, and on August 20 following, the town solicitor was instructed "to prepare for the next meeting of Council a bylaw and agreement authorizing Mr. Prince to erect poles and string wire within the municipality on conditions agreed on between him and Council."

Actually, Prince wasn't the first to generate electricity in the community. According to Norway-born Theodore Strom, who had charge of the Prince plant from its beginning, a small company was operating two dynamos "in the alley back of the Bank of Montreal," and trying to block Peter Prince's plans. But the man from Wisconsin secured qualified approval, hurriedly bought squared cedar timbers for light poles, strung wire and beat the contract deadline by 48 hours.

Prince's generator went into service on September 5, 1889, and then he went forward with the organization of his Calgary Water Power Company. A while later, on behalf of the new comnany, he was making a deal with the City to light the streets at a price of $7 a month for each arc light for a term of five years. "Should the City desire to take over our lighting at the expiration of a term of five years," wrote Prince, "they are to take our plant at prices to be settled by arbitration." (Letter to Council, May 25, 1894)

The water-generated power had its shortcomings. When stream flow was high everything went well, but at low water the lights became dim or went out. To provide for the winter season when the river was frozen over, the company built a steam plant in which waste from the saw-mill was the chief fuel.

But there were other pioneer difficulties and the relations between company and city were not always harmonious. In February, 1895, the City Council was threatening to terminate its agreement with the company, and in November Mr. Prince was writing to warn of court action "if the Council refuses to pay our accounts ... by the end of the month."

There was no termination of contract and no court action; but a few years later, 1905, the City did establish its own municipal electric light and power plant — a steam plant on 9th Avenue West. According to one narrator, "the price of light went down and the taxes went up."

The old Calgary Water Power Company continued as a local producer until 1928, when its capital stock was bought by Calgary Power Company, which had been in existence since 1909 and had constructed its first up-stream plant on the Bow River system in 1911. Gradually the production and distribution of electrical energy were being consolidated with two agencies. From 1928 the Calgary Power Company was the sole supplier for city needs, and from 1938 the city utility was the sole distributor.

From its birth the Calgary Power was a vigorous organization. The first plant at Horseshoe Falls, 55 miles west of Calgary and furnishing 20,000 horse power, was intended largely to meet the needs of the Canada Cement Company at Exshaw; but there being an excess of power, a transmission line to Calgary was constructed and one by one new producing units were added. The Horseshoe Falls plant was followed by the Kananaskis Falls plant providing 12,000 horse power.

These two up-river plants, along with the Calgary Water Power steam plant in the city and the city-owned steam plant, accommodated Calgary needs for a few years and then the Ghost River was harnessed for power in 1929. In the early years of the Second World War Calgary had a new nitrogen plant, and this along with demand from military establishments and growing population made further development necessary. Plant number four was Cascade, adding 23,000 horse power in 1942. Barrier was next; and then, with the discovery of oil at Leduc and the accompanying growth of industry, the Spray Lakes project was added to the Calgary Power system. Next came Bearspaw, Pocaterra, Inter-Lakes, a steam plant at Wabamun; and the end is not yet.

In 1958, with 5,000 miles of transmission lines carrying power far beyond the city from which the Company took its name, Calgary Power had 30,000 farm customers, some indication of the widespread acceptance of rural electrification. Nothing was doing as much to relieve the traditional hardships associated with country living as those power lines with leads to farm homes and stables. The kerosene lamp, the ice-box, and the hand crank on the washing machine were disappearing as they had done earlier from urban homes, because the resources of wild mountain water were efficiently harnessed to work for Alberta people scores of miles away.

The modern Calgary Power Company, with a dozen big plants — eleven of them hydro — furnishing power for industrial and domestic needs in widespread sections of the country, is a far cry from the service provided by Peter Prince for his five courageous customers in 1889. "Calgary Power's hundred million-dollar investment in Alberta is a measure of its belief in the Province's past, present and future."

And what of Peter Prince, the man of action who was still playing a good game of golf at the age of 88? He died in Calgary after an association of 56 years, and the City recounted its debt to his imagination and enterprise.

A TRILLION CUBIC FEET

Natural gas was one of the magic forces contributing to Calgary progress. While people in most Canadian towns and cities were still carrying ashes from basements and kitchens, Calgary citizens were enjoying the convenience and economy of gas piped from nearby fields.

Toward the end of 1957 the company which had piped its first gas to the city 45 years earlier was serving 71,172 customers in Calgary and 48 other Southern Alberta communities. Its pipelines extended for 1422 miles and it could report gas reserves of nearly a trillion cubic feet, approximately 21 times its sales in the preceding year.

Like the Bull Sale, Stampede and oil industry, natural gas played its colorful part in the story of Calgary.

While Calgary was still an urban infant a few imaginative souls expressed their hunches that gas and oil were hiding somewhere under prairie and foothills sod. The C.P.R. discovered natural gas at Alderson, north-west of Medicine Hat, about 1890 and Calgarians had premonitions about the same kind of resource treasure under their feet. Enviously they watched the Town of Medicine Hat drill and make a good strike at just a little more than 1000 feet in depth. Citizens meeting on Stephen Avenue agreed that if their town had a good supply of natural gas it would become the Wonder City of Canada — and lots selling at $100 would immediately be worth $500.

At a meeting of the Calgary Town Council on February 12, 1892, an enthusiastic delegation from the Board of Trade was present to invite the Corporation to co-operate in drilling some test wells. The elected gentlemen were interested and ready to gamble. Three weeks later a committee composed of mayor and three aldermen reported in favor of participating in an exploratory program.

The report had two compelling points: first, that President William Van Horne had offered the use of C.P.R. drilling machinery; and second, that "A company has been formed of our citizens with a subscribed capital of $3400, upon the condition the Corporation of the Town of Calgary subscribe $3000, the Corporation and subscribers to share in any discovery that may be made in proportion to the money invested. We recommend that the Town grant $3000 to be invested in a test well."

Council approved and drilling began. As work progressed, instalment payments of $300 were made by the town treasurer; and the mayor and councillors became so optimistic about the outcome that they took steps to select a site for a huge smelter which some enterprising business organization would be in a hurry to build as soon as the Calgary gas roared in from the new well.

But, sad to say, the drilling venture was a failure. When the drill-bit reached a depth of 1500 feet the well caved in and the press reported that the Town's loss would be $3000 and that of private citizens, $4200.

Local promoters turned their thoughts to coal, at least until about 1902, when Ontario-born Archibald Wayne Dingman, with experience in oil exploration in the State of Pennsylvania, arrived in Calgary and repeated confidently, "Sure, the gas is here; all we've got to do is find the stuff and lay some pipes."

Before long he was organizing the Calgary Natural Gas Company; and the official minutes show that City Council, on May 29, 1905, authorized "negotiations with Mr. Dingman in regard to the question of granting him the right to supply petroleum and other natural products to citizens of Calgary."

Mr. Dingman, whose name is remembered chiefly for his part in the Discovery Well at Turner Valley in 1914, was granted a natural gas franchise. There was just one disturbing obstacle at that time in 1905; it was that Dingman had no gas — certainly no natural gas. But he was optimistic about finding it; and in the next year his company drilled on the Sarcee Indian Reserve, about 12 miles from the City. Drilling continued for 14 months, and by the end of September, 1907, Calgary residents were assured of "an unfailing supply of natural gas."

To celebrate the success, Manager Dingman conducted a party to the well. Two primitive automobiles were made available for the journey. "In Mr. A. A. Dick's auto were Mr. I. K. Kerr, president of the company, Senator Lougheed, Mr. A. E. Cross and Mr. William Pearce. In the second, the speedy car, belonging to Calgary Colonization and Irrigation Company were Mr. Dingman, Mr. F. Higgs and the newspaper men. The return trip of twelve miles was made in 45 minutes which is going some when the nature of the road is considered."

The optimism, however, was unjustified. Drilling ceased at a depth of 3400 feet. The "unfailing supply of natural gas" failed rapidly and in February, 1908, the well was being abandoned.

The next drilling was close to the present Inglewood Bird Sanctuary, on the Major James Walker property, and there the company struck gas at 3414 feet. From that well gas was piped to meet the needs of the Calgary Brewery and some homes in East Calgary. By general admission, however, the supply was still limited and it was for another giant in the industry, Eugene Coste, to provide gas for general use. In 1908 Geologist and Engineer Coste made important discoveries at Bow Island, beyond Lethbridge, and set about to make the product available to the people of Lethbridge and Calgary.

Gaining control of the Calgary Natural Gas Company and also a small company organized to sell artificial gas in Calgary, Coste formed the Canadian Western Natural Gas, Heat, Light and Power Company and promised to meet every Calgary need.

On July 17, 1912, exactly 20 years after the Town Council was paying for a test hole, gas from Bow Island reached the city through the company's 171-mile pipeline. While 12,000 citizens assembled on 9th Avenue East to celebrate the occasion, the Calgary night was illuminated by a flare reaching 100 feet in the air. At exactly 10 p.m. Company President Coste gave the signal to open the valve and ignite the flare. As the flame shot into the night sky spectators held their breath. The magnitude of the new force was evident and people for many miles around could see that Calgary, at last, had the gas for which its citizens had long hoped.

After 15 minutes of watching the flaring, with spectators duly impressed, members of City Council and representatives of the triumphant Gas Company retired to the Empress Cafe to banquet and make speeches and congratulate themselves. The Bow Island reserves were "practically inexhaustible" it was told, and President Coste explained that Calgary at that moment had 80 miles of gas mains ready to serve the 4000 signed subscribers. It was, indeed, a landmark in the history of natural gas to serve Calgary customers.

Bow Island continued to furnish the bulk of Calgary's gas until 1922 when a pipeline from Turner Valley was ready for service. In 1923 the newly-discovered Foremost field was linked with the Gas Company's system, and in 1924 Turner Valley's notable Royalite Number 4 well blew in to boost the assessment of the Valley reserves. Turner Valley then became the chief source of Calgary's gas supply.

When conservation measures were introduced as provincial policy in the early '30's, Turner Valley surplus gas, instead of being wasted in flares, was pumped to Bow Island and forced into the ground to enlarge the reserves there. Thus Bow Island became a storage field capable of meeting peak requirements.

In the course of time other fields were brought into the system, and in 1956 Jumping Pound, West of Calgary, furnished 40 percent of Company gas, with Turner Valley supplying 58 percent. And as demand continued to grow, Company officers cast their eyes toward the Carbon field, 55 miles north-east of Calgary, and made plans to spend nine and one-half million dollars in developing the project.

It made an impressive record but scarcely more so than the story of the developer, Eugene Coste, who was president and managing director from 1912 to 1921. He was born at Amherstburg, Ontario, in 1859, the son of Napoleon Coste who, as a contractor, played a big part in constructing the Suez Canal and was reported to have piloted the first ship through.

Eugene was educated in France and received degrees in science and mining engineering. Returning to Canada he joined the Geological Survey, and later, in private practice, had the distinction of bringing the first two commercial gas wells into production in Ontaro, one in Welland County and one in Essex.

Hailed the "Father" of the natural gas industry of Canada, Eugene Coste died on January 23, 1940. He died in Toronto but Calgary clung tenaciously to its claim upon him.

Coste House in the Mount Royal district, formerly the mansion-like residence of Eugene Coste, is a reminder. It is Calgary's cultural centre. After the 28-room house was acquired by the City and faced an uncertain future, it became the headquarters of Calgary's Allied Arts Council and its numerous affiliated organizations. The plan was good, as thousands of citizens attending art and craft exhibitions there annually would testify. And happily, the Coste name was retained, reminding Calgarians of the industrial pioneer whose 171-mile pipeline terminating at Calgary in 1912 was said to be the longest in the world at the time.

Ultimately, users were inclined to take natural gas for granted. It was unfailing, it was economical, and it required a minimum of attention. But modern users should be reminded that gas wasn't delivered at homes and factories without struggles typical of those in all pioneer enterprises.

THE STAMPEDE

To many people, even in remote parts of the North American Continent the word Calgary suggests Stampede and Stampede suggests Calgary — just as ham suggests eggs.

Calgary has become a big city — some residents say it is getting too big — but, better than most centres, it has retained its rural and pioneer associations. Its Exhibition and Stampede furnish an example. Instead of being overshadowed by the upsurge of oil and industry, the big summer annual has increased in prominence and won ever greater international recognition.

THE STAMPEDE

The exhibition part of the summer show resembles that of many other cities, but the Stampede is unique. In its basis it is still an expression of something out of the Old West, telling stories of the range that never grow old. For the thousands of people converging upon Calgary in early July of any year, the Stampede is the chief attraction. When the big week ended in 1958 the attendance stood at 545,960, another in an almost consistent series of attendance records; and directors asked again: "How long can we do it, getting bigger every year?"

For at least that week each year, Calgary, with strong rangeland traditions at any time, becomes the undisputed cowboy capital of the world. Clothes, conduct and traffic rules are changed to suit the occasion. When it's Stampede Week in the old Cow Town, it's a time for blue jeans, colored shirts and white hats. And anyone who hasn't come honestly by a pair of bowed legs or can't produce a reasonable imitation, is in danger of feeling a humiliating inferiority.

The big Stampede of 1912 was held at Victoria Park, but was not in any way a part of the Exhibition program of that time. The union occurred in 1923; and only then did the Calgary summer show begin to develop as a blend of agriculture, industry and rodeo, unlike that found elsewhere.

Once again Guy Weadick was managing the Stampede part of the show and the program was one to attract contestants and spectators.

A rodeo innovation on Weadick's 1923 program was the chuckwagon race, but nobody at that time could have dreamed of it growing in fame and popularity until it had one of the highest ratings in outdoor entertainment anywhere. At some of the earliest rodeo performances, Burns and Cross chuckwagons served flapjacks in front of the grandstand and indulged in unscheduled races back to the barns. It was this that suggested the "Rangeland Derby," and immortalized the roundup cook's wagon.

At first there was plenty of latitude in rules, but in 1923 the wagons raced from a standing start, made a figure "8", circled the track at a gallop, pulled up in the centrefield, unhitched, set up the cook stoves and started fire. The first wagon outfit to show smoke was the winner. And the first prize was $15.

The race rules were changed a good deal and Calgary found itself with the wildest horse race conducted anywhere — with the possible exception of the mountain-side race at Williams Lake in British Columbia.

Each outfit consisted of a chuckwagon weighing not less than 1350 pounds, hauled by a four-horse team and flanked by four outriders. It meant eight horses for each entry; and with four outfits per heat, 32 horses participated in each dusty and dangerous race. Starting from standing positions, outriders loaded camp stoves and tent poles, as drivers, without use of whips, started their teams around the barrels to hit the track at top speed. Anything could happen — wheels come off, wagons turn over, harness break, outfits pile up — but strangely enough, in the long history of Calgary chuckwagon racing, no contestant was ever fatally injured.

In the races of 1923 the chuckwagon owned by Dan Riley — later Senator Dan Riley — of High River won the championship. But things changed. Most of the horses at that time were range cayuses and not famous for speed. As competition became keener and contestants hoped to qualify for a prize-winner's share of the big purse — $18,000 in 1957 — the drivers wanted Thoroughbreds. Grandsons of Man O' War and other Thoroughbred notables found themselves in chuckwagon harness at Calgary.

The most notable name in chuckwagon racing was that of Dick Cosgrave, who ranched at Rosebud, north-east of Calgary. In point of familiarity around Calgary, it was one to rate at least as high as names like Babe Ruth and Joe Louis. Cosgrave's record before retiring from wagon racing in 1947 to become Arena Director of the Calgary Stampede was ten world championships in the "Rangeland Derby."

In other respects, also, the Calgary Stampede has acquired special character. Nowhere do the bronchos buck more explosively and no area has produced more outstanding riders, like the "Three Petes" — Pete Vandermeer, Pete Le Grandeur and Pete Knight. There have been many others whose names will not be forgotten. Pete Knight from Crossfield was hailed as one of the greatest rodeo riders of all time. Four times he won the world championship for bucking horse riding with saddle and was on his way to a fifth championship when killed by a bad horse in California in 1937.

Indeed, the contests in calf roping, steer decorating, wild cow milking, bull riding and so on have been equally impressive and, as those who have attended the Calgary Stampede events year after year have discovered, there are no dull moments.

And nowhere does the spirit of a rodeo permeate more completely an entire city. That in itself is one reason for rodeo fans from distant parts of the continent converging upon Calgary each year in the month of July — in July when the spirit of Guy Weadick seems to be everywhere in the City.

THE BULL SALE

When a modern Calgarian has boasted adequately about the Stampede, he'll probably have something to say about the Bull Sale. Like the Mardi Gras and the World Series, the Calgary Bull Sale has acquired an internationally recognized individuality and fame. It has become the great cattleman's classic in a region where people are proud of their cow-country traditions. Long ago that annual event was pronounced the biggest thing of its kind in the world, and its position has not diminished in either prestige or practical importance.

When the Calgary Bull Sale of 1958 was concluded, the totals from 58 annual events stood at 30,696 bulls sold for a return of $10,690,105. It was one of the most distinctive sale records in the cattle world.

To cattlemen over a large section of the West, the Calgary Bull Sale has remained the place at which the real significance of the cattle industry came clearly into view. Over the years, when prices averaged higher, the health of the industry was acknowledged; when bidding was slow and prices lower, cattlemen shared concern. And even for thousands of people who have had no direct connection with cattle raising, the Bull Sale has had an attraction ranking with a hockey final or the last night of a horse show. Those who have crowded enthusiastically into the judging pavilion on an afternoon or evening when important championships were being decided were urban dwellers as well as rural.

Although the Calgary sale entries have been from the Province of Alberta, the buyers have always been from far afield, and the judges through the years have been men of international distinction. In 1956 the judge of Shorthorn and Aberdeen-Angus cattle came from Argentina. He was Dr. Carlos Guererro, graduate in law from Oxford University, who chose ranching in his native land and could tell about 30,000 cattle and 30,000 sheep on the ranch holdings operated in partnership with his brother. But even a ranch total of 60,000 cattle and sheep, Dr. Guererro admitted, was no more unique than Calgary's Bull Sale. After listening with evident fascination to the lingo of half a dozen auctineers — all talking at once, more or less — the man from South America said, "They're better entertainment than an opera." Perhaps the rapid-fire performance of auctioneers, working through each day from Monday or Tuesday to Friday, with not even an intermission at noontime, has accounted for part of the interest shown by the fifteen or twenty thousand people who have attended annually.

The Calgary Bull Sale had its birth in 1901, four years before the Provinces of Alberta and Saskatchewan were created. In its origin it was the Territorial Cattle Breeders' Association Sale and not very imposing. Sixty-four bulls, cows and heifers sold at prices averaging $84.17 per head. Most of the entries were Shorthorns; three were Aberdeen-Angus and the Hereford breed was without a single representative.

According to the Association's announcement printed prior to the second annual event on May 14, 1902, "It may be taken for granted that the Annual Sale institution has come to stay in Western Canada. Every one of the breeders who entered stock for sale in 1901 is enthusiastically in favor of these sales as a permanent institution and there has yet to be a single objection or complaint recorded by any of the purchasers. Last year's sale was somewhat defective in point of management. It was an entirely new and untried venture. The forthcoming auction sale and cattle show will be a vast improvement."

The Association, with Territorial Government support, not only paid the freight on animals shipped to the sale but also deliver-ed them freight-free to the buyers' nearest stations in the North West Territories, "West of Moose Jaw."

For the second annual event, in 1902, a Stallion Show was added, with classes for Thoroughbreds, Standardbreds, Hackneys, Clydesdales, Shires, Percherons and Suffolk Punch. And to further distinguish the program of that second year, the first Hereford cattle appeared, but all except one of the representatives of that

THE BULL SALE

breed were entered by the Mossom Boyd Farm at Prince Albert. The Mossom Boyd Company, with farms at Bobcaygeon in Ontario and Prince Albert in the Territories, not only pioneered with Herefords in Western Canada but was one of the leaders in developing the Polled Hereford strain on the continent. One of the Prince Albert breeding triumphs was the production of the bull called Bullion 4th, recognized internationally as one of the greatest foundation sires of the Polled breed.

As the Territories were being carved into two new provinces in 1905, a strenuous Battle of the Breeds was shaping up, with Herefords challenging Shorthorns, Galloways, Aberdeen-Angus, Highland and even Devons for ranch country supremacy. The Calgary Bull Sale arena was to be the scene of many of the skirmishes, and in that particular year 68 percent of the cattle entered were Shorthorns, 25 percent were Herefords, five percent Galloways and five head were Aberdeen Angus. Fifty years later the proportions had changed greatly — 73 percent Herefords, 16 percent Shorthorns, 11 percent Aberdeen-Angus and no Galloways.

There were other significant contrasts; in the sale of 1905 the 340 pure bred cattle representing four breeds brought an average price of $69.28. In recent years the average has been consistently over $500, and in 1951, when commercial beef prices were at record peaks, the Calgary Bull Sale average reached the spectacular level of $1120.

Quite obviously the sales through the years were in the nature of barometers of the livestock economy. The lowest average prices were in 1908 when range and farm herds were still feeling the crippling losses from a severe winter one year earlier. Then there were low prices in 1923 which coincided with post-war slump, and again in 1933 when it took a better than usual steer to bring three cents a pound on the depression-riddled market.

Likewise, the record high prices in 1951 coincided with market quotations running close to 35 cents a pound for good steers — when a fat critter was so valuable that men in the underworld found it more profitable to steal cattle than to rob banks. At least, that was the report from Vancouver and should be convincing.

Some of the exciting moments at Calgary sales came when grand champion bulls or popular favorites were in the ring and cattlemen, trying to remain inconspicuous in the big crowd, were matching their bids in the hope of gaining ownership. On occasions the excitement was such that men with limited budgets bid beyond their means and then faced the embarrassment of having to borrow to make settlement.

Often there were $5000 bulls at Calgary, sometimes $8000 bulls, and in 1955 a Shorthorn bred by A. R. Cross of Midnapore and bought by Claude Gallinger of Edmonton established a new record at $10,000.

There have been other bull sales across the nation, all serving useful purposes in bringing buyers and sellers together, but there has been only one Calgary Bull Sale. For a week each year, as agricultural people gather for the great cattlemen's festival, popular conversation on 8th Avenue and in hotel lobbies turns inevitably to Herefords, Shorthorns, Aberdeen-Angus and the best place to buy blue jeans. The sale has been a link in a long chain of operations providing beef for Canadians tables. And Calgary, with all its new bigness, industry and oil-millionaires, is still the "Cow Capital" of the West.

THE WHITE HAT

The white hat of ranchland proportions has become the symbol of modern Calgary — bright, broad and distinctive. Modelled jauntily by Mayor Donald Hugh Mackay, the glamorous headpiece is a made-in-Calgary product, and a thousand like it have been presented officially to a thousand distinguished visitors from many parts of the world, reminders of the spirit of the storybook City of the Foothills.

Many of the most famous heads of the present generation have been formally hatted with the Calgary emblem: The Duke of Edinburgh; Princess Margaret; Sir Winston Churchill; Governor General Vincent Massey; Governor-General Lord Alexander; Prime Minister Louis St. Laurent; Prime Minister John Diefenbaker; Ezra Taft Benson; the Governor of Texas; the Lord Mayor of London; Jack Dempsey; Premiers; Ambassadors; High Commissioners and so on. Calgary hats are found and prized in high places.

THE WHITE HAT

Probably nobody in history has presented more hats than the Mayor of Calgary — or received more in return. "The hat I treasure most," he has admitted, "is the one Guy Weadick brought for me from Arizona." But there was a silk "topper" from the Mayor of Worthing in England; a bowler hat from Toronto; a French beret from Montreal; a sou' wester from Halifax and a boater from Vancouver.

When Her Royal Highness The Princess Elizabeth and The Duke of Edinburgh visited Calgary in 1951, the Mayor, wearing a natty white hat, met them at the train. The Princess, eying the headpiece, asked: "Is that the hat the British Hat Industry made for you?"

The Mayor had not anticipated that question and confessed: "No, Your Highness; this is a Calgary hat."

"I'm disappointed," she replied. "I thought you'd be wearing our hat today."

The Mayor acted promptly and sent a motorcycle roaring through the city to get the appropriate headpiece. Thereafter for the period of the royal visit, he wore the heavy hat with extremely broad brim and high Australian crown, made by England's best hatters, expressly for the Mayor of Calgary.

Gradually the white hat has become synonymous with Calgary, even far from Alberta. To the annual meeting of the Federation of Mayors and Municipalities in Montreal a visiting representative from Houston, Texas, brought his brightest western clothes but hesitated to wear them in the cosmopolitan Eastern city. Mustering courage, however, he donned a white hat and colored shirt and ventured onto the street. To his surprise, he was greeted on every hand with friendly smiles and exclamations — "Ah, Calgary!" Returning to the hotel, slightly chagrined, he protested, "They all thought I was Mackay; they've never heard of Texas."

Exactly 65 years after a shapeless community elected black-whiskered George Murdoch as its first mayor, a Calgary with population of 125,000 elected 35-year-old, white-hatted Donald Mackay. The latter event was in 1949, and after eight subsequent years of sensational growth sparked by oil and gas development, the city passed the population mark of 200,000 and the Man in the White Hat was still mayor.

His policies haven't escaped criticism and there are those people who say too much effort has been devoted to white hat activities and not enough to civic housekeeping. But relentlessly Mackay has proclaimed the charms of his foothills city and won for it a special sort of admiration.

Don Mackay is the first native son of Alberta to occupy the Mayor's chair. He was born at Lethbridge, March 22, 1914, but almost at once the family moved to Calgary and there Donald began his formal education, starting at Stanley Jones School. The family moved again — to Drumheller, where the lad completed public and high school grades. Returning to Calgary he worked for the Albertan newspaper. The first job consisted of knocking at doors to sell circulation, but his mind was set on bigger things. He became a cub reporter in the Sports Department and then sport announcer for the Albertan's radio station, CJCJ.

Mackay's spontaneity and his enthusiasm for home-town athletes made him an immediate success as a sportscaster. He could make radio listeners sit on the edges of chairs and inter-mittently break living-room decorum with outbursts of wild cheers. When the Calgary Stampeders won over Hamilton in the Allan Cup hockey final in 1946, radio listeners got the impression that Announcer Mackay was on skates and taking part in every play. Many people confessed they'd rather listen to Mackay than watch the game from a ringside seat. And when the Stampede foot-ball team invaded Toronto in 1948 and again in '49, the smiling Mackay was the proper person to be Master of Ceremonies for the Calgary contingent.

In the latter year Toronto people watching with undisguised astonishment whispered, "Is that fellow with the white hat really the Mayor of Calgary? He's awfully young! And he's pretty gay!" Actually he had been elected only a few hours earlier and not until half way over the air route to Toronto did he get confirmation of his success at the polls.

He had been promoted to the position of radio station manager in 1943 and came increasingly into the public eye. Successively he was Calgary president of the Junior Chamber of Commerce, Alberta president and Canadian president. And in 1945 he entered public life, being elected to the office of alderman. Two years later he was returned — topped the aldermanic poll — and in the fall of 1949 came out for Mayor and won over former-Mayor James Watson and two other candidates. Repeatedly he was re-elected to preside in that Council Chamber into which he had made his earliest entry as Drumheller's boy-representative to the Tuxis Boy's Parliament.

As Mayor, Don Mackay has not been like any who preceded him — nor like any elsewhere, for that matter. He has never been noted for silence on matters of public concern, and it was but a short time until he was one of the best-known mayors in Canada. Nobody could welcome the "visiting firemen" like Mackay, and nobody could cover more meetings and sod-turnings and official openings in 24 hours.

Not only did he become president of the Canadian Federation of Mayors and Municipalities in 1954, but he has been almost constantly in the news at home — promoting a fabulous civic centre for his city, endorsing an ambitious program of bingo games for charity, driving in an ostrich race at the Exhibition Corral, plunging into a contest for the national leadership of his political party, or something else commanding the front pages. Now and then a section of the citizens have expressed horror, but the Mayor's hat and voice have been as prominent as ever.

Even Mackay's family is distinctive like his white hat. He married Mary Josephine Quist of Claresholm in 1938 and the first five children were daughters. The sixth child had to be a boy, and Calgarians on 8th Avenue were as much interested as though the newcomer were to be one of their own. The sixth was a boy. The Mayor was absent when the baby arrived; but on his return to the City, Starr's Ambulance with police escort met the plane and, after the grinning and healthy Mayor had been placed firmly on an ambulance stretcher, the sirens wailed and he was whisked through city streets to the maternity ward at the General Hospital to see his son — Donald Hugh John Mackay.

There have been setbacks, of course, as there are in the lives of all public figures. Twice he has been defeated in federal elections. The second time was in June, 1957, but four months later he was re-elected Mayor of Calgary, defeating three other candidates in a landslide victory. "He may be temperamental," one of his friends said, "but he's got all the bounce of a rubber ball."

Modern Calgary has found the Mayor's white hat quite becoming to its intensely Western personality, but the stylish thing hasn't told the full story about serious city planning and the problems born of unusual growth in the years after 1947.

Actually, there were four Calgarys — Fort Calgary, Town of Calgary, City of Calgary and then something else which emerged after the oil discoveries at Leduc.

Until 1947 Turner Valley, as Canada's leading oil field, was frequently in the news and Calgary exercised a paternal watchfulness. Valley production reached peak performance of 30,000 barrels a day in 1942 — by all the Canadian standards, quite a wonderful achievement. But bigger — much bigger things were ahead to justify the optimism of pioneer Calgary promoters like Herron, Dingman, Pearce and others. Fields of equal or greater worth must exist elsewhere in the Province, they had reasoned.

Pursuing the costly search, the Imperial Oil Company drilled 133 consecutive dry holes at a cost in excess of 13 million dollars. The 134th was Imperial Leduc Number One, blowing in early in 1947 to signal a new economic era for the Province.

Leduc was 175 miles from Calgary but most of the oil companies were already established with offices in the southern city and Calgary continued to be the administrative centre. Gas and oil production had moved northward and discoveries were being made farther and farther from Turner Valley, but Calgary people continued to see their City as the real "beating heart" of the Canadian industry. And 250 companies with their offices in Calgary seemed to add weight to the contention.

When Leduc's discovery well was making news, Calgary was a city of roughly 100,000. In the next eleven dramatic years the population doubled; City area was enlarged to 75 square miles and paved streets, sidewalks and sewer mains were extended by hundreds of miles. Housing developments, like an oil slick creeping over the surface of a pond, spread in all directions.

As the City celebrated the seventy-fifth anniversary of the arrival of the railroad, and streets had advanced from the travois to the Cadillac stage, the record was something to justify a Texas-type of boasting. And ahead were still bigger things. Already ranking ninth in population among the cities of Canada, and fourth in money transactions, the planners could foretell half a million people living close to the confluence of Elbow and Bow by the year 1984, when citizens would be celebrating the hundredth anniversary of the formation of the first Town Council.

THE WHITE HAT

Indeed, the seers could recognize much more in the Greater Calgary of the future; they could see extensive industries attracted by abundance and economy of power; they could see a greatly expanded University development serving the southern section of the Province, benevolent ideals with finer cultural interests and growing appreciation for the quality of local traditions.

Chinook winds will still be moderating the winters in those years ahead; the mountain playground at Banff will still be an unequalled attraction; the nearby soil supporting farming and ranching will still be productive; and somebody will be wearing a white hat to proclaim a justifiable pride in Calgary, one of the brightest gems in the Crown of Canadian Cities.

INDEX

INDEX

INDEX

Van Horne, William, 42, 44, 108
Victoria Park, 75
Vigilantes, 23

Wainwright, 146
Walker, Major James, 31, 52, 62, 65, 72, 75, 146, 229
Walker, Rev. William, 168
War, 174
Weadick, Guy, 155, 159, 232
Whiskey, 87

White hat, 237
William Pearce Scheme, 109
Williams, Jesse, 71
Wood, C. E. D., 47
Woodsworth, J. S., 203

Young, J. J., 132
Young Mens' Club, 152, 200

Zoo, 215